CONVEYANCING SOLUTIONS
1: ENQUIRIES BEFORE CONTRACT

AUSTRALIA AND NEW ZEALAND
The Law Book Company Ltd.
Sydney : Melbourne : Perth

CANADA AND U.S.A.
The Carswell Company Ltd.
Agincourt, Ontario

INDIA
N.M. Tripathi Private Ltd.
Bombay
and
Eastern Law House Private Ltd.
Calcutta and Delhi
M.P.P. House
Bangalore

ISRAEL
Steimatzky's Agency Ltd.
Jerusalem : Tel Aviv : Haifa

MALAYSIA : SINGAPORE : BRUNEI
Malayan Law Journal (Pte.) Ltd.
Singapore and Kuala Lumpur

PAKISTAN
Pakistan Law House
Karachi

CONVEYANCING SOLUTIONS
1: ENQUIRIES BEFORE CONTRACT

RUTH ANNAND, B.A.

Solicitor,
Lecturer in Law, University of Bristol

BRIAN CAIN, LL.B.

Solicitor

LONDON SWEET & MAXWELL 1986

Published in 1986 by
Sweet & Maxwell Limited
11 New Fetter Lane, London
Computerset by Promenade Graphics Limited, Cheltenham
Printed in Great Britain by
Robert Hartnoll (1985) Limited
Bodmin, Cornwall

British Library Cataloguing in Publication Data
Annand, Ruth
Enquiries before contract.—
(Conveyancing solutions)
1. Conveyancing—England
I. Title II. Cain, Brian III. Series
344.2064'38 KD979

ISBN 0-421-34810-0

CONTENTS

Table of Cases
Table of Statutes

1 INTRODUCTION **1**

General **1**
Conveyancing procedure **1**
Enquiries before contract **3**

2 PRELIMINARY ENQUIRIES OF THE VENDOR **5**

Introduction **5**
Legal status of the replies **6**
The standard enquiries before contract **15**
General and leasehold **15**
Leasehold **54**
Buying property subject to tenancies and licences **66**
Standard additional enquiries **68**
Other additional enquiries **70**

3 ENQUIRIES OF LOCAL AUTHORITIES **71**

Introduction **71**
When to make the enquiries **71**
Fees **72**
Describing the property **72**
Value of the local authority's replies **73**
Local authority's liability for negligent replies **73**
Compulsory acquisition **74**
Public highways **75**
New housing developments **77**
Diversion and closure of roads and footpaths **78**
Public footpaths **79**
Noise abatement **79**
Smokeless zones **80**
Housing **80**
Sewers **81**
Registered land **83**
Long term planning policy **83**
Building Regulations **86**
Planning permission **87**
Completion, enforcement and stop notices **92**
Tree preservation orders **96**
Section 169 of the Town and Country Planning Act 1971 **96**
Control of advertising **98**
Listed buildings **99**
Conservation areas **104**
Areas of outstanding natural beauty **105**
Urban development areas **106**

Enterprise zones **107**
Improvement areas **108**
Rates **108**
Informal notices **109**
Pipelines **109**

4 OTHER SOURCES OF INFORMATION **111**

Personal inspections **111**
Subsidence **112**
Railway fences and tunnels **115**
Water **116**
Electricity **118**
Gas **119**
Telecommunications **120**
Pipelines **122**
Survey **122**

APPENDICES

A Con 29 (Long), Oyez, Enquiries Before Contract **127**
B Convey. 1, Unilaw, Enquiries Prior to Contract for Sale **131**
C (General) Form Q1, Shaw & Sons, Preliminary Enquiries **135**
D (Leasehold) Form Q2, Shaw & Sons, Preliminary Enquiries **139**
E Con 291, Oyez, General Tenancy Enquiries **143**
F Con 292, Oyez, Agricultural Tenacy Enquiries **147**
G Con 29, Oyez, Supplementary Enquiries Before Contract **151**
H Form Q7, Shaw & Sons, Information Memo **153**
J Additional Enquiries Before Contract, Bristol Law Society **157**
K Flat Purchase Enquiries, Bristol Law Society **159**
L Con 29A, Oyez, Enquiries of District Councils **161**
M Con 29D, Oyez, Enquiries of Local Authority **169**
N The Law Society's Code for Completion by Post **177**
O The Law Society's Contract for Sale (1984 Revision) **179**
P The National Contract of Sale Twentieth Edition **183**

Index **187**

TABLE OF CASES

Aldrington Garages Ltd. *v.* Fielder (1978) 247 E.G. 557; 37 P. & C.R. 461, C.A. 42
Amalgamated Investment & Property Co. Ltd. *v.* Walker (John) & Sons Ltd. [1977] 1 W.L.R. 164; 32 P. & C.R. 278, C.A. 100
Andover Corporation *v.* Mundy [1955] J.P.L. 518 79
Argy Trading Development Co. Ltd. *v.* Lapid Developments Ltd. [1977] 1 W.L.R. 444; [1977] 3 All E.R. 785; [1977] 1 Lloyd's Rep. 67 64
Ashby *v.* Secretary of State for the Environment [1980] 1 W.L.R. 673; 124 S.J. 185; [1980] 1 All E.R. 508; 78 L.G.R. 226; [1980] J.P.L. 178; 40 P. & C.R. 362, C.A.; affirming (1978) 37 P. & C.R. 197; 77 L.G.R. 222; 122 S.J. 524; [1978] J.P.L. 761 78
Ashcroft *v.* Mersey Regional Health Authority [1983] 2 All E.R. 245; affirmed [1985] 2 All E.R. 96, C.A. 4
Austerberry *v.* Oldham Corporation (1885) 29 Ch.D. 750; 55 L.J.Ch. 633; 53 L.J. 543; 49 J.P. 532; 33 W.R. 807; 1 T.L.R. 473, C.A. 55
Avon Finance Co. Ltd. *v.* Bridger (1979) 123 S.J. 705; [1985] 2 All E.R. 281, C.A. 39

Bain *v.* Fothergill (1874) L.R. 7 H.L. 158; 43 L.J.Ex. 243; 31 L.T. 387; 39 J.P. 228; 23 W.R. 261, H.L. 12
Balco Transport Services Ltd. *v.* Secretary of State for the Environment (1986) 130 S.J. 52; 276 E.G. 447; 135 New L.J. 936; 83 L.S.Gaz. 123, C.A.; affirming [1985] J.P.L. 722 45
Barnes *v.* City of London Real Property Co. Ltd. [1918] 2 Ch. 18; 87 L.J.Ch. 601; 119 L.T. 293; 34 T.L.R. 361 60
Becker *v.* Partridge [1966] 2 Q.B. 155; [1966] 2 W.L.R. 803; 110 S.J. 187; [1966] 2 All E.R. 266, C.A. 67
Bell *v.* Lever Brothers Ltd. [1932] A.C. 161; 101 L.J.K.B. 129; 146 L.T. 258; 48 T.L.R. 133; 76 S.J. 50; [1931] All E.R. Rep. 1; 37 Com.Cas. 98, H.L. 5
Bendall *v.* McWhirter [1952] 2 Q.B. 466; [1952] 1 T.L.R. 1332; 96 S.J. 344; [1952] 1 All E.R. 1307; [1952] C.L.Y. 257 41
Berkley *v.* Pavlett (1976) 241 E.G. 911; 242 E.G. 39 49
Binions *v.* Evans [1972] Ch. 359; [1972] 2 W.L.R. 729; 116 S.J. 122; [1972] 2 All E.R. 70; 23 P. & C.R. 192, C.A. 41
Blacklocks *v.* J.B. Developments (Godalming) Ltd. *See* Brickwall Farm, *Re*.
Boland. *See* Williams & Glyn's Bank Ltd. *v.* Boland.
Bolton *v.* Puley (1982) 267 E.G. 1161; 133 New L.J. 558 124
Boyle's claim, *Re* [1961] 1 W.L.R. 339; 105 S.J. 155; [1961] 1 All E.R. 620 38
Bradburn *v.* Lindsay [1983] 2 All E.R. 408; 268 E.G. 152 .... 16, 17
Braybrooks *v.* Whaley [1919] 1 K.B. 435; 88 L.J.K.B. 577; 120 L.T. 281; 63 S.J. 373, D.C. 12
Brewer and Hankin's Contract, *Re* (1899) 80 L.T. 127 30
Brickwall Farm, *Re* [1982] Ch. 183; [1981] 3 W.L.R. 554; 125 S.J. 356; [1981] 3 All E.R. 392; 42 P. & C.R. 27 40
Bridges *v.* Mees [1957] Ch. 475; [1957] 3 W.L.R. 215; 101 S.J. 555; [1957] 2 All E.R. 577 .... 40, 42

Brikom Investments *v.* Carr [1979] Q.B. 467; [1979] 2 W.L.R. 737; 123 S.J. 182; [1979] 2 All E.R. 753; 251 E.G. 359; 38 P. & C.R. 326; [1982] M.L.R. 21, C.A. .. 40
Bristol & West Building Society *v.* Henning [1985] 1 W.L.R. 778; 129 S.J. 363; [1985] 2 All E.R. 606; 50 P. & C.R. 237; 17 H.L.R. 432; 135 New L.J. 508; 82 L.S.Gaz. 1788, C.A. 37
Burn *v.* Secretary of State for the Environment (1971) 219 E.G. 586, D.C. 93
Burns *v.* Burns [1984] Ch. 317; [1984] 2 W.L.R. 582; [1984] 1 All E.R. 244; 14 Fam.Law 244; 128 S.J. 173; 81 L.S.Gaz. 893, C.A. 37

Cann *v.* Willson (1888) 39 Ch.D. 39; 57 L.J.Ch. 1034; 59 L.T. 723; 37 W.R. 23; 4 T.L.R. 588; 32 S.J. 542 123
Caunce *v.* Caunce [1969] 1 W.L.R. 286; 113 S.J. 204; [1969] 1 All E.R. 722; 20 P. & C.R. 877 35
Celsteel Ltd. *v.* Alton Habe Holdings Ltd. [1985] 1 W.L.R. 204; 129 S.J. 115; [1982] 2 All E.R. 562; 49 P. & C.R. 165; 82 L.S.Gaz. 1168 .... 32, 33, 41
Chewood's Registered Land, *Re* [1933] Ch. 574; 102 L.J.Ch. 289; 149 L.T. 70; 49 T.L.R. 320; [1933] All E.R. 946 42
City of London Building Society *v.* Flegg [1986] 2 W.L.R. 616; 130 S.J. 300; [1986] 1 All E.R. 989; 136 New L.J. 311; 83 L.S.Gaz. 1394, C.A. 36, 37, 38
Clore *v.* Theatrical Properties Ltd. [1936] 3 All E.R. 483, C.A. 26
Coats Patons (Retail) Ltd. *v.* Birmingham Corporation (1971) 115 S.J. 757; 69 L.G.R. 356 .... 8, 73, 74
Coldunell Ltd. *v.* Gallon [1986] 2 W.L.R. 466; [1986] 1 All E.R. 429; [1986] F.L.R. 183; (1986) 83 L.S.Gaz. 520, C.A. 39
Collins *v.* Jones (Hugh) (1977) 241 E.G. 837 11
Computastaff Ltd. *v.* Ingleden Brown Bennison and Garrett (1983) 268 E.G. 906; (1983) 133 New L.J. 598 .... 3, 52
Cook *v.* Minion (1978) 37 P. & C.R. 58; [1979] J.P.L. 305 32
—— *v.* Taylor [1942] Ch. 349; 111 L.J.Ch. 214; 167 L.T. 87; 58 T.L.R. 278; 86 S.J. 217 .... 39, 53, 66
Cornish *v.* Midland Bank [1985] 3 All E.R. 513; 135 New L.J. 869, 1985 F.L.R. 298, C.A. 39
Crabb *v.* Arun District Council [1976] Ch. 179; [1975] 3 W.L.R. 847; 119 S.J. 711; [1975] 3 All E.R. 865; 32 P. & C.R. 70, C.A. 32
Cremdean Properties Ltd. *v.* Nash (1977) 244 E.G. 547, C.A.; affirming (1977) 241 E.G. 837 .... 10, 14
Cumberland Consolidated Holdings Ltd. *v.* Ireland [1946] K.B. 264; 115 L.J.K.B. 301; 174 L.T. 257; 62 T.L.R. 215; [1946] 1 All E.R. 284 53

Daniel, *Re*, Daniel *v.* Vassall [1917] 2 Ch. 405; 87 L.J.Ch. 69; 117 L.T. 472; 33 T.L.R. 503; 61 S.J. 646 12
Dawson *v.* Brickman (1850) 3 M. & G. 53; 42 E.R. 181 16
Day *v.* Singleton [1899] 2 Ch. 320; 68 L.J.Ch. 593; 81 L.T. 306; 48 W.R. 18; 43 S.J. 671, C.A. 12
Daymond *v.* South West Water Authority [1976] A.C. 609; [1975] 3 W.L.R. 865; 119 S.J. 846; [1976] 1 All E.R. 39; 74 L.G.R. 128, H.L. 25
Dean *v.* Andrews (1985) 135 New L.J. 728 49
Derry *v.* Peek (1889) 14 App.Cas. 337; 58 L.J.Ch. 864; 61 L.T. 265; 54 J.P. 148; 38 W.R. 33; 5 T.L.R. 625; 1 Meg. 292, H.L.; reversing (1887) 37 Ch.D. 541, C.A. 7, 14

D'Eyncourt *v.* Gregory (1866) L.R. 3 Eq. 382; 36 L.J.Ch. 107; 15 W.R. 186 49
Duke of Westminster *v.* Guild [1985] Q.B. 688; [1984] 3 W.L.R. 630; 128 S.J. 581; [1984] 3 All E.R. 144; 48 P. & C.R. 42; 267 E.G. 763, C.A. 60
Drewell *v.* Towler (1832) 3 B. & Ad. 735; 1 L.J.K.B. 228; 110 E.R. 268 31
Dutton *v.* Bognor Regis Urban District Council [1972] 1 Q.B. 373; [1972] 2 W.L.R. 299; 116 S.J. 16; 70 L.G.R. 57, *sub nom.* Dutton *v.* Bognor Regis United Building Co. [1972] 1 All E.R. 462; [1972] 1 Lloyd's Rep. 227, C.A.; affirming [1971] 2 All E.R. 1003 87

Edmondton Corporation *v.* Knowles (W.M.) Ltd. (1961) 60 L.G.R. 124 60
Edward Wong Finance Co. Ltd. *v.* Johnson Stokes and Master. *See* Wong (Edward) Finance Co. Ltd. *v.* Johnson Stokes and Master.
Epps *v.* Esso Petroleum Co. Ltd. [1973] 1 W.L.R. 1071; 117 S.J. 430; [1973] 2 All E.R. 465; 25 P. & C.R. 402 41
Errington *v.* Errington and Woods [1952] 1 K.B. 290; [1952] 1 T.L.R. 231; 96 S.J. 119; [1952] 1 All E.R. 149, C.A. 41
—— *v.* Martell-Wilson (1980) 130 New L.J. 545 12
Esso Petroleum Co. Ltd. *v.* Mardon [1976] Q.B. 801; 2 Build.L.R. 82, C.A. 7, 14

Federated Homes Ltd. *v.* Mill Lodge Properties Ltd. [1980] 1 W.L.R. 594; 124 S.J. 412; [1980] 1 All E.R. 371; 39 P. & C.R. 576; 254 E.G. 39; [1985] Conv. 177, C.A. 22
Fisher *v.* Knowles (1982) 262 E.G. 1083 124
Flegg. *See* City of London Building Society *v.* Flegg.

George Mitchell (Chesterhall) Ltd. *v.* Finney Lock Seeds Ltd. *See* Mitchell (George) (Chesterhall) Ltd. *v.* Finney Lock Seeds Ltd.
Gilchester Properties Ltd. *v.* Gomm [1948] W.N. 71; 64 T.L.R. 235; 92 S.J. 220; [1948] 1 All E.R. 493 11
Goody *v.* Baring [1956] 1 W.L.R. 448; 100 S.J. 320; [1956] 2 All E.R. 11 .... 3, 5
Gordon *v.* Selico Co. Ltd. (1986) 18 H.L.R. 5
Gosling *v.* Woolf [1893] 1 Q.B. 39; 68 L.T. 89; 41 W.R. 106; 5 R. 81 65
Grant *v.* Edwards [1986] 3 W.L.R. 114; 130 S.J. 408; [1986] 2 All E.R. 426; (1986) 136 New L.J. 439; (1986) 83 L.S.Gaz. 1996, C.A. 37
Greasley *v.* Cooke [1980] 1 W.L.R. 1306; 124 S.J. 629; [1980] 3 All E.R. 710, C.A. 32
Great Portland Estates plc *v.* Westminster City Council. *See* Westminster City Council *v.* Great Portland Estates.

Halsall *v.* Brizzell [1957] Ch. 169; [1957] 2 W.L.R. 123; 101 S.J. 88; [1957] 1 All E.R. 371 32
Hamp *v.* Bygrave (1983) 266 E.G. 720 49
Hancock *v.* Brazier (Anerly) Ltd. [1966] 1 W.L.R. 1317; [1966] 2 All E.R. 901, C.A.; affirming 110 S.J. 368; [1966] 2 All E.R. 1 22
Hedley Byrne & Co. Ltd. *v.* Heller & Partners Ltd. [1964] A.C. 465; [1963] 3 W.L.R. 101; 107 S.J. 454; [1963] 2 All E.R. 575; [1963] 1 Lloyd's Rep. 485, H.L.; affirming [1962] 1 Q.B. 396; [1961] 3 W.L.R. 1225; 105 S.J. 910; [1961] 3 All E.R. 891, C.A.; affirming *The Times*, December 21, 1960 .... 3, 7, 8, 13
Heywood *v.* Mallalieu (1883) 25 Ch.D. 357; 53 L.J.Ch. 492; 49 L.T. 658; 32 W.R. 538 30

Hill *v.* Harris [1965] 2 Q.B. 601; [1965] 2 W.L.R. 1331; 109 S.J. 333; [1965] 2 All E.R. 358, C.A. 3, 5, 122
Hodgson *v.* Marks [1971] Ch. 892; [1971] 2 W.L.R. 1263; 115 S.J. 224; [1971] 2 All E.R. 684; 22 P. & C.R. 586, C.A.; reversing [1970] 3 W.L.R. 956; 114 S.J. 770; [1970] 3 All E.R. 513; 21 P. & C.R. 737 .... 38, 40
Holland *v.* Hodgson (1872) L.R. 7 C.P. 328; 41 L.J.C.P. 146; 26 L.T. 709; 20 W.R. 990, Ex.Ch. 48
Holmes *v.* Bradfield Rural District Council [1949] 2 K.B. 1; [1949] L.J.R. 978; 65 T.L.R. 195; 113 J.P. 140; 93 S.J. 183; [1949] 1 All E.R. 381; 47 L.G.R. 278, D.C 91
—— *v.* Kennard (1984) 128 S.J. 854; 49 P. & C.R. 202; 82 L.S.Gaz. 363, C.A.; reversing (1983) 127 S.J. 172 3
Hone *v.* Benson (1978) 248 E.G. 1013 .... 5, 16, 122
Hopgood *v.* Brown [1955] 1 W.L.R. 213; 99 S.J. 168; [1955] 1 All E.R. 550, C.A. 18, 26, 32
Hunt *v.* Luck [1902] 1 Ch. 428; 71 L.J.Ch. 239; 86 L.T. 68; 50 W.R. 291; 18 T.L.R. 265; 46 S.J. 229, C.A. 40, 66

Inwards *v.* Baker [1965] 2 Q.B. 29; [1965] 2 W.L.R. 212; 109 S.J. 75; [1965] 1 All E.R. 446, C.A. 32
Ives (E.R.) Investment Ltd. *v.* High [1967] 2 Q.B. 379; [1967] 2 W.L.R. 789; *sub nom.* Ives (E.R.) Investments *v.* High, 110 S.J. 963; [1967] 1 All E.R. 504; [1966] C.L.Y. 6674, C.A. 32, 33

Johnson *v.* Humphrey [1946] 1 All E.R. 460; 174 L.T. 324; 90 S.J. 211 54
Joyner *v.* Guildford Corporation (1954) 5 P. & C.R. 30 93

Kingsworth Finance Co. Ltd. *v.* Tizard [1986] 1 W.L.R. 783; [1986] 2 All E.R. 54; 130 S.J. 244; 51 P. & C.R. 296 .... 35, 39

Ladenbau, (G. & K.) (U.K.) Ltd. *v.* Crawley & de Reya [1978] 1 W.L.R. 266; [1978] 1 All E.R. 682 .... 4, 32
Leigh *v.* Taylor [1902] A.C. 157; 71 L.J.Ch. 272; 86 L.T. 239; 50 W.R. 623; 18 T.L.R. 293; 46 S.J. 264, H.L.; affirming, *sub nom. Re* De Falbe, Ward *v.* Taylor [1901] 1 Ch. 523, C.A. 49
Liverpool Corporation *v.* Irwin [1977] A.C. 239; 238 E.G. 879; 13 H.L.R. 38, H.L. 60
London & Cheshire Insurance Co. *v.* Laplagrene Property Co. Ltd. [1971] Ch. 499; [1971] 2 W.L.R. 257; 114 S.J. 912; [1971] 1 All E.R. 766; 22 P. & C.R. 108 40
LTSS Paint and Supply Services *v.* Hackney London Borough Council [1976] Q.B. 663; [1976] 2 W.L.R. 253; 119 S.J. 866; [1976] 1 All E.R. 311; 31 P. & C.R. 133; 74 L.G.R. 210, C.A.; reversing [1975] 1 W.L.R. 138, D.C. 45, 46
Lyus *v.* Prowsa Developments Ltd. [1982] 1 W.L.R. 1044; 126 S.J. 102; [1982] 2 All E.R. 953; 44 P. & C.R. 213 33

Malhotra *v.* Choudhury [1980] Ch. 52; [1978] 3 W.L.R. 825; 122 S.J. 681; [1979] 1 All E.R. 186, C.A. 12
Marchant *v.* Capital and Counties Property Co. Ltd. (1982) 263 E.G. 661 16
—— *v.* Casewell & Redgrave Ltd. (1976) 240 E.G. 127; [1976] J.P.L. 752 22
Midland Bank Ltd. *v.* Dobson (1985) 135 New L.J. 751, C.A. 37
—— *v.* Farmpride Hatcheries Ltd. (1981) 260 E.G. 493, C.A. 35, 41

Midland Bank Trust Ltd. *v.* Green [1980] Ch. 590; (1981) A.C. 513; 125 S.J. 33, H.L.; reversing [1979] 3 W.L.R. 167; 123 S.J. 388; [1979] 3 All E.R. 28; 39 P. & C.R. 265, C.A.; reversing [1978] 3 W.L.R. 149; 121 S.J. 794; [1978] 3 All E.R. 555 .... 34, 41
Midland Railway Co. *v.* Wright [1901] 1 Ch. 738; 70 L.J.Ch. 411; 84 L.T. 225; 49 W.R. 474; 17 T.L.R. 261; 45 S.J. 311 30
Mitchell *v.* Beacon Estates (Finsbury Park) Ltd. (1949) 1 P. & C.R. 32 43
Mitchell (George) (Chesterhall) Ltd. *v.* Finney Lock Seeds Ltd. [1983] 2 A.C. 803; [1983] 3 W.L.R. 163; [1983] 2 All E.R. 737; [1983] 2 Lloyd's Rep. 272; [1983] Com.L.R. 209, H.L. affirming; [1982] 3 W.L.R. 1036; 126 S.J. 689; [1983] 1 All E.R.108; [1983] 1 Lloyd's Rep. 168; 79 L.S.Gaz. 1444; [1981] 1 Lloyd's Rep. 476, C.A. 9
Muskett *v.* Hill (1839) 5 Bing. N.C. 694; 7 Scott 855; 9 L.J.C.P. 201; 132 E.R. 1267 26
Mustafa *v.* Baptist Union Corporation Ltd. (1983) 266 E.G. 812 11

National Provincial Bank *v.* Ainsworth [1965] A.C. 1175; [1965] 3 W.L.R. 1; 109 S.J. 415; [1965] 2 All E.R. 472, H.L.; reversing *sub nom.* National Provincial Bank *v.* Hastings Car Mart [1964] Ch. 665; [1964] 2 W.L.R. 751; 108 S.J. 115; [1964] 1 All E.R. 688, C.A.; upholding [1964] Ch. 9; [1963] 2 W.L.R. 1015; 107 S.J. 295; [1963] 2 All E.R. 204 .... 40, 41
National Westminster Bank plc *v.* Morgan [1985] A.C. 686; [1985] 2 W.L.R. 588; 129 S.J. 205; [1985] 1 All E.R. 821; 17 H.L.R. 360; F.L.R. 266; 135 New L.J. 254; 82 L.S.Gaz. 1485, H.L.; reversing [1983] 3 All E.R. 85; 133 New L.J. 378, C.A. 39
Neilson *v.* Poole (1969) 20 P. & C.R. 909 18
New Windsor Corporation *v.* Mellor [1975] Ch. 380; [1975] 3 W.L.R. 25; 119 S.J. 440; [1975] 3 All E.R. 44; 73 L.G.R. 337; 30 P. & C.R. 429, C.A.; affirming [1974] 1 W.L.R. 1504; 118 S.J. 580; [1974] 2 All E.R. 510; 72 L.G.R. 682 31
Nocton *v.* Ashburton (Lord) [1914] A.C. 932; 83 L.J.Ch. 784; 111 L.T. 641; [1914–15] All E.R. Rep. 45 7
North-West Leicester District Council *v.* Secretary of State for the Environment (1983) 46 P. & C.R. 154; [1982] J.P.L. 777 .... 47, 89

Overbrooke Estates Ltd. *v.* Glencombe Properties Ltd. [1974] 1 W.L.R. 1335; 118 S.J. 775; [1974] 3 All E.R. 511 11

Paddington Building Society *v.* Mendelsohn (unreported, April 2, 1985) 37
Panorama Developments (Guildford) Ltd. *v.* Fidelis Furnishing Fabrics Ltd. [1971] 2 Q.B. 711; [1971] 3 W.L.R. 440; 115 S.J. 483; [1971] 3 All E.R. 16, C.A. 38
Peaktop Properties (Hampstead) Ltd. *v.* Camden London Borough Council (1983) 46 P. & C.R. 177; [1984] L.G.R. 101, C.A.; reversing (1983) 23 R.V.R. 8; 44 P. & C.R. 233; 262 E.G. 239; [1982] J.P.L. 453 97
Peffer *v.* Rigg [1977] 1 W.L.R. 285; [1978] 3 All E.R. 745; 242 E.G. 123 34
Perry *v.* Phillips (Sidney) & Son [1982] 1 W.L.R. 1297; 126 S.J. 626; [1982] 3 All E.R. 705; 22 Build.L.R. 120; 263 E.G. 888; 79 L.S.Gaz. 1175, C.A. reversing [1982] 1 All E.R. 1005; [1981] 260 E.G. 389 124
Philips *v.* Ward [1956] 1 W.L.R. 471; 100 S.J. 317; [1956] 1 All E.R. 874, C.A. 124
Phillips *v.* Lamdin [1949] 2 K.B. 33; [1949] L.J.R. 1293; 93 S.J. 320; [1949] 1 All E.R. 770 48
Phillips Products Ltd. *v.* Hyland (1985) 129 S.J. 47; [1985] Tr.L. 98; 82 L.S.Gaz. 681, C.A. 9

Phipps *v.* Pears [1965] 1 Q.B. 76; [1964] 2 W.L.R. 996; 108 S.J. 236; [1964] 2 All E.R. 35, C.A. 17
Pirelli General Cable Works Ltd. *v.* Faber (Oscar) & Partners [1983] 2 A.C. 1; [1983] 2 W.L.R. 6; 127 S.J. 16; [1983] 1 All E.R. 65; 265 E.G. 979; 133 New L.J. 63, H.L.; reversing (1982) 263 E.G. 879, C.A. 22
Poster *v.* Slough Estates Ltd. [1969] 1 Ch. 495; [1968] 1 W.L.R. 1515; 112 S.J. 705; [1968] 3 All E.R. 257; 19 P. & C.R. 841; [1968] J.P.L. 687 32

Raintree Ltd. *v.* Holmes & Hills (1984) 134 New L.J. 522 .... 3, 5
Resolute Maritime Inc. *v.* Nippon Kaiji Kyokai (The Skepas) [1983] 1 W.L.R. 857; 127 S.J. 491; [1983] 2 All E.R. 1; [1983] 1 Lloyd's Rep. 431; 133 New L.J. 401 ... 13
Royal Crescent, *Re* [1973] J.P.L. 27 105

Salvin's Indenture *Re*, Pitt *v.* Durham County Water Board [1938] 2 All E.R. 498; 82 S.J. 395; 36 L.G.R. 388 26
Sharneyford Supplies Ltd. *v.* Edge [1985] 3 W.L.R. 1; 129 S.J. 316; [1985] 1 All E.R. 976; 50 P. & C.R. 343; 35 New L.J. 288; 82 L.S.Gaz. 2081 .... 4, 12, 13, 14
Sharpe, *Re* [1980] 1 W.L.R. 219; 124 S.J. 147; 39 P. & C.R. 459; *sub nom.* Sharpe (a bankrupt), *Re ex p.* Trustee of the Bankrupt *v.* Sharpe [1980] 1 All E.R. 198 38
Sidney *v.* Buddery (1949) 1 P. & C.R. 34 43
Simpson *v.* Grove Tompkins & Co. (1982) 126 S.J. 347, C.A. 4, 5
Somma *v.* Hazelhurst [1978] 1 W.L.R. 1014; 122 S.J. 280; [1978] 2 All E.R. 1011; 37 P. & C.R. 391; [1978] J.P.L. 554; *sub nom.* Somma *v.* Hazelhurst; Somma *v.* Savelli (1978) 246 E.G. 311, C.A. 42
South West Water Authority *v.* Rumbles [1985] A.C. 609; [1985] 2 W.L.R. 405; 129 S.J. 130; [1985] 1 All E.R. 513; 83 L.G.R. 297; 25 R.V.R. 66; [1985] J.P.L. 476; 82 L.S.Gaz. 1173, H.L.; reversing [1984] 1 W.L.R. 800; 128 S.J. 400; [1984] 2 All E.R. 240; 82 L.G.R. 502; 24 R.V.R. 130; [1985] J.P.L. 115; 81 L.S.Gaz. 2299, C.A. 25
South Western General Property Co. Ltd. *v.* Marton (1982) 263 E.G. 1090 9
Spyer *v.* Phillipson [1931] 2 Ch. 183; 100 L.J.Ch. 245; 144 L.T. 626; 74 S.J. 787, C.A. 49
Strand Securities Ltd. *v.* Caswell [1965] Ch. 958; [1965] 2 W.L.R. 958; 109 S.J. 131; [1965] 1 All E.R. 820, C.A.; reversing [1965] Ch. 373; [1964] 3 W.L.R. 619; 108 S.J. 502; [1964] 2 All E.R. 956 .... 41, 66
Street *v.* Mountford [1985] A.C. 809; [1985] 2 W.L.R. 877; 129 S.J. 348; [1985] 2 All E.R. 289; 50 P. & C.R. 258; 274 E.G. 821; 17 H.L.R. 402; 135 New L.J. 460; 82 L.S.Gaz. 2087, H.L.; reversing (1984) 128 S.J. 483; 49 P. & C.R. 324; 16 H.L.R. 27; 271 E.G. 1153; 81 L.S.Gaz. 1844, C.A. 42
Sturolson & Co. *v.* Weniz (1984) 17 H.L.R. 140; 272 E.G. 326, C.A. 42
Suffolk County Council *v.* Mason [1979] A.C. 705; [1979] 2 W.L.R. 571; 123 S.J. 285; [1979] 2 All E.R. 369; 77 L.G.R. 621; 39 P. & C.R. 20; [1979] J.P.L. 529, H.L.; affirming [1978] 1 W.L.R. 716; 122 S.J. 349; [1978] 2 All E.R. 618; 76 L.G.R. 569; 37 P. & C.R. 21; [1978] J.P.L. 372, C.A.; reversing (1977) 121 S.J. 375; [1977] J.P.L. 442 79

Taylors Fashions Ltd. *v.* Liverpool Victoria Trustees Co. Ltd. [1981] Q.B. 133; [1981] 2 W.L.R. 576; [1981] 1 All E.R. 897; [1981] Com.L.R. 34; (1979) 251 E.G. 159 . 32
Terrene *v.* Nelson [1937] 3 All E.R. 739; 157 L.T. 254; 53 T.L.R. 963; 81 S.J. 649 5

Terunnanse v. Terunnanse [1968] A.C. 1086; [1968] 2 W.L.R. 1125; [1968] 1 All E.R. 651; *sub nom.* Terunnanse v. Terunnanse (1968) 112 S.J. 134, P.C. 26
Thames Water Authority v. Blue and White Launderettes Ltd. [1980] 1 W.L.R. 700; 124 S.J. 100; 78 L.G.R. 237; [1980] J.P.L. 402, C.A. 27
Tollemache and Cobbold Breweries Ltd. v. Reynolds (1983) 268 E.G. 52, C.A. 16, 17
Tredegas (Viscount) v. Harwood [1929] A.C. 72; 97 L.J.Ch. 392; 139 L.T. 642; 44 T.L.R. 790, H.L. 64

Vale of Glamorgan Borough Council v. Palmer [1984] J.P.L. 334; [1983] Crim.L.R. 334; 81 L.G.R. 678, D.C. 19

Wadsworth v. Lydall [1981] 1 W.L.R. 598; 125 S.J. 309; [1981] 2 All E.R. 401, C.A. ... 4
Walker v. Boyle (1981) 125 S.J. 724; [1982] 1 W.L.R. 495; [1982] 1 All E.R. 634; 44 P. & C.R. 20; 261 E.G. 1090; 79 L.S.Gaz. 954 .... 8, 10
Ward v. Kirkland [1967] Ch. 194; [1966] 1 W.L.R. 601; 110 S.J. 289; [1966] 1 All E.R. 609 .... 31, 32
Watts v. Spence [1976] Ch. 165; [1975] 2 W.L.R. 1039; 119 S.J. 168; [1975] 2 All E.R. 528; 29 P. & C.R. 501 .... 12, 13
Webb v. Pollmount [1966] Ch. 584; [1966] 2 W.L.R. 543; 109 S.J. 1029; [1966] 1 All E.R. 481; [1965] C.L.Y. 2179 40
Westminster City Council v. Great Portland Estates [1985] A.C. 661; [1984] 3 W.L.R. 1035; 128 S.J. 784; [1984] 3 All E.R. 744; 49 P. & C.R. 34; [1985] J.P.L. 108; 81 L.S.Gaz. 3501, H.L.; reversing (1983) 49 P. & C.R. 20; [1984] J.P.L. 510, C.A. 86
—— v. Haymarket Publishing Ltd. [1981] 1 W.L.R. 677; 125 S.J. 220; [1981] 2 All E.R. 555; 42 P. & C.R. 29; 258 E.G. 641; 80 L.G.R. 528; [1981] J.P.L. 751, C.A.; affirming [1980] 1 W.L.R. 683; 123 S.J. 804; [1980] 1 All E.R. 289; 40 P. & C.R. 130; 78 L.G.R. 206; 253 E.G. 805 50
White v. Bijou Mansions Ltd. [1938] Ch. 351; 107 L.J.Ch. 212; 158 L.T. 338; 54 T.L.R. 458; 82 S.J. 135; [1938] 1 All E.R. 546 65
Williams v. Usherwood (1983) 45 P. & C.R. 235, C.A. 29
Williams & Glyn's Bank Ltd. v. Boland [1981] A.C. 487; [1980] 3 W.L.R. 138; 124 S.J. 443; [1980] 2 All E.R. 408; 40 P. & C.R. 451, H.L.; affirming [1979] Ch. 312; [1979] 2 W.L.R. 550; 123 S.J. 183; [1979] 2 All E.R. 697; 38 P. & C.R. 622, C.A.; reversing (1978) 36 P. & C.R. 448; 77 L.S.Gaz. 1242; [1980] Conv. 427; [1981] 2 Business L.R. 90; 32 N.I.L.Q. 3 .... 3, 34, 35, 36, 37, 38, 39
Wilson v. Bloomfield (1979) 123 S.J. 860, C.A. 4, 14, 18
Woodstead Finance v. Petrou (1986) 136 New L.J. 188, C.A. 39
Woolwich Equitable Building Society v. Marshall [1952] Ch. 1; [1951] 2 T.L.R. 783; [1951] 2 All E.R. 769 40
Wright, *Re* [1985] R.A. 21 51

Yandle & Sons v. Sutton [1922] 2 Ch. 199; 91 L.J.Ch. 567; 127 L.T. 783 5
Yianni v. Evans (Edwin) & Sons [1981] 3 W.L.R. 843; [1982] Q.B. 438; 259 E.G. 969; 125 S.J. 694 123
Young v. Secretary of State for the Environment [1983] 2 A.C. 662; [1983] 3 W.L.R. 382; 127 S.J. 537; [1983] 2 All E.R. 1105; 47 P. & C.R. 165; [1983] J.P.L. 667; 81 L.G.R. 779; 269 E.G. 219, H.L.; affirming (1983) 81 L.G.R. 389; [1983] J.P.L. 465; 80 L.S. Gaz. 2443, C.A. 41

TABLE OF STATUTES

1925 Law of Property Act (15 & 16 Geo. 5, c. 20)—
s. 14 .... 36, 40
s. 25 65
s. 44(5) 65
s. 45(2) 59
s. 53(1)(*a*) 38
(*c*) 38
s. 62 26
(1) 48
s. 76(1)(*a*) 59
(*b*) 59
s. 78 22
s. 146 58
s. 199(1)(ii)(*a*) 35
(*b*) 35
Sched. 2, Pt. I 59
Pt. II 59
Land Registration Act (15 & 16 Geo. 5, c. 21)—
s. 20 65
(1) 33
s. 24 59
s. 34(4) 33
s. 49(1) 32
s. 54(1) 32
s. 59(6) 33
s. 70(1) 30, 32, 42
(1)(*a*) 33, 111
(*f*) 111
(*g*) 34, 38, 39, 40, 41, 42, 111
(*k*) 42, 111
s. 110 65
Land Charges Act (15 & 16 Geo. 5, c. 22) 32, 41
s. 15 19
1927 Landlord and Tenant Act (17 & 18 Geo. 5, c. 36)—
s. 19(2) 57
1936 Public Health Act (26 Geo. 5 & 1 Edw. 8, c. 49)—
s. 18 82
s. 20 81
s. 24 82
1936 Public Health Act—*cont.*
s. 37 82
s. 38 82
1937 Public Health (Drainage of Trade Premises) Act (1 Edw. 8 & 1 Geo. 6, c. 40) 27
Coal (Registration of Ownership) Act (1 Edw. 8 & 1 Geo. 6, c. 56) 112
1938 Coal Act (1 & 2 Geo. 6, Ch. 52) 112
1939 London Building Acts (Amendment) Act (2 & 3 Geo. 6, c. xcvii) 17
1943 Coal Act (6 & 7 Geo. 6, c. 38) 112
1946 Coal Industry Nationalisation Act (9 & 10 Geo. 6, c. 59) 112
1947 Town and Country Planning Act (10 & 11 Geo. 6, c. 51) 45
1949 National Parks and Access to the Countryside Act (12, 13 & 14 Geo. 6, c. 97) 31
ss. 27–38 79
s. 87 105
1950 Coal Mining (Subsidence) Act (14 Geo. 6, c. 23) 113
1956 Clean Air Act (4 & 5 Eliz. 2, c. 52)—
s. 11 80
1957 Electricity Act (5 & 6 Eliz. 2, c. 48) 118
Coal Mining (Subsidence) Act (5 & 6 Eliz. 2, c. 59) 113
1961 Land Compensation Act (9 & 10 Eliz. 2, c. 33)—
s. 15 98
Public Health Act (9 & 10 Eliz. 2, c. 64) 27, 82
s. 12 82
s. 13 82
s. 29 17
1962 Building Societies Act (10 & 11 Eliz. 2, c. 37)—
s. 25 122

1962 Pipelines Act (10 & 11 Eliz. 2, c. 58) ... 122
s. 35 ... 109
1963 Water Resources Act (c. 38) ... 117
s. 32 ... 27
1965 Gas Act (c. 36) ... 119
1967 Misrepresentation Act (c. 7) ... 3, 8, 10, 12
s. 2 ... 3
(1) ... 7, 12, 13
(2) ... 7
s. 3 ... 3, 8, 9, 10, 11, 14, 15, 67, 74
s. 4 ... 3
General Rate Act (c. 9)—
s. 16 ... 50
s. 17 ... 50, 108, 109
s. 55 ... 50
s. 56 ... 50
s. 69 ... 51
s. 115 ... 50
Sched. 1 ... 50, 108
Matrimonial Homes Act (c. 75) ... 3
Leasehold Reform Act (c. 88) . 55, 59
1971 Town and Country Planning Act (c. 78) ... 85, 100
s. 22 ... 44, 101, 104
s. 22(1) ... 88
s. 23 ... 44
(*a*) ... 46
s. 34 ... 88
s. 44 ... 92
(2) ... 92
(3)(*a*) ... 92
(*b*) ... 93
s. 45 ... 91
s. 46 ... 91
s. 51 ... 91
s. 52 ... 105
s. 53 ... 88
s. 54 ... 101, 103, 104
(1) ... 99
s. 55(1) ... 102
(4) ... 102
s. 56(5) ... 101
s. 58 ... 99, 101
(1) ... 103
s. 60 ... 96
s. 87 ... 44, 89, 93
(1) ... 44
1971 Town and Country Planning Act—*cont.*
s. 87—*cont.*
(3) ... 44
(5) ... 93
(6) ... 93
s. 88 ... 94
(1) ... 94
s. 88A ... 94
s. 88B ... 94
s. 89 ... 93
(6) ... 93
s. 90 ... 93, 95
s. 92A ... 94
s. 96 ... 102
(3) ... 102
s. 98 ... 102
s. 101 ... 105
s. 114 ... 99, 103
s. 115 ... 99, 103, 105
s. 117 ... 103
s. 142 ... 106
s. 144 ... 106
s. 169 ... 96, 97, 98
s. 171 ... 101
s. 173 ... 104
s. 177 ... 96
s. 178 ... 91
s. 180 ... 91
(1) ... 45
s. 181 ... 92
s. 190 ... 102
ss. 209–210 ... 78
s. 242 ... 91
s. 244(1) ... 86
s. 245 ... 91
s. 277 ... 104
s. 290 ... 91, 98
Sched. 8 ... 103
Pt. II ... 96, 97
Scheds. 8–18 ... 97
Sched. 11 ... 101
1972 Gas Act (c. 60) ... 119
s. 32 ... 109
Land Charges Act (c. 61) ... 41, 65
1973 Land Compensation Act (c. 26)—
s. 71 ... 92
Water Act (c. 37) ... 116
s. 30 ... 25

1974 Local Government Act (c. 7)—
s. 21(*b*) 51
s. 21 51
(*a*) 51
Town and Country (Amenities) Act (c. 32) 104
1974 Control of Pollution Act (c. 40) 27
s. 63 79
s. 65 80
s. 67 79
Housing Act (c. 44)—
s. 118 59
1975 Coal Industry Act (c. 56)—
s. 2 113
Local Land Charges Act (c. 76) 19
s. 10(3) 73
1976 Water Charges Act (c. 9)—
s. 2 25
1977 Rent Act (c. 42) 58, 67
s. 4 58
s. 5(4) 58
Unfair Contract Terms Act (c. 50)—
s. 2 .... 14, 15
s. 8 .... 8, 74
s. 11 74
s. 11(1) 8
1978 Inner Urban Areas Act (c. 50)—
s. 4 108
1980 Housing Act (c. 51) 59
Limitation Act (c. 58)—
s. 2 74
s. 5 74
s. 11 74
s. 14 74
Local Government, Planning and Land Act (c. 65) ... 85, 96, 100
s. 134 106
s. 165 107
s. 166 107
s. 179 107
Sched. 15 101
Sched. 32 107
Highways Act (c. 66) 78
s. 1 75
1980 Highways Act—*cont.*
s. 36 75
s. 37 76
s. 38 77
ss. 116–118 78
s. 205 75
s. 228 76
1981 British Telecommunications Act (c. 38) 120
Local Government and Planning (Amendment) Act (c. 41) 44, 96
Wildlife and Countryside Act (c. 69) 31
s. 61 79
Sched. 17 79
Pt. II 79
1982 Supply of Goods and Services Act (c. 29)—
s. 13 4
s. 14 4
s. 18(1) 4
1983 Matrimonial Homes Act (c. 19) 3
Mobile Homes Act (c. 34) 70
1984 Registered Homes Act (c. 23) .. 80
1985 Town and Country Planning (Compensation) Act (c. 19)—
s. 1(2) 97
Local Government Act (c. 57)—
Sched. 1 83
Administration of Justice Act (c. 61)—
s. 1 4
s. 5 1
s. 7 1
Housing Act (c. 68)—
s. 253 81
s. 346 80
s. 347 80
Landlord and Tenant Act (c. 70) 63
ss. 1–3 57
s. 18 62
ss. 18–25 .... 59, 62, 65
s. 29 61

1 INTRODUCTION

General

This is the first in a series of conveyancing manuals for practitioners. The idea for the series was formulated at a time of growing public dissatisfaction with the system of residential conveyancing. Now the Administration of Justice Act 1985 contains provisions which extend the procedures for dealing with complaints against solicitors[1] and allow licensed non-solicitors to undertake conveyancing for reward.[2] The manuals will concentrate in the main on residential conveyancing, although much of what will be said applies equally to commercial and agricultural conveyancing. References to "solicitor" should be read as including licensed conveyancers where appropriate.

There follows, in chart form, a basic description of the conveyancing process. The topics covered by this manual—enquiries before contract—are identified in bold type.

Conveyancing procedure

PRELIMINARY

Preliminary agreement to buy

Vendor and Purchaser instruct solicitors

Vendor's solicitor	*Purchaser's solicitor*
Sends draft contract with copy Register entries and filed plan and, or other copy documents to →	
	Peruses draft contract and other documents Private surveyor instructed Application for mortgage made Searches Public Index Map (unregistered land) Makes local land charges search and **enquiries of the local authority**
←	**Raises enquiries before contract**
Answers enquiries before contract → (refers to client where necessary)	
	Search of Commons Register and, or Register of rents? **Other enquiries?** Considers replies to searches and enquiries with client together with mortgage offer and surveyor's report
Agrees contract Obtains vendor's signature to contract	Agrees contract Obtains purchaser's signature to contract and deposit

[1] s.5.
[2] s.7.

EXCHANGE OF CONTRACTS

Insurance is necessary as from date of contract as risk passes to purchaser
Protection of contract by registration?

Supplies abstract of title or authority to inspect Register →

Investigates title
← Prepares draft conveyance or transfer and requisitions on title. Reserves right to raise further requisitions on behalf of mortgagee

Notifies mortgagee of redemption and obtains redemption figure and "daily rate"

Replies to requisitions and approves conveyance or transfer →

CONTRACT TO COMPLETION

If not acting for mortgagee—sends all documents to mortgagee's solicitor; receives mortgagee's requisitions and draft mortgage from mortgagee's solicitor, replies to mortgagee's requisitions by raising further requisitions with vendor's solicitor if necessary; mortgagee agrees loan
If acting for purchaser and mortgagee—reports on vendor's title to mortgagee; drafts mortgage

Replies to any additional requisitions →

Makes land charges search or official search of register (and "Bankruptcy only" land charges search if necessary)
Search of Companies register?

Prepares completion statement →

Mortgage executed
← Dispatches engrossed conveyance or transfer (sometimes bearing purchaser's signature)

Makes final arrangements for completion

Confirms arrangements for completion
Obtains completion moneys from mortgagee and purchaser

COMPLETION

AFTER COMPLETION

Redeems mortgage
Accounts to client

If not acting for mortgagee sends all documents to mortgagee's solicitor
Otherwise attends to stamping and registration where appropriate

Forwards receipted mortgage or Form 53 →

Conveyancing committee's recommendation

As part of their package for reducing to three weeks the length of a normal house or flat purchase, the Farrand Committee "strongly recommended" that vendors should supply to purchasers replies to enquiries of the local authority and standard preliminary enquiries.[3] The objections to "Vendor's enquiries" are that they quickly become out of date and that the vendor's idea of what enquiries should be made may not correspond with the purchaser's.

Enquiries before contract

The past 20 years have seen the conveyancer's pre-contract work assume mammoth proportions. Several factors have contributed to this—the rule of *caveat emptor*, ever-increasing public control over private ownership of property, the passing of the Misrepresentation Act 1967, *Williams & Glyn's Bank Ltd.* v. *Boland and Brown*,[4] and recent developments in the law of professional negligence.[5] Each of these factors will be explored in the following pages. Here our particular concern is with professional negligence.

Proper enquiries

A purchaser's solicitor is obliged to make such enquiries before contract as are appropriate to the transaction in hand[6] and to discuss the replies with the purchaser.[7] Two types of enquiries are appropriate to most transactions and are made using standard forms, namely preliminary enquiries of the vendor and enquiries of the local authority. These are dealt with in Sections 2 and 3 respectively. In addition less usual enquiries may have to be made, depending on the status of the purchaser (private person or developer) and the geographical location of the property to be purchased. Section 4 looks at other sources of information.

Negligence

Failure to make these enquiries on the purchaser's behalf may lead to liability in negligence. Three recent cases involving the two "usual" enquiries can be cited by way of example. In *Computastaff Ltd.* v. *Ingledew Brown Bennison & Garrett*[8] the purchaser's solicitors were held to be negligent in not checking the stated rateable value of the property in replies to preliminary enquiries with the vendor's solicitors, after it had been queried by the purchaser. In *Raintree Ltd.* v. *Holmes & Hills*[9] solicitors acting for a development company negligently forgot to check the currency of a planning permission relating to the land purchased. It was due to expire shortly after completion. And in *Holmes* v. *Kennard*[10] the purchasers' solicitors failed to appreciate that since February 14, 1983 a spouse's rights to occupy the matrimonial home[11] can only be protected by the entry of a

[3] Second Report of the Conveyancing Committee, 1985, para. 9.4.
[4] [1981] A.C. 487.
[5] Beginning with *Hedley Byrne & Co. Ltd.* v. *Heller & Partners Ltd.* [1964] A.C. 465.
[6] *Goody* v. *Baring* [1956] 1 W.L.R. 448.
[7] *Hill* v. *Harris* [1965] 2 Q.B. 601.
[8] (1983) 268 E.G. 906.
[9] (1984) 134 New L.J. 522.
[10] (1985) 49 P. & C.R. 202.
[11] Under the Matrimonial Homes Act 1983, replacing the Matrimonial Homes Act 1967 (as amended).

notice on the register of title. Their oversight resulted in their being held liable in negligence to their clients. When it comes to enquiries other than those in standard form the position appears to be that liability in negligence is only avoided by acting in accordance with the best conveyancing practice accepted by the profession.[12] This can of course lead to difficulties where the practitioner is not familiar with the area in which the property is situated, and the advice of a local estate agent or surveyor might usefully be sought. The onus of proving that he has acted with due professional care rests on the practitioner.[13]

A vendor's solicitor who negligently gives an incorrect answer to enquiries may be liable to the vendor. In *Sharneyford Supplies Ltd.* v. *Edge*[14] the vendor was entitled to be indemnified by his solicitor for the loss he had suffered because of the latter's negligent statement in reply to an enquiry to the effect that the vendor's tenants were licensees.

Liability to third parties

Whether acting for purchaser or vendor liability may lie not only to one's client, but also to third parties. In *Wilson* v. *Bloomfield*[15] the Court of Appeal accepted as arguable the purchaser's contention that the vendor's solicitors owed him a duty of care in answering enquiries before contract.

Statutory provisions

Attention is also drawn to the Supply of Goods and Services Act 1982, which implies certain terms into contracts for services, including one for the provision of conveyancing services.[16] Section 13 of the Act implies the term that the supplier will carry out the service with reasonable care and skill, according to section 14, within a reasonable time. It is not thought that the Act increases or alters in any way the common law liability of solicitors acting in conveyancing transactions, as outlined above. It should also be noted that section 1 of the Administration of Justice Act 1985 gives the Council of the Law Society power to order a solicitor to remit or repay part or all of his costs, or to take specified action in the client's interests, where it is considered that the solicitor has provided inadequate professional services.

Sometimes it is impossible for enquiries to be made before contracts are exchanged, either because the solicitor is not instructed until after contract, which occurs in some sales by auction, or because the client wishes to enter into the contract immediately. In such a case enquiries should be carried out as soon as possible after the date of the contract.[17] Both sets of standard conditions allow for the contract to be made subject to the purchaser obtaining satisfactory replies to his enquiries. Law Society condition 4 and National condition 5 may be incorporated into the contract by special condition if the parties so desire.

[12] *G. & K. Ladenbau (U.K.) Ltd.* v. *Crawley & de Reya* [1978] 1 W.L.R. 266.
[13] *Ashcroft* v. *Mersey Regional Health Authority* [1983] 2 All E.R. 245.
[14] [1985] 1 All E.R. 976.
[15] (1979) 123 S.J. 860; and see *Wadsworth* v. *Lydall* [1981] 1 W.L.R. 598.
[16] s.13 and s.18(1).
[17] See *Simpson* v. *Grove Tompkins & Co.* (1982) 126 S.J. 347.

2 PRELIMINARY ENQUIRIES OF THE VENDOR

Introduction

Caveat emptor

The general rule in the law of contract is that a vendor is under no duty to disclose material facts to a prospective purchaser: "the failure to disclose a material fact which might influence the mind of a prudent contractor does not give the right to avoid the contract."[1] This *caveat emptor* rule applies to sales of land[2] with one exception: a vendor must disclose latent defects in his title, that is incumbrances and other adverse matters of title which a purchaser could not reasonably discover for himself by inspecting the property.[3]

Function of preliminary enquiries

The function of preliminary inquiries is to discover information materially affecting the property for sale. This fact is often forgotten in practice today. On the one hand purchasers' solicitors, for fear of being negligent,[4] send off "standard" additional questions as a matter of routine. On the other hand, because untrue answers may bring the vendor liability in misrepresentation or his solicitor liability in negligence, replies to enquiries, additional or otherwise, can be "no more informative than an official communique."[5] And it is indeed mean justice that a practice devised by solicitors solely to improve the lot of purchasers should now be used against them to deprive them of

[1] *Bell* v. *Lever Brothers Ltd.* [1932] A.C. 161 at 227.

[2] *Terrene* v. *Nelson* [1937] 3 All E.R. 739 at 744.

[3] *Yandle & Sons* v. *Sutton* [1922] 2 Ch. 199 (right of way). Law Society condition 5(1) additionally requires the vendor to disclose any patent easements and other rights of which he knows or ought to know other than those known to the purchaser at the date of the contract or which a prudent purchaser would have discovered by that date by making the usual searches and enquiries. And see *Hone* v. *Benson* (1978) 248 E.G. 1013 where "amateur builder"-vendors owed a duty of care to their purchasers in respect of an allegedly faulty central heating system constructed and installed by them on the property. Lord Grantchester said in *Sakkas* v. *Donford Ltd.* (1982) 46 P. & C.R. 290 at 302 that a vendor was liable to disclose *material facts adversely affecting the property sold*. This was however *obiter* and seems wider than the established rule which is limited to latent defects in title. Also see *Gordon* v. *Selico Co. Ltd.* (1986) 18 H.L.R. 219, which suggests that the *caveat emptor* rule has no application whatsoever where a purchaser is induced by fraud to enter into a contract for purchase. The vendors had fraudulently concealed the presence of dry rot in a flat (by a cosmetic building work) prior to granting a lease of it to the purchasers. The vendors were ordered to pay the purchasers damages in deceit for fraudulently misrepresenting that the flat was free from dry rot.

[4] A purchaser's solicitor should make usual enquiries; *Goody* v. *Baring* [1956] 1 W.L.R. 448 (failure to enquire as to terms of tenancies), *Raintree Ltd.* v. *Holmes & Hills* (1984) 134 New L.J. 522 (failure to check currency of planning permission) and communicate the replies to his client; *Hill* v. *Harris* [1965] 2 Q.B. 601. But see *Simpson* v. *Grove Tompkins & Co.* (1982) 126 S.J. 347—purchaser's solicitor negligent in losing purchase through delay before contract.

[5] H. W. Wilkinson (1980) 130 New L.J. 1215, and see J. E. Adams [1983] Conv. 341.

their conveyancing monopoly, being instanced as a prime example of the delay, expense and futility involved in a present day conveyancing transaction.

Improved usage of preliminary enquiries

Many suggestions have been made for the improved usage of preliminary enquiries. The Farrand Committee rejected imposing a general legal duty of disclosure on vendors, but recommended requiring vendors in practice or by statute to supply to purchasers with the draft contract replies to standard preliminary enquiries.[6] Other suggestions include that vendors' solicitors be entitled to charge the purchaser for answering additional enquiries above a certain number, or alternatively that the Law Society lay down guidelines as to the types of matters on which enquiries should or should not be entertained, the purchaser being entitled to an unequivocal rely to those questions which the Law Society regards as acceptable. No one suggests abandoning preliminary enquiries altogether. Perhaps the simplest solution is for the purchaser's solicitor to ask only those questions, additional or standard, which are pertinent to the purchase in hand, and for the vendor's solicitor to be as helpful as possible in delivering the replies.

Standard forms

The climate is such that even Oyez's 40 year monopoly over the standard forms of enquiries before contract is now challenged. Two "pirate" sets of standard preliminary enquiries have appeared on the market, one produced by the Unilaw Group of Publishers,[6a] the other by Shaw & Sons Ltd.[6b] We shall look in detail at the form with which the majority of readers are most familiar—Oyez's Con 29 (Long)[7] Enquiries Before Contract—which was substantially modernised in 1984 and revised in April 1985 to take account of the abolition of development land tax. Variations on the other two forms will be mentioned as appropriate. (The forms themselves appear in the Appendices.)

Legal status of the replies

First then the terms on which the replies are given. Con 29 contains this disclaimer of responsibility:

The disclaimer

> "These replies, except in the case of any enquiry expressly requiring a reply from the Vendor's solicitors, are given on behalf of the proposed Vendor and without responsibility on the part of his solicitors their partners or employees. They are believed to be correct but the accuracy is not guaranteed and they do not obviate the need to make appropriate searches, enquiries and inspections."

The disclaimer consists of two parts, each serving a different purpose. For the sake of clarity the second half of the disclaimer will be discussed first.

[6] The Second Report of the Conveyancing Committee (1985), Part II.

[6a] Viz. Stephen Cox & Co. (Law Stationers) Ltd., Holbrook & Gration Ltd., Jordan & Sons Ltd., Meredith Ray & Littler Ltd., Services to Lawyers Ltd. and Dennis Welbourn Ltd. And see J. E. Adams (1985) 135 New L.J. 170.

[6b] Format and Stat-plus also produce standard forms of enquiries before contract but confines of space have led us to choose Unilaw and Shaw & Sons Ltd.'s forms for comment in the text.

[7] Oyez also produce a Con 29 (Short) which basically covers the same ground as Con 29 (Long) but leasehold enquiries are omitted.

"THEY [the replies] ARE BELIEVED TO BE CORRECT BUT THE[8] ACCURACY IS NOT GUARANTEED AND THEY DO NOT OBVIATE THE NEED TO MAKE APPROPRIATE SEARCHES, ENQUIRIES AND INSPECTIONS."

This part of the disclaimer is aimed at relieving the *VENDOR* of liability for misrepresentation.

Misrepresentation

A misrepresentation is an untrue statement of fact made by one party to a contract to the other, which while not forming a term of the contract, induces the other to enter into the contract.

At one time rescission of the contract *and* damages could only be obtained when the misrepresentation was made fraudulently ("1. knowingly or 2. without belief in its truth, or 3. recklessly, careless whether it be true or false."[9]) For non-fraudulent misrepresentation (negligent or innocent) rescission was the only remedy and it was generally too late if the contract had been completed by conveyance. To this there was one important exception. Equity, utilising the general doctrine of "constructive fraud," allowed damages to be recovered for negligent misrepresentation (one made without reasonable cause for believing it to be true) where the parties stood in a fiduciary relationship.[10]

Hedley Byrne v. Heller

In 1963 the House of Lords decided the famous case of *Hedley Byrne & Co. Ltd.* v. *Heller & Partners Ltd.*[11] and added another exception to the general rule for non-fraudulent misrepresentation. Where a "special relationship" exists between the parties an action would lie in tort for negligent misstatement (not negligent misrepresentation *stricto sensu*). Thus in *Esso Petroleum Co. Ltd.* v. *Mardon*[12] the plaintiff[13] company let a garage to M. One of the company's agents, an experienced salesman, told M. that the turnover would be approximately 200,000 gallons a year. In the event, it was found to be less than half of that. It was held that the plaintiffs owed a duty of care to M. since they knew he would rely on their estimates in deciding to take a lease of the garage. The advice was clearly inaccurate because the salesman had negligently failed to take into account all the relevant factors. The plaintiffs were liable for M.'s loss.

Negligent misstatement

The Misrepresentation Act 1967

The Misrepresentation Act 1967 now gives the representee more valuable remedies. Those relating to fraudulent misrepresentation remain the same, but where a misrepresentation is made negligently the representee may sue for damages either instead of or as well as rescinding, even after conveyance.[14] No duty of care need be shown and it is for the representor to prove that he had reasonable grounds to believe, and did believe that the facts represented were true. An innocent misrepresentation also entitles the representee to rescind the contract but does not give him the additional right to claim

[8] Should this not be "their"?
[9] *Derry* v. *Peek* (1889) 14 App.Cas. 337, *per* Lord Herschell at 374.
[10] *Nocton* v. *Lord Ashburton* [1914] A.C. 932.
[11] [1964] A.C. 465.
[12] [1976] Q.B. 801.
[13] The defendant, M., was counterclaiming to the company's claim for arrears of rent under the lease.
[14] s.2(1) and (2).

damages. The court can award damages in lieu of rescission for both negligent[15] and innocent misrepresentation.

Nevertheless negligent misstatement should not be forgotten. An action at common law might well be preferred for any of the following reasons. First under *Hedley Byrne & Co. Ltd.* v. *Heller & Partners Ltd.*[16] the plaintiff does not have to prove that a "misrepresentation" has been made, only a misstatement. Secondly, if a "special relationship" is shown heavier damages may be awarded. And thirdly, the 1967 Act only applies "where a person has entered into a contract"—what if the contract is never entered into or is void *ab initio* for mistake as a result of the statements?

Suppose the vendor, his solicitor or other agent misrepresents the true state of affairs in replies to preliminary enquiries, for example, regarding existing boundary disputes as in *Walker* v. *Boyle*,[17] how far will the disclaimer protect him?

How far does the disclaimer protect the vendor?

The first point to note is that the disclaimer is conditional upon belief (presumably the vendor's) in the correctness of the replies. If belief is lacking the disclaimer is inoperative.[18] In *Coats Paton (Retail) Ltd.* v. *Birmingham Corporation*[19] the defendant corporation issued a wrong reply to a supplemental enquiry to a local search. Their disclaimer stated that the replies were furnished after appropriate enquiries and in the belief that they were in accordance with available information but on the understanding that they were not legally liable for them. The appropriate enquiries had not been made, the disclaimer was conditional upon this being done, and the corporation were liable for the plaintiffs' loss as a result of the reply.

Secondly, the clause must be read in the light of section 3 of the Misrepresentation Act 1967, which, as altered by section 8 of the Unfair Contract Terms Act 1977 now reads:

> "If a contract contains a term which would exclude or restrict
> (*a*) any liability to which a party to a contract may be subject by reason of any misrepresentation made by him before the contract was made; or
> (*b*) any remedy available to another party to the contract by reason of such misrepresentation that term shall be of no effect except in so far as it satisfies the requirement of reasonableness as stated in section 11(1) of the Unfair Contract Terms Act 1977. . . . "

Requirement of reasonableness

Section 11(1) of the Unfair Contract Terms Act provides that "reasonableness" means that "the term shall have been a fair and reasonable one to be included, having regard to the circumstances which were, or ought reasonably to have been known to or in the contemplation of the parties when the contract was made." It is for the vendor to show that the clause is reasonable. Because the court in each case must have regard to the circumstances in which the contract was made, the Con 29

[15] s.2(2).
[16] [1964] A.C. 465.
[17] [1982] 1 W.L.R. 495.
[18] *Re Englefield Holdings Ltd. and Sinclair's Contract* [1962] 1 W.L.R. 1119.
[19] (1971) 69 L.G.R. 356.

clause may be reasonable in one case and unreasonable in another.[20] The circumstances of the case in *South Western General Property Co. Ltd.* v. *Marton*[21] were that an innocent misrepresentation was made in an auction catalogue when it described land as "Long Leasehold Building Land" and disclosed a particular refusal of planning permission for a proposed house on grounds of design, but failed to mention that planning permission was unlikely to be given for any dwelling on the site, because it was within a conservation area and any infill development would be detrimental to the visual amenities of the local community. Disclaimer clauses in the catalogue stated (*inter alia*) that the property was believed to be correctly described and that "any intending purchaser must satisfy himself by inspection or otherwise as to the correctness of each statement contained in the particulars." The purchaser, Mr. Marton, was a builder who was looking for land on which to build a home for himself and his family. He only got the auction catalogue from the auctioneers the day before the auction and looked at the site the morning of it. Time prevented him from making the usual searches and enquiries but having read the auction catalogue and talked with the auctioneers before the sale he was confident that if he submitted plans for a house which was in character with the area, he would be allowed to build. In deciding whether or not the disclaimer clauses protected the vendors, Mr. Croom Johnson pointed out that people do attend auctions at short notice and do not have time to make enquiries of the vendor's solicitors and local authority. He said that he had to consider whether these conditions were reasonable to be included in a contract, "not with property speculators in mind in which case they might very well be reasonable, but in a case such as a householder like Mr. Marton who is very clearly concerned, if he wants to buy for himself, with planning matters." And he concluded that for the parties to *this* contract and the circumstances in which *this* contract was made: "The [vendors] have not satisfied me that these are terms which are fair and reasonable to have been included in the contract . . . at the time of this auction. These terms if they were included, would exclude liability for failure to tell the purchaser more than only a part of the facts which were among the most material to the whole contract of sale." The vendors could not rely on the disclaimers.

George Mitchell (Chesterhall) Ltd. v. Finney Lock Seeds Ltd.

The only real guideline as to the requirement of "reasonableness" given by the courts so far is more in the nature of a warning to those who are aggrieved at a first instance decision that a clause is unreasonable. In *George Mitchell (Chesterhall) Ltd.* v. *Finney Lock Seeds Ltd.*[22] the House of Lords said that an appellate court should only interfere with the original decision if it was based on some erroneous principle or was "plainly and obviously wrong."

Preliminary enquiries not part of contract?

It has been argued that the disclaimer on Con 29 is not caught by section 3 of the Misrepresentation Act as preliminary enquiries are not part of the contract. This argument was effectively annihilated by Lord Justice Bridge in *Cremdean*

[20] See generally H. W. Wilkinson [1984] Conv. 12–21.
[21] (1982) 263 E.G. 1090.
[22] [1983] 2 A.C. 803, followed recently in *Phillips Products Ltd.* v. *Hyland* (1985) 129 S.J. 47.

Properties Ltd. v. *Nash*,[23] where he said of a similar exclusion clause that if it was not contractual it could not help the vendor and if it was contractual it would offend section 3.

Con 29 warns the purchaser that the accuracy of the replies is not guaranteed and that he should rely on his own searches, enquiries and inspections. Shaw & Sons Ltd. throw the burden of verifying the replies on the purchaser, he "must verify all replies to the extent that the same admit of independent verification by inspection, examination, survey, searches, or otherwise." In *Cremdean Properties Ltd.* v. *Nash*[24] it was argued that this type of clause (the latter variety) contained in auction particulars prevented from being a representation of fact, the vendor's statement in the particulars that the premises sold had outline planning permission for a development of about 17,900 square feet of office space; the Misrepresentation Act did not apply. Lord Justice Bridge, in the Court of Appeal, thought the clause had the opposite effect; it was saying that the vendor was making a representation, which he believed was true but invited the purchaser to verify. The call on the purchaser to conduct his own investigations was only relevant to the question of whether the purchaser did rely on the statement. The clause was a purported exclusion of liability for misrepresentation and therefore fell within section 3. Lord Justice Scarman felt that to hold otherwise would be to dash the Misrepresentation Act to pieces.

Attempts to deny making of representation of fact

Walker v. Boyle

A similar approach was adopted by Dillon J. in *Walker* v. *Boyle*.[25] Mrs. Boyle's solicitors stated in reply to a preliminary enquiry that no disputes affected the property sold. Mrs. Boyle was however in the middle of an argument with a neighbour over the position of a boundary fence. When Mr. Walker discovered this he claimed rescission of the contract and return of the deposit. The reply was made on the 1980 version of Con 29 which used this disclaimer: "These replies on behalf of the vendor are believed to be correct but the accuracy is not guaranteed and they do not obviate the need to make appropriate searches, enquiries and inspections." The judge held that the disclaimer was inadequate to deprive the reply of the quality of being a representation of fact. Any vendor would know that the replies he gave to preliminary enquiries were likely to be relied on by a purchaser. The disclaimer should be ignored.

Attempts to deny reliance

Shaw & Sons Ltd. purport to deny another essential ingredient of an actionable misrepresentation, namely "reliance." Their introductory "Notes" state that "the replies are not given by the Vendor to induce the Purchaser to enter into any Agreement." Although this type of clause is yet untested it too is probably doomed to failure, especially in the light of Lord Justice Bridge's comment in *Cremdean* v. *Nash*[26]: "that if the ingenuity of a draftsman could devise language [which would have the effect of bringing about a situation in law as if no representation at all had ever been made],[27] I am extremely doubtful whether

[23] (1977) 244 E.G. 547 discussed in (1978) 128 New L.J. 79.
[24] (1977) 244 E.G. 547.
[25] [1982] 1 W.L.R. 495 and see case note by K. Hodkinson, [1982] Conv. 46.
[26] (1977) 244 E.G. 547 at 551.
[27] Borrowed from earlier in the judgment.

the court would allow it to operate so as to defeat section 3."

In view of what has been said above it is also unlikely that qualifying replies with words such as "so far as the vendor knows" will relieve the vendor of liability for misrepresentation, despite the older authority of *Gilchester Properties Ltd.* v. *Gomm.*[28] Nevertheless to guard against the possibility of that decision being followed, *Emmet on Title*[29] advises the purchaser: "if it is proposed to rely on [the replies] the vendor should be called on to insert a term in the contract warranting their accuracy."

Using an agent

There is one way a vendor can avoid liability for misrepresentation, and that is "by channelling every statement through the disinfecting medium of an agent."[30] It was held in *Overbrooke Estates Ltd.* v. *Glencombe Properties Ltd.*[31] that it was permissible and not contrary to section 3 for a vendor by means of sale particulars to limit the ostensible authority of his agents to make representations about the property being sold. There one of the general conditions of a sale by auction read: "The Vendors do not make or give and neither the Auctioneers nor any person in the employment of the Auctioneers has any authority to make or give any representation or warranty in relation to [the property]." The purchasers claimed that the auctioneers told them before the sale that the local authority had no proposals for the property and that this induced them to enter into the contract. They later found out that a clearance programme might affect the property and refused to complete. An order of specific performance was granted against them. The condition effectively protected the vendor, even if the auctioneers did make the alleged statement. The purchasers bought knowing that anything the auctioneers said could not bind the vendor. *Overbrooke* was applied in *Collins* v. *Hugh Jones.*[32] The purchaser bought a property having been misled by the vendor's estate agents over the possibility of building another storey. The agent's sale particulars included a statement that: "The vendor does not make or give, and neither [the estate agents] or any person in their employment has any authority to make or give, any representation or warranty whatever in relation to this property." It was held that the agents' statement established their own lack of authority to make any representations. These decisions have been criticised on the ground that they mean, "a veritable convoy of coach and fours can trundle through the 1967 statute."[33] Furthermore such a formula prefacing replies to preliminary enquiries is hardly conducive to the smooth running of a conveyancing transaction. It must be noted that an *Overbrooke* type clause will not work if the vendor gives his agent authority to make representations about the property.

Incidentally, the *Overbrooke* formula back-fired in *Mustafa* v. *Baptist Union Corporation Ltd.*[34] The auction particulars of a

[28] [1948] 1 All E.R. 493.
[29] (18th ed.), p. 11.
[30] J. E. Adams [1981] Conv. 326 at 328.
[31] [1974] 1 W.L.R. 1335 and see H. W. Wilkinson (1978) 128 New L.J. 79.
[32] (1977) 241 E.G. 837.
[33] J. E. Adams [1981] Conv. 326 at 328 and see H. W. Wilkinson [1984] Conv. 12.
[34] (1983) 266 E.G. 812.

house failed to mention the existence of a blocked-off room with external access only, let to a neighbour.[35] The purchaser succeeded in claims for rescission and damages. In reply to the vendors' argument that the purchaser could have discovered that the room was tenanted by asking the auctioneers, the court said that even the most prudent purchaser could not be expected to make enquiries of an agent who was held out to have no authority to make statements about the property.

Damages for non-fraudulent misrepresentation to be assessed on tortious basis

The measure of damages under the Misrepresentation Act is tortious rather than contractual. Damages for loss of bargain are not normally available.[36] This view was recently endorsed by Mervyn Davies J. in *Sharneyford Supplies Ltd.* v. *Edge*.[37] The vendor contracted to sell a maggot farm to the purchasers with vacant possession. He was unable to give vacant possession on completion because the farm was occupied by periodic tenants. The purchasers sued the vendor for breach of contract and non-fraudulent misrepresentation—his solicitor had stated in reply to a preliminary enquiry that the tenants had no security of tenure and that the farm would be vacated before completion. It was held that the vendor had done all he could to complete the conveyance[38] and consequently the purchasers' contractual damages were limited by the rule in *Bain* v. *Fothergill*[39] to their conveyancing costs. Their claim for £131,544 loss of profits was excluded. Nor could they recover this sum in an action for negligent misrepresentation. Here they had hoped to rely on *Watts* v. *Spence*[40] where Graham J. held that the fact that the vendor entered into a contract of sale amounted to a negligent misrepresentation that he could convey the property.[41] Damages awarded to the purchaser under section 2(1) of the 1967 Act included a sum for loss of bargain even though *Bain's* rule limited the damages for breach of contract. Mervyn Davies J. in *Sharneyford* refused to follow the previous decision. He said: "An action on the new statutory right [s.2(1) of the Misrepresentation Act] is an action in which damages will be measured as in tort, not contract; and in tort, as I understand, loss of bargain damages may not, in every case, be recoverable."[42] The purchasers could only have been awarded substantial damages if they had proved deceit (fraudulent misrepresentation). Deceit would have removed the *Bain* bar on their recovering *contractual* damages for loss of bargain.[43] The new statutory tort of negligent misrepresentation does not have the same effect. It has nothing to do with the rule in *Bain* v. *Fothergill*.

No damages for loss of maggot business

[35] The Psychiatric Rehabilitation Association!

[36] McGregor, *Damages* (14th ed.), paras. 1486–1489.

[37] [1985] 1 All E.R. 976. H. W. Wilkinson (1985) 135 New L.J. 676.

[38] This is questionable because the vendor could have paid the tenants the £12,000 they demanded to quit the farm. See *Re Daniel* [1917] 2 Ch. 405.

[39] (1874) L.R. 7 H.L. 158. The rule limits the damages recoverable by a purchaser where the contract is broken because the vendor, provided he is acting in good faith, cannot make good title. The purchaser is only entitled to return of his deposit and expenses incurred in investigating the vendor's title.

[40] [1976] Ch. 165 followed in *Errington* v. *Martell-Wilson* (1980) 130 New L.J. 545.

[41] The vendor was only one of two joint tenants and the other would not concur in the sale.

[42] [1985] 1 All E.R. 976 at 990.

[43] *Day* v. *Singleton* [1919] 1 K.B. 435, *Malhotra* v. *Choudhury* [1980] Ch. 52.

Sharneyford seems[44] to have put paid to the usefulness of trying to extract from vendors in reply to preliminary enquiries, express statements about their good titles free from incumbrances, a practice which grew up in the wake of *Watts* v. *Spence*[45] and which is reflected in Shaw & Sons Ltd.'s general enquiry 3(a): "Is the Vendor aware of any title imperfections (major or minor) which might cause problems."

Loss of bargain damages may still be recoverable in domestic conveyancing

However it has been suggested[46] that tortious damages for non-fraudulent misrepresentation could include an element for loss of bargain in residential conveyancing. The example is given of a purchaser who contracts to buy a house for £30,000. The deal goes off when the vendor is found liable of negligent misrepresentation under section 2(1) of the 1967 Act. The tort method of assessing damages is to put the purchaser in the position he would have been in had the misrepresentation not been made. His position was having the purchasing power to buy the vendor's type of house for £30,000. If there has been an increase in prices and an equivalent house would now cost £32,000 then the purchaser's damages should be £2,000. This would of course not help *Sharneyford* type purchasers. They were claiming for the profits they expected from use of the land. This necessitates a contractual method of calculation which puts the purchaser in the position he would have been in if the statement in the contract had been true.

Damages for loss of bargain or no, it should be more than apparent that those acting for vendors should warn them of the importance of giving accurate replies to preliminary enquiries.

Loss suffered by others in chain

They should further be made aware of the possibility that loss suffered by others in the purchase and sale chain of whom the vendor knows (perhaps even ought reasonably to have known of) might be recoverable from him as damages if the loss of his own sale through misrepresentation causes them to lose their contracts.[47]

Agents not within s.2(1)

Two more points before we revert back to the opening words of the disclaimer. First, in *Resolute Maritime Inc.* v. *Nippon Kaiji Kyokai (The Skopas)*[48] the following question of law was considered as a preliminary issue: "If an agent, acting in his express or ostensible authority, makes a statement which is untrue in circumstances where he did not have reasonable ground to believe that it was true, can he [the agent] be held liable under section 2(1) of the Misrepresentation Act 1967." Mustill J. answered "No." He held that the purpose of the Act was to fill the gap in the remedies for misrepresentation available to a contracting party before 1967, that is that as a general rule he could not claim damages from the other contracting party for a non-fraudulent misrepresentation made by that other or his agent. Agents were already liable for their own negligent statements under the principle laid down in *Hedley Byrne & Co. Ltd.* v. *Heller & Partners Ltd.*[49] The importance of the decision

[44] It is understood that the purchasers intend to appeal.
[45] [1976] Ch. 165.
[46] M. P. Thompson [1985] Conv. 137–146.
[47] *Wadsworth* v. *Lydall* [1981] 1 W.L.R. 598; T. M. Aldridge (1981) 125 S.J. 732.
[48] [1983] 1 W.L.R. 857.
[49] [1964] A.C. 465.

for present purposes is that if the purchaser wishes to pursue his remedies under the Act for a non-fraudulent representation made by the vendor's solicitor or other agent (innocent or negligent) then he must proceed directly against the vendor. The vendor, who is thus subjected to liability will be able to gain an indemnity from his agent in the tort of negligence if the misrepresentation was made negligently. This in fact occurred in *Sharneyford*. But where the misrepresentation was made by the agent innocently, the vendor has no comeback.

Disclaimer and vendor's negligent misstatement

Secondly, does the disclaimer shield the vendor if the purchaser sues him for negligent misstatement? It is likely that section 3 will apply to the disclaimer even though the vendor may not have made a misrepresentation *stricto sensu*; a statement of opinion perhaps as in *Esso Petroleum Co. Ltd.* v. *Mardon*.[50] In *Cremdean Properties Ltd.* v. *Nash*,[51] Lord Justice Bridge said that for the purposes of section 3 "representation" should be given a wide interpretation. If section 3 was excluded the disclaimer might still be subjected to the "reasonableness" test by section 2 of the Unfair Contract Terms Act 1977, as a clause excluding liability for negligence, but only if the vendor was acting in the course of business.[52] Since to found an action in negligent misstatement the purchaser has to show a "special relationship" it might well be that the misstatement was made in the course of a business transaction.

> "THESE REPLIES, *EXCEPT IN THE CASE OF AN ENQUIRY EXPRESSLY REQUIRING A REPLY FROM THE VENDOR'S SOLICITORS*, ARE GIVEN ON BEHALF OF THE PROPOSED VENDOR AND WITHOUT RESPONSIBILITY ON THE PART OF HIS SOLICITORS THEIR PARTNERS OR EMPLOYEES."

Purported exclusion of vendor's solicitors liability for negligence

The object of this part of the disclaimer is to protect the vendor's solicitor from liability in tort to the purchaser for negligent misstatements about the property. The first point to note is that if the vendor's solicitor makes a reply fraudulently he will be liable to the purchaser in the tort of deceit.[53] Secondly, if he has reasonable cause to believe his statement to be true he attracts no liability. Only where he has no such reasonable cause can he be guilty of negligence.

Wilson v. Bloomfield

The clause was introduced into the disclaimer on the advice of the Council of the Law Society as a result of the decision in *Wilson* v. *Bloomfield*.[54] The purchaser was told in replies to preliminary enquiries that there were no boundary disputes. There were. The purchaser, *inter alia*, sued the vendor's solicitors for damages in negligence; they knew that he would rely on their replies being accurate, they should have known of the boundary dispute and they therefore owed him a duty of care. The solicitors were unsuccessful both at first instance and in the Court of Appeal in getting the claim against them struck out of

[50] [1976] Q.B. 801.
[51] (1977) 244 E.G. 547.
[52] s.1(3).
[53] *Derry* v. *Peek* (1889) 14 App. Cas. 337.
[54] (1979) 123 S.J. 860.

the purchaser's action; he had an arguable point in law. The decision led to the fear that a vendor's solicitor could be liable to a purchaser (even though represented by his own solicitor) in negligence if he knows or ought reasonably to have foreseen that the purchaser would rely on his careless statement.[55] Presumably this duty of care could be owed to others in the conveyancing chain.

Some[56] have expressed doubts as to whether the clause falls within the purview of section 3, arguing that it is not a contractual term. However it is probably caught by section 2 of the Unfair Contract Terms Act 1977 because it purports to exclude liability for negligence. A solicitor clearly answers preliminary inquiries in the course of his business. The effectiveness of the clause will therefore depend on its reasonableness in any particular case.

Amendment in 1984 revision of Con 29

The words in italics, "except in the case of any enquiry expressly requiring a reply from the Vendor's solicitors" were added in the 1984 revision to meet accusations[57] that it is unfair to expect a vendor to shoulder liability for answers that only his solicitor can give. The obvious example is the new enquiry 12(B): "The Purchaser's solicitors wish to complete by adopting the Law Society's Code for Completion by Post (1984 edition). Do the Vendor's solicitors agree?" Neither of the other two forms incorporate this exception to the blanket denial of responsibility which they claim.

Finally it must be said that if the vendor's solicitor answers enquiries that are within the vendor's province himself, in other words does not refer them to his client, then he cannot have reasonable grounds for believing his replies to be true, and cannot use the disclaimer to cloak his fault.

The standard enquiries before contract

General and Leasehold

Layout

All three forms boast a similar layout. Oyez and Unilaw include their general and leasehold and a space for additional enquiries on one form. Shaw & Sons Ltd. prefer the purchaser to send separate sheets of leasehold and additional enquiries (left blank for the purchaser to draft his own) with their master form of general enquiries. Let us now look at the enquiries themselves, with those on Con 29 forming a framework for discussion.

1. Boundaries[58] (Unilaw, 1; Shaw & Sons Ltd., 4)

(A) To whom do all the boundary walls, fences, hedges and ditches belong?

(B) If no definite indications exist, which has the Vendor maintained or regarded as his responsibility?

[55] As will be the case in most conveyancing transactions.

[56] J. E. Adams [1982] Conv. 236, and on previous wording H. W. Wilkinson (1967) 117 New L.J. 975; (1970) 67 L.S. Gaz. 257.

[57] H. W. Wilkinson (1980) 130 New L.J. 1215.

[58] See generally T. M. Aldridge *Boundaries, Walls and Fences* (5th ed.).

Vendor's contractual obligation re boundaries

Under an open contract it is doubtful that the vendor is under a duty to define the ownership of the boundaries of the property for sale.[59] The standard conditions of sale[60] resolve this doubt in favour of the vendor. He is under no obligation to warrant or provide any evidence as to the boundaries. The purchaser must glean what information he can on the subject before making the contract. The vendor's solicitor will normally answer the question by reference to the title deeds or register of title. With regard to the latter it should not be forgotten that Land Registry filed plans indicate general boundaries only,[61] unless they are noted as fixed, and cannot be relied upon in a boundary dispute.

Oyez recognise that ownership and maintenance of boundaries do not necessarily go hand in hand, a fact not fully appreciated by the draftsmen of the other two forms. Unilaw asks: "Has the property mooring rights attached to its river boundary?" "Altogether too esoteric for inclusion in a general form"[62] says Professor J. E. Adams, with whom we must agree.

Plans

Unilaw also ask for a plan showing the maintenance of boundaries and the situation and length of party walls. If a plan, detailing ownership or maintenance of boundaries, is supplied, care must be taken to see that it is accurate. In *Jackson* v. *Bishop and Walter Thomas Properties Ltd.*[63] plots on a "luxurious and high class building development" in Hampshire were sold by reference to an inaccurate site plan. The result was that part of the same plot was sold twice, the second purchaser getting less land than he bargained for. He had completed his purchase, so that the developers' liability was for breach of the implied covenants for title. But it was further held that the developers owed a duty of care to the purchaser to ensure that the site plan was accurate. And dicta suggest that he could also have been guilty of misrepresentation even though a note on the site plan warned: "The plot boundaries as shown may be subject to adjustments." Nor is the case necessarily limited to developers. According to Fay J. in *Hone* v. *Benson*[64]: "no valid distinction or no distinction of principle can be drawn between the case of a vendor who is a professional builder, or for that matter a professional estate developer, and a vendor who is a private individual. . . . " As a final warning, in the *Jackson* case, the developers' solicitors were asked in preliminary enquiries to colour the plot being sold. This they did on the incorrect plan. The court treated it as a representation binding on the vendors.

Party walls

Unilaw's enquiry into the situation of party walls could usefully be incorporated into the other two forms. Two 1983 cases *Bradburn* v. *Lindsay*[65] and *Tollemache and Cobbold Breweries Ltd.* v. *Reynolds*[66] make it clear that adjoining

[59] *Dawson* v. *Brinckman* (1850) 3 M. & G. 53.
[60] Law Society condition 13, National condition 13, reproduced in Apps. O and P.
[61] Land Registration Rules 1925, rr. 278 and 279.
[62] (1985) 135 New L.J. 171.
[63] [1982] Conv. 324.
[64] (1978) 248 E.G. 1013 at 1013–1014.
[65] [1983] 2 All E.R. 408 but see *Marchant* v. *Capital and Counties Property Co. Ltd.* (1982) 263 E.G. 661.
[66] (1983) 268 E.G. 52.

landowners owe each other not only a duty of support but also a duty not to make alterations to a party wall so as to adversely affect its weather-resisting qualities. Remedies lie in injunction, declaration, or damages depending on the facts of the case. In *Bradburn* the defendant's property was demolished,[67] in *Tollemache* destroyed by fire, both leaving a party wall exposed to the elements. The principle is equally applicable to where construction work has the same effect. However it does not apply unless the properties are linked by a party wall. It was decided in *Phipps* v. *Pears*[68] that where A's house stood very close to B's house (but was detached) and afforded it considerable protection, and damp entered B's wall when A's house was pulled down, then B had no remedy at common law.[69] There was no easement of weather proofing.[70] Party walls in London[71] are subject to special rules and indeed special definitions and reference should be made to the London Building Acts (Amendment) Act 1939.

2. Disputes (Unilaw, 1; Shaw & Sons Ltd., 7)

(A) Is the Vendor aware of any past or current disputes regarding boundaries, easements, covenants or other matters relating to the property or its use?

(B) During the last three years, has the Vendor complained or had cause to complain about the state and condition, or the manner of use, of any adjoining or neighbouring property? If so, please give particulars.

Boundaries most fruitful cause of disputes

Most solicitors feel that a general enquiry on disputes like 2(A) above is justified because no purchaser can be expected to buy himself into a legal wrangle. Some delete "or other matters" before replying, another[72] always answers: "we habitually advise vendors not to answer." Despite the width of the enquiry it is a well-known fact that boundaries are the most fruitful source of litigation between neighbours.[73] This is recognised by Unilaw who link the two in their first question and omit any general enquiry on disputes. The Farrand Committee[74] saw no solution to the problem of boundary disputes. They agreed that better plans would bring more certainty to conveyancing, but reminded us that: "accurate plans can only show the physical boundaries—they can do nothing to guarantee the legal boundaries which depend upon agreement between neighbours as well as between vendors and purchasers."[75]

67 By the local authority because of the defendant's neglect but it would not have affected the outcome of the case had she removed the house herself.

68 [1965] 1 Q.B. 76.

69 But see s.29 of the Public Health Act 1961. A local authority may serve notice to have a building shored up, weatherproofed or repaired when a person has begun or intends to begin the demolition of the adjacent building and this work will affect the first building. The owner of the first building may be called upon to contribute towards the work.

70 For a discussion of the cases mentioned in this paragraph see H. W. Wilkinson (1983) 133 New L.J. 1121, P. Jackson [1984] Conv. 54.

71 The Inner London boroughs, the City of London and the Temples.

72 Professor J. E. Adams.

73 See Fifth Annual Report of the Lay Observer 1979 where Maj. Gen. J. C. R. Allen said: "I have been surprised by the frequency of these disputes and I have been appalled by the extreme bitterness which they so often generate."

74 The Second Report of the Conveyancing Committee, January 1985. See 4.62–4.63 and 6.43–6.47.

75 *Ibid.* 6.43.

Reform? Fixed boundaries in registered land?[76] "The perennial problem with such a proposal is the need to obtain prior agreement as to the precise boundaries from neighbours" Expensive, even if possible, and bound to cause a spate of boundary disputes between neighbours. Further, even if agreed, boundaries can be altered informally later.[77] The Committee, like the Law Commission in their Report on Land Registration,[78] were in favour of the retention of the general boundaries rule. They did however suggest for consideration clarifying the status of boundaries. One idea they did not seem to favour because it could waken sleeping disputes, was to replace or supplement enquiry 2(A) by a question asking whether the boundaries are agreed, and if not the extent and nature of any disagreements. Making such an enquiry would also incur additional expense and delay.

Wilson v. Bloomfield We have already mentioned the case of *Wilson* v. *Bloomfield*,[79] which illustrates that vendors' solicitors should be wary of answering this enquiry without direct reference to their clients. To recap, the solicitors replied to enquiries before contract that their client was not aware of any boundary disputes. There were such disputes and they were sued by the purchaser on the basis that they knew he would rely on their replies being accurate and therefore owed a duty of care to him. The Court of Appeal decided that the purchaser had an arguable point of law.

Enquiry 2(B) new Enquiry 2(B) was newly added to the form in the 1984 revision, the idea being to give the purchaser as much advance warning as possible of potential trouble with neighbours. The three year period has no legal significance. It was just thought a suitable back-period for making such enquiries.

3. Notices (Unilaw, 2; Shaw & Sons Ltd., 7)

> Please give particulars of all notices relating to the property, or to matters likely to affect its use or enjoyment, that the Vendor (or to his knowledge, any predecessor in title) has given or received.

Overlap with local searches? Enquiry 3 could be criticised for overlapping the purchaser's local searches[80] but in truth it supplements them. Suppose the local authority is intending to widen the road fronting the property for sale. They will have served the vendor with notice of their proposals. The purchaser's enquiries of the local authority will show that a notice has been served and where it can be inspected but may not give further details.[81] Here the purchaser is saving time and trouble by asking the vendor in advance for a copy of the notice.

[76] *Ibid*. 4.62–4.63 and 6.44.

[77] By agreement, estoppel or adverse possession, see *Hopgood* v. *Brown* [1955] 1 W.L.R. 213 and *Neilson* v. *Poole* (1969) 20 P. & C.R. 909.

[78] (1983) Law.Com. No. 125.

[79] (1979) 123 S.J. 860.

[80] Used in the wider sense to include a local land charges search and enquiries of the local authority.

[81] See below, pp. 92–96.

Non-registration of local landcharge no defence to criminal prosecution

Local searches would not have helped the purchaser in the type of situation which arose in *Vale of Glamorgan Borough Council* v. *Palmer*,[82] whereas a revealing reply to this enquiry would. A landowner was prosecuted for contravening a tree preservation order which had not been registered as a local land charge. Nor had a map relating to it been deposited as required by the Town and Country (Tree Preservation Order) Regulations 1950. The divisional court held that because a map had not been deposited in accordance with the regulations, the order was invalid and could not be contravened. But it added that non-registration as a local land charge did not matter. That was required for civil matters only and can have no effect on criminal liability whatsoever. Significance for purchasers? In cases before the Local Land Charges Act 1975, as this case was, section 15 of the Land Charges Act 1925 provided that an unregistered local land charge was void against a purchaser of a legal estate for money or money's worth. Apparently that now means void, unless the purchaser contravenes a restriction and is prosecuted. Local land charges created after the 1975 Act are not void for non-registration. Instead the purchaser is entitled to compensation. Would that compensation include a fine for recovery? Unlikely.[83]

The enquiry also embraces notices relating to private actions. Examples might be a writ served by or against a neighbour for private nuisance or a notice of claim served on the National House-Building Council for a defect in the property covered by their Scheme.

Comparison with standard conditions of sale

Readers may care to link this enquiry and its answers, to the vendor's disclosure obligations under the standard conditions of sale. By Law Society condition 5(1): "The vendor warrants that he has disclosed to the purchaser the existence of all easements, rights, privileges and liabilities affecting the property, of which the vendor knows or ought to know, other than the existence of those known to the purchaser at the date of the contract, or which a prudent purchaser would have discovered by that date." National condition 14 imposes on him the much lesser liability of disclosing: "all latent easements and latent liabilities known to the vendor to affect the property. . . . " Where the Law Society's contract for sale is used enquiry 3 is in fact unnecessary, at least so far as written notices are concerned. Condition 3(3)(*a*) requires him to disclose the contents of any *written* communications relating to any "relevant matter" received by or known to the vendor, before contracts are exchanged. The condition is wider than the enquiry in that it is not restricted to notices received or given by the vendor; narrower because it does not include oral notices. "Relevant matters" are defined by Law Society condition 3(2) as:

(a) A requirement[84] of, or matter capable of registration by, a "competent authority." A "competent authority" means[85]

[82] (1983) 81 L.G.R. 678.

[83] But query whether there is sufficient *mens rea* for criminal liability unless the purchaser has actual knowledge.

[84] By condition 3(1)(*b*) "requirement" includes (whether or not subject to confirmation) any notice, order or proposal.

[85] Condition 3(1)(*a*).

a local authority or other body exercising powers under statute or Royal charter, for example government departments.

(b) All matters disclosed or reasonably expected to be disclosed by searches and as a result of enquiries formal or informal, and whether made in person, by writing or orally by or for the purchaser or which a prudent purchaser ought to make. This category includes local land charges, local authority proposals relating to the property and matters covered by standard preliminary enquiries.

(c) All notices served by or on behalf of a reversioner, a tenant or sub-tenant, or the owner or occupier of any adjoining or neighbouring property.

Under the National conditions the vendor is only required to disclose planning matters of which he is aware. This would include things like the notice of a road widening scheme, used earlier as an example.

Before concluding the discussion on notices we feel that it is worth mentioning Shaw & Sons Ltd.'s equivalent enquiry because of its commendable brevity. They link disputes and notices in one question and ask:

> "Does the Vendor know of
> (b) any notice received from any source."

4. Guarantees, etc. (Unilaw, 3; Shaw & Sons Ltd., 8)

(A) Please supply a copy of any of the following of which the Purchaser is to have the benefit:
agreement, covenant, guarantee, warranty, bond, certificate, indemnity and insurance policy, relating to any of the following matters:

the construction of the property, or any part of it, or of any building of which it forms part;
any repair or replacement of, or treatment or improvement to the fabric of the property;
the maintenance of any access way;
the construction costs of any road (including lighting, drainage and crossovers) to which the property fronts, and the charges for adopting any such road as maintainable at the public expense;
a defective title;
breach of any restrictive covenant.

(B)(i) What defects or other matters have become apparent, or adverse claims have been made by third parties, which might give rise to a claim under any document mentioned in (A)?

(ii) Has notice of such defect, matter or adverse claim been given? If so, please give particulars.

(iii) Please give particulars of any such claims already made, whether or not already settled.

Con 29. Enquiry 4 restyled in 1984

Although the content remains the same, Oyez inform us[86] that enquiry 4 has been restyled and rephrased in an effort to

[86] Oyez Forms Information Service announcement, October 5, 1984.

simplify its structure. Be that as it may, the advantage of the old enquiry 4 was that Part (A) drew the vendor's attention to the precise nature of the documents, copies of which the purchaser wanted, and to which the questions in Part (B) applied. Now vendors' solicitors will in many cases find it necessary to enumerate them for clients, so that none are forgotten.

National House Building Council's scheme

It may be beneficial to list the most common "Guarantees" revealed by this type of enquiry. Part (A) of the old enquiry 4 provides a useful reminder. 4(A)(i) asked for copies of the agreement and certificate or insurance policy with notice of insurance cover where the property is covered by the National House-Building Council's scheme.[87] (The equivalent request in the new enquiry comes from the words "agreement . . . certificate . . . insurance policy, relating to . . . the construction of the property. . . . ") Basically the scheme, which is insurance based, applies to houses, bungalows, maisonettes and flats, built, converted or renewed and sold with the benefit of the scheme by builder/developer-vendors who are registered with the Council. It gives 10 years protection to original and subsequent purchasers of new houses, against non-completion of the building and defects or damage which later occur. Purchasers of conversions are protected for seven years. The main drawback of the 1975–79 scheme (which only applied to new dwellings) was that the insurance cover given by the Council was not inflation-linked. The first purchaser could counteract this problem by buying "top-up cover." This was not available to second or subsequent purchasers, although if taken up by the first purchaser, was automatically transferred to them. Solicitors acting for second purchasers of new homes therefore had to check the extent of insurance cover in preliminary enquiries. Great changes were made to the scheme for new dwellings in 1979. Chief among these was that insurance cover became inflation-linked. So if property is being sold with the benefit of a 1979 agreement (H.B.5 (1979)) the extent of cover need not be checked; if with the benefit of a 1977 agreement (H.B.5 (1977)) "Top up cover" is important. The Council's scheme was extended to conversions in December 1983. (The documentation is distinguishable by its bright orange colour). Insurance cover is not inflation linked. No "top up cover" is available at present but we are informed[88] that it may be in the near future.

Is express assignment of N.H.B.C agreement necessary?

Both the original and conversion National House-Building Council schemes require the owner to first pursue his remedies against the developer/builder-vendor where the defect or damage occurs during "the Initial Guarantee Period"—two years from the date of the original purchase for new homes, one year for conversions. One grey area within the scheme has always been: Is an express assignment of the benefit of the agreement vital to enable a second purchaser to sue the builder/developer for breach of the agreement? After all the agreement is only made between the builder/developer vendor and the *first* purchaser. The Council's rules have consistently contained a provision

[87] See generally Tapping and Rolfe, *Guarantees for New Homes* (2nd ed., 1981), and Annand and Cain, *Modern Conveyancing* (1984), Chap. 10, and J. E. Adams (1980) 130 New L.J. 171 and 196.

[88] By the Council's legal department, August 1985.

prohibiting registered vendors from taking objection in proceedings or otherwise to the fact that the benefit of the agreement has not been assigned to the purchaser making the claim. Now clause 10 of both agreements states: "The Vendor undertakes that he shall not seek to deny liability under this Agreement on the ground that it has not been assigned." Should the builder/developer plead the lack of assignment as a defence to a purchaser's claim, he would lay himself open to disciplinary proceedings and probably removal of his name from the Council's register, but the possibility of having to meet a large claim might well outweigh the unpleasantness of these sanctions. Then the purchaser would have to rely on the decision in *Marchant* v. *Caswell and Redgrave Ltd.*[89] and the doubtful use of section 78 of the Law of Property Act 1925 to make the benefit of the agreement run with the land, or claim that the builder/developer is estopped from relying on the lack of assignment because of the undertaking he has given in Clause 10. The assignment point could also be important where the purchaser is forced to sue the builder/developer on his common law obligations[90] because the particular defect or damage is not covered by the scheme or because it occurs outside the 10 year period.[91] In view of this many solicitors acting for second purchasers of new homes (or conversions) prefer to take an express assignment of the benefit of the agreement. Readers might like to know that the Council's overall liability presently stands at £30 million.[92]

N.H.B.C. Building Control Services Ltd.

A new building control system has been introduced for new dwellings.[92a] A developer or builder may opt for N.H.B.C. Building Control Services Ltd., a wholly-owned subsidiary of the N.H.B.C., to carry out building control supervision instead of the local authority. Submission by N.H.B.C. Building Control Services Ltd. and the developer or builder of an "initial notice" to the local authority will become the statutory equivalent to building regulation consent. The N.H.B.C. guarantee that building regulation work will be completed satisfactorily and that if, exceptionally, the initial certificate is cancelled and a final certificate cannot be issued, the purchaser who has exchanged contracts will not be financially prejudiced. The N.H.B.C. also provide extra insurance for new dwellings when its subsidiary has carried out building control. The cover is contained in a new section IV of the House Purchaser's Insurance Policy 1985 issued

[89] (1976) 240 E.G. 127, followed in *Federated Homes Ltd.* v. *Mill Lodge Properties Ltd.* [1980] 1 W.L.R. 594.

[90] Clause 3 of the Agreement (new homes and conversions) provides: "The Vendor warrants to the Purchaser that the Dwelling has been or will be built in an efficient and workmanlike manner and of proper materials and so as to be fit for habitation," repeating the rule in *Hancock* v. *Brazier (Anerly) Ltd.* [1966] 1 W.L.R. 1317.

[91] If the purchaser founds his claim in negligence (limitation might bar his contractual claim) express assignment of the benefit of the Agreement is essential unless the damage is still continuing. A cause of action in negligence vests in the owner of the dwelling when the damage occurs (*Pirelli General Cable Works Ltd.* v. *Oscar Faber & Partners* [1983] 2 A.C. 1) and does not pass to a purchaser.

[92] For dwellings with agreements bearing the number N.96000 and higher.

[92a] The Building (Approved Inspectors, etc.) Regulations 1985 (S.I. 1985 No. 1086); (1986) 83 L.S. Gaz. 15.

for all dwellings registered for inspection after November 11, 1985 (Part IV only applies where N.H.B.C. Building Control Services Ltd. does the building control).

The N.H.B.C. say[92b] that existing conveyancing procedures will only be slightly affected. In response to enquiry 4 the new insurance policy will be handed over and the purchaser's solicitor will know whether section IV applies by the reply to enquiry 9 on Con 29, which will show an "initial notice" or building regulation consent for the dwelling.

The new building control system does not apply to flats more than four storeys or mixed developments (flats above shops, for example).

Part 4(A)(ii) of the former enquiry asked whether any insurance policy had been taken out to cover any defect in title or breach of restrictive covenant (now " . . . insurance policy . . . relating to . . . defective title; breach of restrictive covenant.")

Title insurance Title insurance has been common in the United States for some time, but is not used extensively here. Most major insurance companies offer insurance against breach of restrictive covenant or defective title, but only after they have satisfied themselves that the particular restrictive covenant cannot or will not be enforced or that the defect in title is purely technical and the risk is minimal. In other words they are happy to insure against "dormant" risks but none will insure against "live" risks. Where insurance is taken out payment is usually by a single premium. The Farrand Committee[93] saw no future in this country for title insurance on the American scale.

Other guarantees 4(A)(iii) was aimed at discovering what guarantees, certificates, insurance policies and so on related to the fabric of the property. Guarantees for new roofs, double glazing, treatment of woodworm or dry rot, new central heating, extensions, damp proofing, electrical wiring *et al.*—these spring into the minds of most vendors on reading an enquiry like 4(A), new or old. They nearly always need to be expressly assigned to the purchaser.

Maintenance of roads, etc. Next, 4(A)(iv) requested a copy of any "agreement or covenant for the maintenance by some other person of any road or footpath over which rights of access to the property are enjoyed," now neatly shortened into "agreement, covenant . . . relating to . . . the . . . maintenance of any access way." Any forthcoming copy will show the purchaser the extent of his obligations in relation to the access way. The final question of the old 4(A) requested documentation relating to the construction of the road fronting the property or sewers under it and details of road charges payable on its adoption as maintainable at the public expense. The equivalent request in the new 4(A) is wider, in that crossovers and lighting are expressly included. The question is particularly important to purchasers of new properties. It will be seen in the next chapter[94] that in the case of new housing developments the builder/developer generally agrees with the local and water authorities to construct the necessary roads and

[92b] Queries on the new scheme should be addressed to the N.H.B.C. Legal Department, Chiltern Avenue, Amersham, Bucks. HP6 5AP. The N.H.B.C. will be issuing a booklet on the new building control system.

[93] The Second Report of the Conveyancing Committee, 1985, para. 6.50–6.52.

[94] See below, pp. 72 and 82.

sewers and maintain them until they are taken over by the relevant authority. (The price of the properties reflecting the cost to the builder/developer.) If the builder/developer fails to complete the construction to the standard specified in the agreement the authority can do the work and charge the frontagers. Where the builder/developer is also in liquidation (as is often the case) the purchasers cannot recoup the cost. For this reason the authorities usually insist that the agreement is supported by a bond; a guarantee. In cases of default the purchasers can then recover their expenses from the bondsman. The purchaser's enquiries of the local authority will reveal the existence of any agreement and bond. The demand here for copies is so that the purchaser can see, first that the construction work is up to standard and second that the bond is adequate to cover any charges he might have to pay.

Bonds

Unilaw's and Shaw & Sons Ltd.'s guarantee questions

Unilaw's and Shaw and Sons Ltd.'s questions on guarantees, etc., look much the same as the old enquiry 4(A). One criticism of both is that they envisage "top-up cover" in the National House-Building scheme to be the norm rather than the exception. Unilaw put their enquiry much more directly: "Has the property the benefit of . . . ?" then follows a list of the guarantees etc. Part of their quest to invent "a form whose questions are more specific and demand specific answers."[95] One commentator[96] sees two difficulties with the question. First, it will gain no more information than 4(A), where the vendor has had major works carried out to the property, which he prefers not to disclose and which are not guaranteed or the guarantees have expired. The general law puts him under no duty to disclose the work and a negative answer to the enquiry cannot involve him in liability for misrepresentation. Secondly, and this applies equally to the other two publishers' questions, if there are guarantees, etc., but the vendor answers, "None," there is technically a misrepresentation but what has the purchaser lost? In the case of major works the commentator suggests that the benefit of having unexpected guarantees might be outweighed by the purchaser having been deprived of pre-contractual knowledge of the works.

Shaw & Sons Ltd. further ask if the vendor has claimed under any insurance policy or guarantee for flooding, subsidence, damp rot or infestation. This is reminiscent of the old "hell and disaster" question 9 on Con 29 which most practitioners found objectionable as more properly suited to the purchaser's survey, and which was dropped from the form in the 1973 revision. In areas where for example flooding or subsidence is known to have occurred and possible resultant damage would not show up on a survey, this question is quite proper, but is probably more suitably phrased as an additional rather than a general enquiry.

Notification of N.H.B.C. claims

It is only necessary to make one comment on Oyez's new enquiry 4(B). To derive any benefit under the National House-Building Council's scheme purchasers (original or subsequent) must notify any claim promptly and in writing to the builder/developer during the "Initial Guarantee Period," and thereafter to the Council. It is therefore very important to a second purchaser of a new or converted property covered by the

[95] Unilaw's advertising leaflet.

[96] J. E. Adams (1985) 135 New L.J. 170.

scheme to ensure before exchange of contracts that the vendor has reported any defect or damage in the proper manner and obtain an undertaking from him to notify any claims arising before completion.

5. Services[97] (Unilaw, 4; Shaw & Sons Ltd., 6).

(A) Does the property have drainage, water, electricity and gas services? Which of them are connected to the mains?
(B) Is the water supply metered?
(C) Do any of the services (except where part of the mains) pass through or over property not included in the sale?
(D) If so please give details of route and particulars of any easement, grant, exception, reservation, wayleave, licence or consent authorising this.
(E) Please supply a copy of any licence to abstract water and of any consent or licence relating to drainage, issued in respect of the property or the activities carried on there.

Enquiry 5 has been expanded[98] to cover water supply meters, water abstraction licences and licences and consents relating to drainage. Like enquiry 1 it demands information not obtainable from the vendor once contracts have been exchanged.

5(A) calls for little comment. The purchaser will probably have the answer anyway, from the estate agent's particulars or the vendor himself. However if you are acting for a purchaser of a lock-up shop with no water, sink or drainage facilities, you might additionally ask how surface water is drained. In *South West Water Authority* v. *Rumbles*[99] the tenant of such a shop on the ground floor of a building, otherwise comprising residential accommodation, objected to a sewerage charge of £196. Surface water ran from the roof of the building down a pipe, into a gulley and then into the water authority's sewer and they claimed that they were entitled to make the charge under section 30 of the Water Act 1973. This, as amended by section 2 of the Water Charges Act 1976,[1] provides that a water authority has power to fix such charges for the services performed, facilities provided, or rights made available, as it thinkss fit. The House of Lords said that the amended section 30 should be given a wide meaning. The tenant had the use of the roof and its drainage facility, even though the residential accommodation separated him from it, and this clearly benefited the shop. The water authority could make the charge.

How is surface water drained?

Route of mains services

Unilaw follow their enquiry "is there mains water, mains electricity, gas, drainage" with the request: "If so, please supply plan showing the running of these services if it is not already dealt with in the contract." Although it is wildly over-optimistic to expect the majority of vendors to comply with this request, the location of mains equipment can be of considerable importance to

[97] See generally, H. W. Wilkinson, *Pipes, Mains, Cables and Sewers* (4th ed., 1984).
[98] In the 1984 revision.
[99] [1985] A.C. 609.
[1] The amendment was made because of *Daymond* v. *South West Water Authority* [1976] A.C. 609 where it was held that a water rate was not payable by a person who is not connected to the water supply. Now a reduced rate can be levied.

a purchaser, especially one who intends to develop or work the land. Water authorities, electricity boards, gas boards and for that matter British Telecom all have powers to acquire and enter onto private land to install, inspect, repair, replace or renew their installations, sometimes at the expense of the landowner. Further it is an offence to damage any of their property or interfere with the provision of their services. Reference for information should however not be made to the vendor but to the authority concerned.[2]

Water supply meters

Most of us pay for our water as a percentage of the general rate. Water authorities will however on request and on payment of a moderate fee (about £30) install a water supply meter on premises. Thereafter the consumer pays a rental fee for the meter and is charged so much per gallon (say 6p) for water used. Having a meter is really only advantageous to those who own property with a high rateable value or consume little water. If a positive reply is given to 5(B) it would be appropriate to enquire further into the present cost of a gallon of water and of renting the meter.

The laying of pipes, etc., by private agreement

5(C) and 5(D) should be read together. They concern the laying of pipes, cables and so on by private agreement, implication or prescription. Take for example a property which is supplied with water from adjoining premises, or drains its foul water through a neighbour's land into a public sewer or drains water from its roof down through a pipe or gulley onto other land. The purchaser needs to know that he will be able to continue to enjoy these rights when he becomes the new owner of the property. Yet once contracts have been exchanged the vendor is under no obligation to disclose any benefits with which the property is sold. Most pipes and so on are laid by easement; the benefit therefore runs with the land. The purchaser's solicitor should however insist that they are included in the description of the property in the contract.[3] This will in due course entitle him to investigate title to them. Not only must he satisfy himself that the easements have been validly created (in accordance with common law or statute) but he must also ensure that they are sufficient in extent for the purchaser's purposes. For example, an easement to drain rainwater through B's land would be no good if the purchaser needs to get rid of sewage. Occasionally the right to lay pipes and so on in land of another is permitted by licence. The benefit of such a licence cannot always be assigned to the purchaser[4] and may need to be renegotiated with the licensor.

Water abstraction licences

The beginning part of 5(E) was included to prevent the valuable asset of a water abstraction licence being lost to the

[2] The rights of these owners are probably easements; *Re Salvin* [1938] 2 All E.R. 498.

[3] Omission is not fatal, as the conveyance will pass all existing easements without express mention (Law of Property Act 1925, s.62).

[4] A bare licence (one without consideration) is personal to the licensee and will cease on assignment; *Terunnanse* v. *Terunnanse* [1968] A.C. 1086. The assignability of a contractual licence depends on the terms of a contract; *Clore* v. *Theatrical Properties Ltd.* [1936] 3 All E.R. 483. A licence coupled with an interest in land (highly unlikely to be encountered in connection with services) is assignable; *Muskett* v. *Hill* (1839) 5 Bing N.C. 694 at 707–708. A licence protected by equity (*e.g.* proprietary estoppel or approbate and reprobate) can be enjoyed and enforced by the successor in title of the licensee; *Hopgood* v. *Brown* [1955] 1 W.L.R. 213.

purchaser. The Water Resources Act 1963 provides that, subject to certain exceptions, a licence is required before any person is entitled to abstract water from any inland water, such as a river or underground strata, in the water authority area. If the holder of a water abstraction licence ceases to be the occupier of the land specified in his licence, then his successor, as occupier of that land, becomes the holder of such licence automatically, but unless that successor gives notice to the relevant water authority of the change of occupation within one month of the date of change of occupation, he will cease to be the holder of that licence which will therefore lapse.[5] A letter[6] sent by Anglian Water Authority to *The Law Society's Gazette* just before the revised Con 29 came out, suggested that notification was not being made on purchasers' behalf, primarily due to the existence of water abstraction licences not being discovered until well after completion. Licences and consents for drainage were added to the form for the sake of completeness, and are more likely to be encountered where non-domestic activities are carried out on the property for sale. Take, for example, the sale of a launderette. Discharge from launderette washing machines is trade effluent[7] and licence or consent should have been obtained from the local water authority to drain this into a sewer.[8] Any drainage licence would of course be in the name of the vendor and it would be sensible to arrange for it to be transferred into the purchaser's name on completion. Neither Unilaw nor Shaw & Sons Ltd. mention licences to abstract water or for drainage expressly, although Unilaw ask about licence fees for water abstraction in their question "Outgoings." Users of these forms should draft an additional enquiry along the lines of 5(E) where the circumstances of the case make one appropriate.

6. Facilities (Unilaw, 5; Shaw & Sons Ltd., 5)

(A) Except in the case of public rights or where particulars have already been given, what rights are there for the use of the following facilities whether enjoyed by the owner or occupier of the property or over the property for the benefit of other property:
- — Access for light and air;
- — Access for pedestrians and vehicles;
- — Emergency escape routes;
- — Pipes and wires for services not dealt with in enquiry 5.
- — Access and facilities for repair and maintenance.

Please supply copies of any relevant documents.

(B) Has any person taken any action to stop (whether immediately or at some future time) the use of any facility? If so, please give particulars.

[5] Water Resources Act 1963, s.32.
[6] (1984) 81 L.S. Gaz. 2425.
[7] *Thames Water Authority* v. *Blue and White Launderettes Ltd.* [1980] 1 W.L.R. 700.
[8] Public Health (Drainage of Trade Premises) Act 1937, Public Health Act 1961; as amended by the Control of Pollution Act 1974.

(C) In respect of maintenance, repair or replacement work on any land or fixtures affording any facility:
(i) What work has been done by the Vendor (or to his knowledge, any predecessor in title) and when?
(ii) What work has the Vendor been called upon to do which has not yet been done?
(iii) What sums has the Vendor contributed to work done by others and when? Is any demand for such sums still outstanding?
(iv) What sums has the Vendor called upon others to contribute and when? Is any demand still outstanding?

Con 29 enquiry 6—new

Six is new.[9] Former enquiries 6 (Exclusive Facilities) and 7 (Shared Facilities) have been combined together to form a single enquiry headed "Facilities," and "the draftsman has taken the opportunity to restyle and re-draft the enquiry to facilitate use." Our concern for the new 6 is the same as for the new 4; in its revised form it is not nearly as readily comprehensible to the lay vendor as were its predecessors. Moreover, there is now an overlap with enquiry 7 (formerly 8). The facilities questions were designed to complete the purchaser's quest (begun by 4) for the "credits" going with the property for sale. Six continues to provide a net to catch benefits escaping revelation under enquiries 4 and 5. But it also asks the vendor to disclose burdens: "What rights are there for use of the following facilities . . . over the property for the benefit of other property . . . ?" Burdens are more appropriately dealt with in the next enquiry. We understand that Oyez's draftsmen find (and have found) the facilities question the most difficult of all the preliminary enquiries to draft. If the current trend towards "plain English"[10] continues, they expect to have to revise it again. Perhaps difficulty in drafting is the reason why Unilaw and Shaw & Sons Ltd. omit a question like 6 from their forms, although they do poach on a bit of its ground. Shaw & Sons Ltd. have a question headed "Access" (5), and Unilaw in "Adverse rights; restrictions etc." ask (5(f)): "Is the Property sold with the benefit of (i) rights of access (ii) rights of air and light (iii) rights of common over other land. If so, please let us have details."

The medley of rights a purchaser can expect to be revealed by enquiry 6 include the right to go onto a neighbour's land to repair an outside wall of the property with any restrictions on or payment for the right, arrangements for the use and maintenance of private sewers, roads, footpaths and so on, and party wall agreements.

Joint driveways

The Court of Appeal recently had to consider the rights of neighbours over a joint driveway. Envisage two houses separated by a drive which is not wide enough for the owner of either to have access to his house or garage without using part of the other's half of the drive. Three possibilities exist. The drive might belong to one of the owners alone, the other having a right of way to gain access to his house; or the two might own the drive jointly holding it on trust for sale for themselves as tenants in common; or each might own part of the drive subject to a right of way over it for his neighbour.

[9] In the 1984 revision.
[10] [1984] Conv. 325.

Williams v. Usherwood

The last possibility was the case in *Williams* v. *Usherwood.*[11] A plan will help to explain the facts:

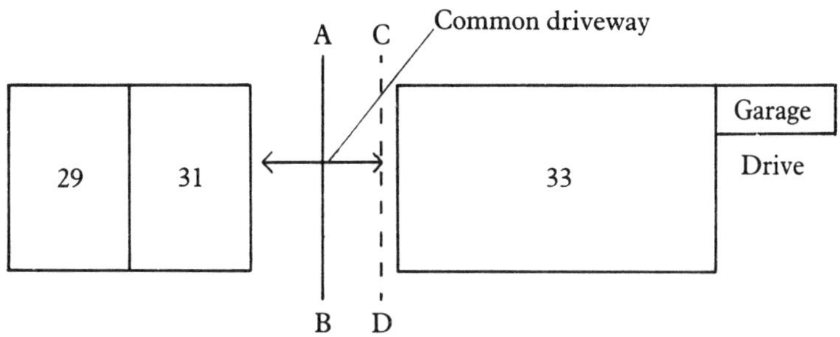

The dispute concerned a driveway running between semi-detached No. 31 and detached No. 33 on a housing estate. When the properties were originally sold in 1935, 2'6" worth of drive was conveyed to No. 33, the rest to No. 31 (marked A–B on the plan). Each conveyance reserved a right of way to the owner and occupier of the property to use the other's part of the drive at all times "with or without motor-cars." The transfer of No. 31 contained a covenant to fence the property but since putting a fence down the middle of the drive would obstruct it, the then owners of Nos. 31 and 33 agreed that the fence should be constructed alongside the outer wall of No. 33 (marked C–D on the plan). This left the eaves and windows, when opened, of No. 33 projecting into the airspace above the fence, and its drains and footings running under the drive. The only cars ever to use the drive were those belonging to No. 31. No. 33 had its own garage and drive on the other side of the property. In 1937 a Mrs. Whitehorne bought No. 31 and it was clear that she thought the boundaries of her house were as fenced. Later as a war-time measure a gate was built in the fence giving No. 33 access to the drive, but from then until it was nailed up in 1952 it was only used by the neighbours to visit each other. In 1952 the then owner of No. 31 built a garage. In 1962 the defendants bought No. 31 (they again believed the extent of the property to be as fenced). They frequently parked cars on the whole width of the drive and resurfaced it in 1974. In 1975 the then owners of No. 33 reopened the gate to gain access to the drive to maintain their outside wall. By 1979 the plaintiffs had bought No. 33. There was a quarrel and they claimed the original right of way granted to them in 1935.

The Court of Appeal, clearly swayed by No. 31's parking of cars, garage-building and resurfacing of the drive, held that the defendants had acquired possessory title to the drive:

> "(a) without dispossessing the plaintiffs of the eaves or projections or fixtures of or on their house and
> (b) subject to a right in the nature of an easement for the plaintiffs and their successors in title to enter on the drive for the purpose of maintenance of the south side of number 33, its windows and fixtures and its drainage apparatus."

[11] (1983) 45 P. & C.R. 235; H. W. Wilkinson (1984) 134 New L.J. 144, M. Dockray [1983] Conv. 396.

This idea of a person acquiring possessory title to the surface of land only, the true owner preserving his other rights in the land, is not new. In *Midland Railway Co.* v. *Wright*[12] someone acquired title by adverse possession to land, subject to the railway's right to tunnel under it.

The moral?

Two points emerge from the case. First despite several changes of ownership of both Nos. 31 and 33, no-one seems to have realised that the boundaries of No. 31 were not as fenced. "The vital necessity of conveyancers perusing the title deeds or land certificate most carefully and explaining them to the client, preferably in writing for greater certainty is clearly shown by the case."[13] Secondly, it is quite usual in housing developments, especially flats, for the garages to be built in a block separate from the dwellings. Each dwelling is allotted a garage and a part of the forecourt, with appropriate rights of access over the estate roads or footpaths. Those without cars must guard against the others acquiring title by adverse possession to their garages.

7. Adverse rights (Unilaw, 5; Shaw & Sons Ltd., 9)

(A) Is the Vendor aware of any rights or informal arrangements specifically affecting the property, other than any disclosed in the draft contract or immediately apparent on inspection, which are exercisable by virtue of an easement, grant, wayleave, licence, consent, agreement relating to an ancient monument or land near it, or otherwise or which are in the nature of public or common rights?

(B)(i) Please give the full names, and ages if under 18, of all persons in actual occupation of the property.

(ii) What legal or equitable interest in the property has each of those persons?

(C) Is the Vendor aware of any other overriding interests as defined by the Land Registration Act 1925, s.70(1)?

Enquiry 7 is probably the most important to the purchaser of all the enquiries. Apart from being renumbered (from 8 to 7) it escaped the 1984 revision unscathed. Before looking at the component parts of the enquiry the reader is asked momentarily to return to the disclosure obligations in the standard conditions of sale.

Disclosure obligations under the standard conditions

It will be remembered that National condition 14 obliges the vendor to inform the purchaser of *any* easements, rights, privileges or liabilities to which the property is subject (even those he is unaware of[14]). Law Society condition 5(1) limits his duty of disclosure to those incumbrances of which he knows or ought to know, other than the existence of those known to the purchaser at the date of the contract, or which a prudent purchaser would have discovered by that date, but extends it to cover patent as well as latent incumbrances. Both sets of conditions state that the property is otherwise to be sold (Law Society condition 5(2)(*b*) and "if the vendor so requires, conveyed") subject to all rights of way, light, drainage and so on.

[12] [1901] 1 Ch. 738.

[13] H. W. Wilkinson (1984) 134 New L.J. 145.

[14] *Heywood* v. *Mallalieu* (1883) 25 Ch.D. 357; *Re Brewer and Hankin's Contract* (1899) 80 L.T. 127.

In making an enquiry like 7 what the purchaser really wants to know is: "Has anyone any adverse rights over the property?" To ask that tempts the recipient to answer: "The vendor knows of none." Hence the enquiry is cast in the form quoted. But what of rights of which the vendor ought to know? Such is the difficulty in drafting an enquiry of this nature.

Many different kinds of rights could be revealed by 7(A). The purchaser then has to decide whether they are of a nature to be binding on him if he purchases. He may demand that they be terminated on completion or he may refuse to contract until they are terminated. The characteristics the rights have in common are that they are unlikely to be referred to in the title deeds, do not therefore appear in the draft contract and are not usually immediately apparent on inspection. Rights of way, water and drainage are common examples. Perhaps less frequently encountered are rights allowing neighbours to hang clothes on a line passing over the vendor's property[15] or permitting them to enter onto the land to repair buildings on adjoining property.[16] Unilaw try to ensure a specific answer to their adverse rights question by listing most of the burdens (common and uncommon) which could affect the property and then asking the vendor which of them do. Mention of a few of these rights demonstrates the wide span of the question: restrictive covenants, positive covenants, rent charges, chancel repair liabilities, corn rents, declarations (?),[17] rights of way, rights for timber extraction, rights to extract water, rights of common. . . .

Overlap with local searches

Some of the information the purchaser is given in reply to 7(A) will be duplicated by his other searches and enquiries. Assume our purchaser is buying property in a rural area. The likelihood of a public path crossing the property is strong. Its relevance to him is that he will not be able to interfere with its enjoyment. Enquiry 1 of Part II[18] of the standard enquiries of the local authority asks the authority for details of any path abutting or crossing the property. A path may be shown on a "definitive map and statement" prepared by the county council under the Wildlife and Countryside Act 1981 or the National Parks and Access to the Countryside Act 1949. Evidence of a public path on such a map is conclusive proof of the public's right to use the path. However the absence of a map showing a path does not prove that there is no public right of way over the land—answer to those who consider enquiries of the vendor redundant. Other information may prompt further searches and enquiries. If, for instance, there are indications that the land may be subject to rights of common, a Commons Registration search[19] should be made before contracts are exchanged. In *New Windsor Corporation* v. *Mellor*[20] a local authority was forced to discontinue use of a piece of land in the middle of New Windsor as a car park because a "customary right" had been established by the "Bachelors of Windsor" to play cricket. The search should be

Rights of common

[15] *Drewell* v. *Towler* (1832) 3 B. & Ad. 735.
[16] *Ward* v. *Kirkland* [1967] Ch. 194.
[17] The writers are unsure as to what this refers.
[18] See below, p. 75.
[19] Form 21. See Annand and Cain, *Modern Conveyancing* (1985), pp. 47–50.
[20] [1975] Ch. 380.

made whether the title is registered or unregistered; rights of common are registrable in the commons register, not at H.M. Land Registry. Furthermore the decision in *G. & K. Ladenbau (U.K.) Ltd.* v. *Crawley & de Reya*[21] establishes that a purchaser's solicitor will be negligent if he fails to make a Commons Registration search in circumstances where he knows or ought to know that rights of common may exist.

Proprietary estoppel or mutual benefit rights in unregistered land

Perhaps the most dangerous third party rights to a purchaser of unregistered land are licences protected in equity by proprietary estoppel[22] or by the doctrine of approbate and reprobrate[23] (mutual benefit and burden). These equities are neither overreachable nor registrable as land charges and will bind all purchasers except a bona fide purchaser of a legal estate for value without actual or constructive notice. Thus in *E.R. Ives Investment Ltd.* v. *High*,[24] the defendant High built a house on his own land. His neighbour then built a block of flats whose foundations encroached on High's land. High and his neighbour agreed orally that the foundations should stay where they were and that High should have a right of way over the neighbour's yard. In reliance on this High built a garage on his own land which could only be reached via the yard. The neighbour sold the block of flats to a purchaser who resold it to the plaintiffs expressly subject to High's right of way. The right of way was not a legal interest as it had not been created by deed, nor had it been registered as an equitable easement or estate contract under the Land Charges Act 1925. The Court of Appeal held that High had a right by estoppel or alternatively by mutual benefit, which not being registrable as a land charge, was binding on the plaintiffs who had purchased the legal estate of the licensor with actual notice.[25]

Estoppel or mutual benefit rights in registered land

In registered land a licence by estoppel or mutual benefit must be protected by the entry of a notice or caution on the register,[26] unless it is an overriding interest. Section 70(1) of the Land Registration Act 1925 gives (amongst others) as overriding interests "drainage rights, . . . watercourses, rights of water and other easements not being equitable easements required to be protected by notice on the register" (para. (*a*)) and "the rights of every person in actual occupation of the land . . . , save where enquiry is made of such person and the rights are not disclosed." (para. (*g*) discussed below). So it has been said: "If (a licensee by estoppel or mutual benefit) is not in possession and does not

[21] [1978] 1 W.L.R. 266.

[22] Instances when this occurred are: *Inwards* v. *Baker* [1965] 2 Q.B. 29 (licence to live in bungalow); *Ward* v. *Kirkland* [1967] Ch. 194 (licence to lay and use drains); *Crabb* v. *Arun D.C.* [1976] Ch. 179 (licence of way); *Taylors Fashions Ltd.* v. *Liverpool Victoria Trustees Co. Ltd.* [1981] Q.B. 133 (licence to renew lease); *Greasley* v. *Cooke* [1980] 1 W.L.R. 1306 (licence to remain in employer's house).

[23] *Halsall* v. *Brizzell* [1957] Ch. 169, he who takes the benefit must accept the burden.

[24] [1967] 2 Q.B. 379.

[25] See also *Hopgood* v. *Brown* [1955] 1 W.L.R. 213 (mutual drainage rights binding on purchaser with constructive notice); *Cook* v. *Minion* (1978) 37 P. & C.R. 58 (position of relaid drains secure against purchaser because of estoppel); and P. N. Todd [1981] Conv. 347.

[26] Land Registration Act 1925, s.49(1), s.54(1). Dicta of Cross J. in *Poster* v. *Slough Estates Ltd.* [1969] 1 Ch. 495 disapproved in *Celsteel Ltd.* v. *Alton House Holdings Ltd.* [1985] 1 W.L.R. 204.

possess water rights he will not have an overriding interest"[27] and "such protection (an overriding interest) would not be accorded to the estoppel licensee in *E.R. Ives Investment Ltd.* v. *High*, when the garage was sited on his own land. Nor would the intermittent user of his right over the licensor's land amount to actual occupation."[28] These statements no longer accurately reflect the law following *Celsteel Ltd.* v. *Alton House Holdings Ltd.*[29] which decided that despite the exception in section 70(1)(*a*) (quoted above) for "equitable easements required to be protected by notice on the register," certain equitable easements *can* be overriding interests. The plaintiff had an equitable right of way over a driveway to reach his garage. Did the easement bind the new registered leasehold proprietor of the driveway? Scott L.J. answered in the affirmative. He interpreted the word "required" in the exception to section 70(1)(*a*) as meaning "need" and came to the conclusion that the plaintiffs right did not "need" to be protected by notice on the register. It was a right openly exercised and enjoyed with other land (the garage) and was an overriding interest within section 70(1)(*a*) by virtue of rule 258 of the Land Registration Rules 1925. Rule 258, insofar as is relevant, provides: "Rights . . . appertaining . . . to land . . . or enjoyed therewith . . . which adversely affect registered land, are overriding interests within section 70 of the Act."

Equitable easements capable of being overriding interests

Constructive trust may protect unregistered minor interests

Lyus v. *Prowsa Developments Ltd.*[30] presents yet more problems to a purchaser of registered land. This time it is not estoppel rights or equitable easements, but unregistered minor interests. The general rule with registered land is that only minor interests protected on the register will bind the purchaser. Section 20(1) of the Land Registration Act 1925 accordingly states that a transferee for value under a registered disposition takes free from unprotected minor interests unless they are overriding interests, and section 59(6) of the Act provides that notice will not make an unprotected minor interest bind a purchaser. In *Lyus* the registered proprietor of a housing estate created a registered charge in favour of a bank. He later contracted to sell plot 29 on the estate to the plaintiffs, who registered a caution. The registered proprietor went bankrupt before completion of the plaintiffs' purchase and the bank exercised its power of sale. Section 34(4) of the Land Registration Act 1925 provides that where a chargee sells under its power of sale, the sale shall operate as a transfer for valuable consideration would have operated, and, as respects the land transferred, the charge and all inferior incumbrances shall be cancelled. As we have seen, the plaintiffs' contract was created and protected on the register *after* the bank's charge was registered. Their contract was not therefore binding on the bank and could not be binding on a purchaser from it. Unfortunately however the bank contracted to sell the estate to the first defendant, expressly subject to the plaintiffs' contract. The first defendant then sold the estate on to the second defendant and their contract stated

[27] H. W. Wilkinson, *Pipes, Mains, Cables and Sewers* (4th ed., 1984), p. 17.
[28] E. H. Burn, *Cheshire and Burn's Modern Law of Real Property* (13th ed., 1982), p. 570.
[29] [1985] 1 W.L.R. 204; M. P. Thompson [1986] Conv. 31.
[30] [1982] 1 W.L.R. 1044; C. T. Emery and B. Smythe (1983) 133 New L.J. 798.

that the estate was sold subject to the plaintiffs' contract, insofar as it was enforceable against the first defendant. Dillon J. held that the second defendant was bound by the plaintiffs' contract on the basis that a constructive trust would be imposed on the first defendant. He thought that "the court may yet intervene to raise a constructive trust on appropriate terms if to leave the defendant retaining the property free from all interest would be tantamount to sanctioning a fraud on the part of the defendant." Here the fraud amounted to the first defendant going back on his promise to buy the estate subject to the plaintiffs' contract.

The importance of the decision[31] from our point of view is that if the purchaser is told about an unprotected minor interest in reply to 7(A) he cannot ignore it if circumstances arise where a constructive trust should be imposed. And if the decision is accepted as correct it could equally well be applied to make a purchaser of unregistered land bound by an unregistered land charge. There is however weighty authority against such a proposition. In *Midland Bank Trust Co. Ltd.* v. *Green*[32] the House of Lords refused to hold that the purchaser was bound by an unregistered option to purchase the property, even though there was actual notice and a collusive sale. Lord Wilberforce expressed the view that it was not a fraud to rely on the rights conferred by statute.

Occupational hazards

As conveyancers will be all too aware, 7(B) was introduced onto Con 29 in the wake of *Williams & Glyn's Bank Ltd.* v. *Boland*.[33] In that case a husband was registered as the sole proprietor of the matrimonial home in which he lived with his wife. She had made substantial contributions to the acquisition of the home entitling her to an equitable interest therein. The husband mortgaged the house to the bank, without telling his wife, to secure the debts of his faltering business. The bank made

Boland

no enquiries of the wife as to her interest, which she had not protected by entering a caution. The combined result of the Court of Appeal and House of Lords decisions was that the husband held the home on trust for sale for himself and his wife as tenants in common and that because she was in actual occupation of it when the Bank's charge was registered she had an overriding interest under section 70(1)(*g*) of the Land Registration Act 1925 which was binding on the bank. Section 70(1)(*g*) protects against a purchaser under a registered disposition: "the rights of every person in actual occupation of the land or in receipt of the rents and profits thereof, save where inquiry is made of such person and the rights are not disclosed." The bank was refused an order of possession against the wife, the husband having defaulted on the payments due under the charge.

Unregistered land

The *Boland* case was concerned with the position of a spouse who is in occupation of and has a beneficial interest in registered land. It has been generally accepted however that the decision extends to protect other persons in a similar position (for example, brothers, aunts mothers-in-law, cohabitees . . .) whether the interest of such person is in registered or

[31] See also *Peffer* v. *Rigg* [1977] 1 W.L.R. 285.
[32] [1981] A.C. 513.
[33] [1981] A.C. 487.

Caunce v. Caunce not followed

unregistered land. The earlier decision in *Caunce* v. *Caunce*[34] to the effect that occupation by a spouse of a legal estate owner does not constitute actual, imputed, or constructive notice to a purchaser or mortgagee of the legal estate in unregistered land of any beneficial interest held by the spouse, because that occupation was consistent with the title offered by the vendor was expressly disapproved of in *Boland*, and was not followed in the subsequent cases of *Midland Bank Ltd.* v. *Farmpride Hatcheries Ltd.*[34a] and *Kingsnorth Finance Co. Ltd.* v. *Tizard.*[35] The facts of the latter case were comparable to *Boland* except that they concerned unregistered land. A matrimonial home in the husband's name was built by husband and wife. He charged the house with Kingsnorth for a loan without disclosing the wife's interest: he said he was single. However Kingsnorth's agent had learnt on inspecting the property earlier that the Tizards were separated and she was living elsewhere. No further enquiries were made as to the marital position. The husband defaulted on the loan and Kingsnorth sought to enforce their charge.

By way of preliminary, Judge John Finlay Q.C. found that the wife had a beneficial half share in the house (as a result of her substantial contribution to its building) and was at all material times in occupation of it despite the separation. He then went on to hold that Kingsnorth had imputed knowledge of the marriage through their agent, despite the husband's assertion that he was single, and should have made further enquiries as to the wife: section 199(1)(ii)(*b*) of the Law of Property Act 1925. These enquiries would have revealed that the wife had an interest in the house; Kingsnorth would then have had notice of that interest and the mortgage was therefore to be held subject to it: section 199(1)(ii)(*a*). The judge added that if proper enquiries had not revealed a wife in occupation, Kingsnorth could have argued that they had no notice of the wife's interest and were not bound by it. Some will say *Tizard* was predictable. Nevertheless it is an important decision. First, it confirms that a person may be in occupation notwithstanding regular and repeated absences. Mrs Tizard spent several nights per week away from the house but did return every day to look after the children and do the housework. Secondly it shows how important careful and extensive enquiries and inspections by the purchaser are, even in the case of unregistered land. Rather worryingly, Judge John Finlay Q.C. doubted whether an inspection to ascertain who was in occupation made at a pre-arranged time with the vendor was sufficient, even though for residential property such an appointment would be essential. Purchasers of unregistered land should not however despair. A purchaser of land with registered title is in a much worse position: he is bound by the mere fact of occupation not the reasonableness of inspection.

[34] [1969] 1 W.L.R. 286.
[34a] (1981) 260 E.G. 493. It is submitted that the decision was wrong because it proceeded on the false basis that the manager had a proprietary interest capable of binding to bank: see R. E. Annand [1982] Conv. 67.
[35] [1986] 2 All E.R. 54.

One question that was left open by *Boland* (and not considered in *Tizard*) was whether the wife's undivided share in the property would have been overreached by the operation of Part I of the Law of Property Act 1925, had the mortgagee been given a receipt by two trustees instead of one (for overreaching to occur the conveyance must be made by trustees for sale). Speculation was ended by the decision of the Court of Appeal in *City of London Building Society* v. *Flegg*.[35a] It was agreed that Mr. and Mrs. Flegg had contributed to the purchase price of property bought in the names of their daughter and son-in-law as legal joint tenants, that they were each beneficially entitled as tenants in common and at all material times were in actual occupation. The daughter and son-in-law were the registered proprietors, had mortgaged the property and then defaulted on the mortgage repayments. At first instance it was held that as there were two registered proprietors the case was different from *Boland* because the overreaching machinery in the Law of Property Act applied. The Court of Appeal disagreed. The reasoning in *Boland* concentrated on the distinction between a minor interest and an overriding interest. Once a minor interest had been elevated to the position of an overriding interest by the fact of actual occupation, it could not be overreached. Whether there was one registered proprietor and therefore one trustee for sale, or two was irrelevant. Furthermore it seems the same result would have been arrived at had the title to the land been unregistered. Section 14 of the Law of Property Act 1925 states that Part I: "shall not prejudicially affect the interest of any person in possession or in actual occupation of land to which he may be entitled in right of possession or occupation." Dillon L.J. thought that these words: "were apt to cover the interest of an equitable tenant in common which was reinforced by his being in possession or actual occupation of the land."

City of London Building Society v. Flegg

It is a pity that the Government failed to introduce its Land Registration and Law of Property Bill[36] into parliament in February 1985. The object of the Bill was to restrict to a minimum the enquiries[37] that were necessary on the purchase of a house, by limiting those occupants who would have overriding interests to the spouse of the owner and producing the same effect in unregistered land by modifying the doctrine of actual or constructive notice in relation to occupants other than spouses. The Bill was unfortunately withdrawn the following April because, as the Lord Chancellor put it, the main purpose of the Bill would have been defeated, if the amendments which had been put down for debate were passed. The main objections to the Bill as expressed in its second reading debate in the House of Lords were:

(a) that its protection was limited to spouses;
(b) that no alternative means of protection would have been

[35a] [1986] 2 W.L.R. 616 (leave to appeal to House of Lords has been granted); D. Hayton (1986) 136 New L.J. 208.

[36] See R. Bonehill (1985) 129 S.J. 309.

[37] In 1985 the Law Society estimated that the additional enquiries arising out of *Boland* cost the house-owning public approximately £6¾ million annually.

available in the case of unregistered land to persons other than spouses (their interests are not registrable as landcharges);

(c) that the alternative means of protection available in the case of registered land, namely the entry on the register of a notice or caution would be of little use, because for example mothers-in-law and grandparents who had contributed towards the purchase or extension of the dwelling-house, would be ignorant of it; and

(d) that the questions of overriding interests and of the protection of co-owners were (and at the time of writing are) still under consideration by the Law Commission.

The impact of *Boland* lessened

On the bright side there are indications that the Court of Appeal are trying to lessen the impact of *Boland* in domestic conveyancing, by restricting the circumstances in which non-spouses can acquire an interest in an owner's property, in the absence of an express declaration of trust or express agreement. In *Burns* v. *Burns*[38] an interest was refused to a mistress who had lived in her lover's house for 19 years, borne him two children and contributed throughout towards the household expenses. More interestingly, the decision in *Bristol & West Building Society* v. *Henning*[39–40] suggests that where as is normal in domestic conveyancing, the property is purchased with the aid of a mortgage, the equitable interest of anyone (spouse or non-spouse) occupying with the purchaser is to be postponed to the mortgage. Browne-Wilkinson L.J. explained in *Henning* that: "There was no way in which the villa could have been bought without the assistance of the mortgage to the society and the mortgage to the society could not be properly granted without giving the society a charge over the whole legal and equitable interest. Since the nature of Mrs. Henning's interest has to be found in the imputed intention of the parties and the imputed intention of the parties must have been that her interest was to be subject to that of the society, it is impossible for Mrs. Henning to establish that she is entitled to some form of equitable interest which gives her rights in priority to the rights of the society."

Effectiveness of enquiries

Given however that for the foreseeable future the law will remain as expressed in *Williams & Glyn's Bank Ltd.* v. *Boland*, how effective are the enquiries presently made on a purchaser's behalf (and interpreted in *Flegg*),[41] 7(B) asks for details of *all* persons in actual occupation of the property other than the vendor and what, if any, interests they have in it. Unilaw[42] and Shaw & Sons Ltd. make the same mistake as most building societies and only enquire about persons over 18 (or possibly 17) living on the property. A minor can hold an equitable interest but cannot validly dispose of it until he reaches majority. Even where enquiry is directed to children, Jill Martin[43] draws attention to the probability of a child beneficiary not comprehending the

[38] [1984] Ch. 317. See also *Grant* v. *Edwards* [1986] 2 All E.R. 431.

[39–40] [1985] 1 W.L.R. 778, and see *Paddington Building Society* v. *Mendelsohn* (unreported, April 2, 1985) and *Midland Bank Ltd.* v. *Dobson* (1985) 135 New. L.J. 751. R. Owen (1985) 82 L.S. Gaz. 3511.

[41] [1980] Conv. 313.

[42] They betray this fact in their information publicity.

[43] [1980] Conv. 371.

enquiry, which problem could of course arise wherever an occupier lacks the capacity legal, physical or mental, to make due disclosure of rights.[44] Identifying those present at this stage of the transaction leaves a gap between the date of the answer and the date of completion or registration.[45] The later date is the one for determining what interests are binding on the purchaser. The reader may like to note in this regard that under National condition 5(4) the purchaser is entitled, on giving reasonable notice, to require that on, or immediately before the time of completion possession of the property or part of it be handed to him or his representative.

Enquiries should be directed to possessor of interest

All three publishers address their enquiries to the vendor. This is no good especially in the case of registered land where the proviso to section 70(1)(*g*) only operates: "where inquiry is made of *such person* and the rights are not disclosed." Thus in *Hodgson* v. *Marks*[46] Russell L.J. remarked: "Reliance upon the untrue *ipse dixit* of the vendor will not suffice." Enquiry must be made of the possessor of the rights for:

> "What is involved is a departure from an easy-going practice of dispensing with inquiries as to occupation beyond that of the vendor and accepting the risks of doing so. To substitute for this a practice of more careful inquiry as to the fact of occupation, and, if necessary, as to the rights of occupiers, cannot, in my view of the matter, be considered as unacceptable."[47]

The purchaser's task is however lightened a little in that he is probably protected if he makes enquiries of the proper person and the rights are not disclosed within a reasonable time.[48] It would be useful if the standard enquiries stipulated a time within which *written* disclosure or non-disclosure should be made: "how far in law and practice could you trust a non-disclosure not by signed writing? Apart from questions of proof, arguably it involves the disposition of an interest within the Law of Property Act 1925, s.53(1)(*a*) or (*c*)."[49]

If the enquiries reveal the existence of a beneficial interest in the property of a sole legal owner the purchaser or mortgagee is alerted to the existence of a trust for sale, and to the fact that the vendor cannot give a valid receipt for the proceeds of sale or other capital moneys. The owner of the beneficial interest should be made to join in the receipt of the money so that proper advantage can be taken of the overreaching machinery provided by the 1925 property legislation. Since *Flegg* the same is apparently true even if there are joint legal proprietors. However present practice on a purchase is merely to require non-owner occupiers with possible beneficial interests to sign the contract; on a mortgage a deed of

[44] As with the aunt in *Re Sharpe* [1980] 1 W.L.R. 219.
[45] *Re Boyle's claim* [1961] 1 W.L.R. 339 and the Land Registration Rules 1925, r. 83(2).
[46] [1971] Ch. 892.
[47] *Per* Lord Wilberforce in *Williams & Glyn's Bank Ltd.* v. *Boland* [1981] A.C. 487 at 508.
[48] *Panorama Developments (Guildford) Ltd.* v. *Fidelis Furnishing Fabrics Ltd.* [1971] 2 Q.B. 711.
[49] [1980] Conv. 315.

Undue influence

release. Apart from being "defective conveyancing"[50] this practice must now be viewed in the light of *Kings North Trust Ltd.* v. *Bell.*[51] Mr. Bell owned a house in which Mrs. Bell had an equitable interest. Kings North agreed to lend him £18,000 secured by a second mortgage on the house provided Mrs. Bell signed a deed of release. Kings North's solicitors sent the deed to Mr. Bell's solicitors who gave it to Mr. Bell to get his wife to sign. Mr. Bell defaulted on the mortgage repayments and the mortgagees sought possession. The Court of Appeal held that Mr. Bell had misled his wife over the true purpose of the loan. She had signed the deed under her husband's influence and retained her rights in priority to the second mortgagees.

Necessity for independent legal advice for those signing consent forms

The relationship of husband and wife, unlike some relationships for example father and son,[52] does not give rise to the presumption of undue influence. But if undue influence is shown then lack of independent legal advice will result in the transaction being set aside. The problem for conveyancers is to know exactly what is meant by undue influence. In the later case of *National Westminster Bank plc* v. *Morgan*[53] Lord Scarman said that for the court to intervene, the transaction must be shown to be to the serious disadvantage[53a] of the person subjected to the influence, but he also warned that there was no precisely defined law setting limits to the equitable jurisdiction of the court to relieve against undue influence. If the present practice of signing the contract or a deed of release is continued it might be advisable for purchasers' or mortgagees' solicitors to ensure that any persons living with the vendor are separately advised.

Other examples of occupational overriding interests

So far our discussion has centred on the occupational hazards presented to a purchaser of a dwelling house. In registered land conveyancers problems are not confined to those illustrated by *Boland et al.* They extend to interests which in the equivalent unregistered land situation would be void for non-registration as land charges. To take a recent example. In *Kling* v. *Keston Properties Ltd.*[54] the plaintiff had a right of pre–emption to call for a long lease of a garage which was converted into an option to purchase when the owner of the garage agreed to lease it to the defendant. The option was held to be an overriding interest within section 70(1)(*g*) and was binding on the defendant, because the plaintiff was in actual occupation of the garage under a licence agreement when the defendant's lease was registered. The decision was hard on the defendant; she had visited the garage twice and found it empty.

Here are examples of just a few of the rights that (when coupled with actual occupation) have been recognised by the courts as overriding interests within section 70(1)(*g*):

(1) The right of occupation and specific performance under a contract to purchase a freehold or leasehold interest;

[50] *Emmet on Title* (18th ed., 1983, by J. T. Farrand), p. 210; J. Martin [1980] Conv. 316–387.

[51] [1986] 1 All E.R. 423, and see P. H. Kenny (1985) 82 L.S.Gaz. 1320.

[52] *Avon Finance Co. Ltd.* v. *Bridger* [1985] 2 All.E.R. 281.

[53] [1985] 2 W.L.R. 288.

[53a] On this see *Cornish* v. *Midland Bank* [1985] 3 All E.R. 513, *Coldunell Ltd.* v. *Gallon* [1986] 2 W.L.R. 466, and *Woodstead Finance Ltd.* v. *Petrou* (1986) 136 New L.J. 188.

[54] (1984) 134 New L.J. 1005.

Bridges v. *Mees*[55]; *Woolwich Equitable Building Society* v. *Marshall*.[56]

(2) The right of a tenant to purchase the freehold reversion of a lease; *Webb* v. *Pollmount*.[57]

(3) The right to an unpaid vendor's lien (where there has been a "sale and leaseback"); *London & Cheshire Insurance Co.* v. *Laplagrene Property Co. Ltd.*[58]

(4) The right of a tenant and his successors under a waiver of rights by the landlord; *Brikom Investments* v. *Carr*.[59]

(5) A right of rectification ancillary to an equitable estate or interest in land; *Blacklocks* v. *J. B. Developments (Godalming) Ltd.*[60]

(6) The rights of a beneficiary under a bare trust *Hodgson* v. *Marks*.[61]

(3) to (6) above are not registrable as land charges in the case of unregistered land. Their validity against subsequent purchasers of the legal estate for value depends upon the doctrine of notice.

The rights of those in receipt of rents and profits

With all the publicity accorded to the *Boland* line of cases it is sometimes forgotten that section 70(1)(*g*) also protects the rights of those in receipt of rents and profits. In *National Provincial Bank Ltd.* v. *Ainsworth*[62] Lord Wilberforce stated that section 70(1)(*g*) amounts to "a statutory application to registered land of the well known rule protecting the rights of persons in occupation." In fact as we shall see it does more than that. The "well known rule" was formulated in *Hunt* v. *Luck*[63] as follows:

(1) a tenant's occupation is notice of all that tenant's rights but *not* of his lessor's title or rights;

(2) *actual* knowledge that the rents are paid by the tenant to some person whose receipt is inconsistent with the title of the vendor is notice of that person's rights

The court rejected the argument that a purchaser would be fixed with constructive notice if he found that there was a tenant in the property and did not bother to make sure that the tenant paid rent to the vendor. But under section 70(1)(*g*) if there is a tenant and he is paying rent to someone other than the vendor, "save where enquiry is made of such person and the rights are not disclosed" (and remember it does not matter how difficult it is to discover that the rent is paid to that other) the purchaser will take subject to the other person's interest because he is in receipt of the rents and profits.

Another difference between registered and unregistered land

This extension of the rule in *Hunt* v. *Luck* in relation to registered land is strange when it is remembered that it was inadvertently excluded in relation to unregistered land. Although nominally preserved by section 14 of the Law of Property Act 1925 it failed to qualify the harsh rules in the Land Charges Act

55 [1957] Ch. 475.
56 [1952] Ch. 1.
57 [1966] Ch. 584.
58 [1971] Ch. 499.
59 [1979] Q.B. 467.
60 [1982] Ch. 183.
61 [1971] Ch. 892.
61a *Williams and Glyn's Bank Ltd.* v. *Boland* [1981] A.C. 487.
62 [1965] A.C. 1175.
63 [1902] 1 Ch. 428.

1925 (now the Land Charges Act 1972) which render void registrable but unregistered interests. As a result the extended application of the rule in registered conveyancing produces a considerable difference in the two systems, part of which we have already seen in the foregoing discussion. The reader will bear with a simple example: Suppose A the fee simple owner agrees to grant a 10 year lease to B who enters into possession. B then agrees to grant a five year lease to C, who is also allowed into possession. Neither transaction is formally completed. A then sells the fee simple to D. In the case of registered land D is bound by both B and C's interests; C's because he is in actual occupation and B's because he is entitled to the receipt of rents. If the land was unregistered D would take free from B's and C's interests unless they were registered as estate contracts under the Land Charges Act 1972, even if D actually knew of them.[64] But perhaps the greatest anomaly of section 70(1)(*g*) is that the recipient of rent appears to be protected even if the payer is not in actual occupation.

Limits on section 70(1)(*g*)

Some limits have been placed on the operation of section 70(1)(*g*). First there must be actual occupation or receipt of rents. In *Epps* v. *Esso Petroleum Co. Ltd.*[65] the regular parking of cars on a strip of land was held not to amount to an overriding interest; it did not amount to actual occupation either in whole or in respect of any defined part or time. Neither was the plaintiff's use of the driveway in *Celsteel Ltd.* v. *Alton House Holdings Ltd.*[66] for the same reason. In *Strand Securities Ltd.* v. *Caswell*[67] a lessee allowed his daughter and her family to occupy a flat as a favour without receiving even a token rent. He was not in receipt of rents and profits for the purposes of section 70(1)(*g*). Second the rights which it is sought to protect must be of such a nature as could have been protected by constructive notice under the old law, that is proprietary as opposed to personal rights. According to Lord Wilberforce in *National Provincial Bank Ltd.* v. *Ainsworth*[68]:

> "To ascertain what rights come within [section 70(1)(*g*)] one must look outside [the Land Registration Act 1925] and see what rights affect purchasers under the general law . . . there is no warrant in the terms of this paragraph or elsewhere in the Act for supposing that the nature of the rights which are to bind a purchaser is to be different excluding personal rights in one case, including them in another."

The rights of a contractual licensee are therefore not capable of falling within section 70(1)(*g*).[69] But what if a contractual licensee

[64] *Midland Bank Trust Co.* v. *Green* [1981] A.C. 513.
[65] [1973] 1 W.L.R. 1071.
[66] [1985] 1 W.L.R. 204.
[67] [1965] Ch. 958.
[68] [1965] A.C. 1175.
[69] There is Court of Appeal authority to the effect that a contractual licence does confer a proprietary interest in land; see *Errington* v. *Errington and Woods* [1952] 1 K.B. 290; *Bendall* v. *McWhirter* [1952] 2 Q.B. 466; *Binions* v. *Evans* [1972] Ch. 359; and *Midland Bank Ltd.* v. *Farmpride Hatcheries Ltd.* (1980) 260 E.G. 493—see R. E. Annand and H. W. Wilkinson [1982] Conv. 67 (1982) 132 New L.J. 68. However in *National Provincial Bank Ltd.* v. *Ainsworth*, above, Lords Wilberforce and Upjohn were against this proposition, as was Russell L.J. in the Court of Appeal [1964] Ch. 665.

is suddenly turned into a tenant? Then he would have an overriding interest under section 70(1)(*g*) or 70(1)(*k*) (leases . . . not exceeding 21 years . . . at a rent).[70] This would be the

Street v. Mountford

surprising result of *Street* v. *Mountford*[71] in the House of Lords in May 1985, where it was held that if the true nature of a transaction was that an occupier was granted exclusive possession of *residential* premises for a term at a rent, the result was a tenancy even though the agreement was called a "licence" and the occupier had signed a declaration that it did not give a tenancy protected by the Rent Act. The licence agreement in this case had granted the appellant exclusive possession but their Lordships also cast doubt upon the effectiveness of the non-exclusive licence which has become so popular with private landlords since the decision in *Somma* v. *Hazelhurst*.[72] *Street* v. *Mountford* is of course limited to the residential sector.

Part (C) although appearing last in Enquiry 7 is also of importance to a purchaser. It requires the vendor to disclose other overriding interests under section 70(1) of the Land Registration Act 1925. Present[73] examples are legal easements and profits,[74] squatters' rights,[75] local land charges[76] and short leases. Obviously 7(C) is only relevant if the title to the property is registered.

8. Restrictions (Unilaw, 5; Shaw & Sons Ltd.—)

(A) Have all restrictions affecting the property or its use been observed up to the date hereof? If not, please give details.

(B) Where such restrictions have in the past required any person's consent or approval of plans, does the Vendor have written evidence of that consent or approval?

The form of enquiry 8 has not been altered since the 1973 revision when part (B) (taken from enquiry 7 of the pre 1973 Con 29) was reworded in a more positive form—"if consent was required, is there written proof?" —instead of—"have all consents been obtained? If not give details."

If the vendor cannot produce necessary consents to building work or alterations to the property, he may still be able to rely on estoppel or limitation to show that they cannot be challenged. It is interesting that neither Unilaw nor Shaw & Sons Ltd. felt that an enquiry like 8 was needed on their general forms of enquiry.

9. Planning, etc (Unilaw, 3; Shaw & Sons Ltd., 10)

(A)(i) When did the present use of the property commence?
(ii) Has this use been continuous since it commenced?

[70] In unregistered land the "tenant" would probably have a periodic legal tenancy.
[71] [1985] A.C. 809.
[72] [1978] 1 W.L.R. 1014. See also *Aldrington Garages Ltd.* v. *Fielder* (1978) 37 P. & C.R. 461; *Sturolson & Co.* v. *Weniz* (1984) 272 E.G. 326.
[73] The Law Commission are presently considering the categories of overriding interests.
[74] Usually unimportant as overriding interests as normally created by deed and noted on the register.
[75] *Re Chowood's Registered land* [1933] Ch. 574; *Bridges* v. *Mees* [1957] Ch. 475.
[76] These would also be revealed by the purchaser's local land charges search.

(B) During the four years immediately prior to receipt of these enquiries:

(i) Were any of the buildings on the property erected, or have any been altered or added to?

(ii) Have any other building, engineering, mining or other operations been carried out in, over or under the property?

(iii) Has any condition or limitation on any planning permission not been complied with? If so, please give details.

(C) Please supply a copy of:

(i) Any planning permission authorising or imposing conditions upon the present use of the property, and the erection or retention of the buildings now on it.

(ii) Any bye-law approval or building regulation consent relating to those buildings.

(iii) Any current fire certificate.

Open contract rule

We can again compare enquiry 9 with enquiries 1 and 5. Under an open contract the vendor is not under a duty to disclose planning matters which affect the enjoyment of the property provided they do not amount to latent defects in title,[77] although in *Sakkas* v. *Donford Ltd.*,[78] Lord Grantchester incidentally[79] held that the vendor had been under a duty to disclose to potential purchasers of a house the *material fact* that the locality had been zoned as a public place. Furthermore in the absence of a term in the contract specifying an authorised use, that is one to which the property may be put without infringing planning law, the vendor does not warrant that the purchaser's intended use of the property is authorised by planning law.[80] So if it is important to the purchaser to have information on these matters he must obtain it at this stage of the transaction or stipulate in the contract for it to be provided.

National condition 15(3) and (4) Law Society condition 3

Both sets of standard conditions amend the common law in favour of the purchaser. National condition 15(4) obliges the vendor to disclose those planning matters affecting the property which he knows about; Law Society condition 3 any written communications relating to planning matters received by or known to him. National condition 15(3) provides that a special condition may express that the property is to be sold on the footing of a specified "authorised use." If this is done and the purchaser then discovers before completion that the specified use is not an authorised one, he may rescind. He may also have an additional right to rescind under optional condition 3. Where the National Contract for Sale is used enquiries as to change of use (but not other development) may therefore be postponed until after contract. If an authorised use is specified by special condition in the Law Society contract the purchaser still has to

[77] In *Sidney* v. *Buddery* (1949) 1 P. & C.R. 34 it was held that the vendor should have told the purchaser that the building being sold was erected under a temporary planning permission and had to be demolished at a future date. This was a latent defect in his title.

[78] (1982) 47 P. & C.R. 149.

[79] The case was decided on National condition 15(4).

[80] *Mitchell* v. *Beacon Estates (Finsbury Park) Ltd.* (1949) 1 P. & C.R. 32.

verify through his own enquiries that this in fact is the authorised use. However he is given the opportunity to rescind specifically in relation to the intended use of the property if optional condition 4 is included in the contract.

When is planning permission required?

Generally speaking planning permission is needed for "development." This is defined as:

(1) the carrying out of building, engineering, mining or other operations in, on, over or under land; or
(2) the making of any material change in the use of any buildings or other land.[81]

It is specifically provided that change of use as a dwelling house to two or more dwellings is a change of use and "development." Certain matters are specified as not being "development" and therefore not requiring planning permission. These include building works which do not change the external appearance of a building and change of use from a use within one class of the current Use Classes Order to another within the same class.[82] Other matters are "development" but do not require planning permission. An example we shall meet later is resumption of the use of land for an immediately preceding lawful use, following the service of an enforcement notice.[83] Development is unauthorised if it is carried on contrary to any condition in a planning permission or without obtaining the necessary planning permission at all. A planning authority's normal remedy for unauthorised development is the issue of an enforcement notice.[84] Essentially the requirements of an enforcement notice are negative: demolish the offending structures or cease the offending uses—and this is not prevented by a subsequent purchase of the property. Unless an enforcement notice has been served the only ways a purchaser can ascertain whether one may be served on him are by inspecting the property himself and enquiries as to the existing use and building or other operations and by seeing that the requisite permissions were obtained and their terms complied with.

Enforcement notices

The 4-year rule

Enquiry 9 is designed to extract this information. The reason why the questions in 9(B) are limited to the four years immediately prior to the receipt of the enquiries, is that an enforcement notice relating to building or other operations may only be issued within four years of the breach having occurred.[85] With one exception a post-1963 material change of use made in breach of planning control remains subject to enforcement proceedings at any time.[86] The exception is a change of use to use as a single dwellinghouse, which is subject to the four year rule. Uses commenced before 1964 without planning permission are immune to enforcement proceedings and are referred to as "established uses."

The combined result of 9(A) and (C) should be that the purchaser discovers whether the present use is lawful (either

[81] Town and Country Planning Act 1971, s.22.
[82] *Ibid.* s.22.
[83] *Ibid.*, s.23.
[84] Pursuant to *ibid.*, s.87.
[85] *Ibid.*, s.87(3).
[86] *Ibid.*, s.87(1), (4) as amended by the Local Government and Planning (Amendment) Act 1981.

because it is covered by planning permission or became authorised under the provisions of the Town and Country Planning Act 1947 (because this was its use on July 1, 1948), or established, and whether it has been continuous since it began. The Law Society have recommended as well as furnishing the purchaser with copy permissions for the present use and buildings, the vendor should supply him with copies of: "outstanding planning permissions including any site layout or access plans . . . *i.e.* all permissions, which have never been implemented by development and permissions which have been implemented within the preceding four years." The Law Society considered that there is "no obligation upon a vendor's solicitor to supply copies of spent permissions, *i.e.* temporary permissions which have expired by effluxion of time, or permissions which have been implemented by development completed more than four years previously."[87] Not so Unilaw! They ask for copies of all planning permissions relating to the property. Their reason: "The planning questions are aimed at obtaining answers to points which would not necessarily be revealed through local searches—for example, unconditional consents to a planning application."[88] It is true that local searches in the narrow sense will now reveal neither conditional nor unconditional permissions, but supplementary enquiries of the local authority will reveal the existence and often the content of both, and if necessary lead on to a search of the planning register.

All permissions

Just because a particular unauthorised development cannot be challenged by enforcement proceedings does not mean that that development is lawful.[89] *Emmet on Title* suggests[90] that the amount of compensation payable might be affected by "unlawful" development should the property later become the subject of a compulsory purchase order. It therefore advocates enquiries as to building and other operations outside the four year limit. *Balco Transport Services Ltd.* v. *Secretary of State for the Environment*[91] seems to say that the position would be exactly the opposite. The case concerned the confirmation of a purchase notice served by *Balco* on the local authority under section 180(1) of the Town and Country Planning Act 1971 on the ground that their land was incapable of reasonably beneficial use in its existing state. The only use to which the land could lawfully be put was agricultural use but such use was impossible unless hardcore, laid by the previous owner without the necessary planning permission, was removed at an estimated cost which would outweigh the benefit of any possible use of the restored land. Since the hardcore was laid more than four years before the purchase notice the local authority had lost their right to issue an enforcement notice requiring its removal. The hardcore was therefore something which the Secretary of State could take into account when deciding whether to confirm or quash the purchase notice. Lord Justice Glidewell said: "But the maxim that a man could not take advantage of his own wrong had no application to

Balco v. Secretary of State for the Environment

[87] (1966) 63 L.S.Gaz. 21.
[88] Information leaflet.
[89] *LTSS Print & Supply Services Ltd.* v. *Hackney London Borough Council* [1967] Q.B. 663.
[90] 18th ed., 1983 (by J. T. Farrand), p. 21.
[91] (1985) 276 E.G. 447.

the question whether the land had become incapable of reasonably beneficial use in its existing state." However he went on to add (*obiter*) that if by the serving of an enforcement notice (even after the purchase notice) a local authority could require a landowner to restore the land to its previous condition and the land in its previous condition would be capable of reasonably beneficial use, then the conditions for the service of a purchase notice were not fulfilled and the notice should not be confirmed.

Young v. Secretary of State for the Environment

Although past unchallengeable "unlawful" building or other operations need not concern a purchaser, an unchallengeable "unlawful" use might. *Young* v. *Secretary of State for the Environment*[92] turned on the effect of section 23(9) of the Town and Country Planning Act 1971, which provides that after the service of an enforcement notice in respect of any development, permission is not required for use for a purpose for which the land "could lawfully have been used if that development had not been carried out." The House of Lords held that the subsection contemplated one "backward step" only, namely to the purpose for which the land was used immediately before the development, the subject of the enforcement notice, took place. If that immediately preceding use was unlawful, planning permission would be needed for any use it was proposed to adopt, except the limited purposes (for example, agriculture) for which no planning permission is required. Furthermore their Lordships tacitly approved the Court of Appeal's ruling in *LTSS Print & Supply Services Ltd.* v. *Hackney London Borough Council*[93] that a "lawful" use means one for which planning permission has been obtained or is not required, not an established use.[94]

Young's case reduces the usefulness of the not uncommon practice of searching the planning history of land on behalf of a commercial client, in case a reversion to a former lawful use is desired. Here is an illustration of just one of the problems the case could cause in practice:

Suppose X wishes to buy land presently used for Use 1. He intends to continue Use 1. Local searches reveal planning permission for Use 1. The vendor is not asked about past developments on the land. It transpires that he changed from Use 1 to Use 2 without planning permission and then back to Use 1 again. No enforcement proceedings were taken in respect of Use 2, so that reversion to Use 1 was a development which needed planning permission. After completion of the purchase an enforcement notice is served on X. His land now has a nil use. He cannot take advantage of section 23(9) because the immediately preceding Use 2 was unlawful. The problem is that even an appropriately framed enquiry would have been no help to X, if the reply had read: "The purchaser should rely on his own searches and inspections."

Future plans

Often a purchaser is not only concerned with establishing that what he is buying is in no way in breach of planning control. He may also want to know that his proposals for the property stand a good chance of being accepted by the planning authority.

92 [1983] 2 A.C. 662; N. Graveson [1984] Conv. 339.

93 [1976] Q.B. 663.

94 A report of a DOE planning appeal suggests that there should be a saving for an established use; see (1985) 274 E.G. 140, DOE ref. T/APP/XO415/C/84/1514–7/P6, March 5, 1985.

This is really part of the more general question of whether the property is suitable for the purchaser's purposes, which both the purchaser and his solicitor will have to consider before exchange of contracts. Here enquiries into the planning history of the property back to 1948 might prove useful or essential. First they will give the purchaser an indication of the planning authority's attitude towards future development. Second ascertainment of the use and extent of development which was lawful on July 1, 1948 may be necessary to determine the extent of enlargement permitted without planning consent. And thirdly the General Development Order 1977 obviates the need to make an express application for planning permission in a large number of cases. Especially relevant to domestic conveyancing is Class I of that order which permits the enlargement, improvement or alteration of a dwelling house provided certain conditions are met. Knowledge of the original size of the building for which permission was granted and any building work carried out on the property (often not only within the past four years) will enable the purchaser hoping to extend a property decide whether he needs express planning permission to implement his plans. In this regard practitioners might find the recent decision in *North-West Leicester District Council* v. *Secretary of State for the Environment*[95] of interest. The case involved the provision in Class I of the Town and Country Planning General Development Order 1977 which permits the enlargement of a dwelling-house provided that, *inter alia*, no part of the building as extended should project beyond the forwardmost part of any wall of the house fronting onto a highway. The house in question was "L" shaped with the bottom part of the "L" projecting towards the road but the position is best indicated by a diagram, thus:

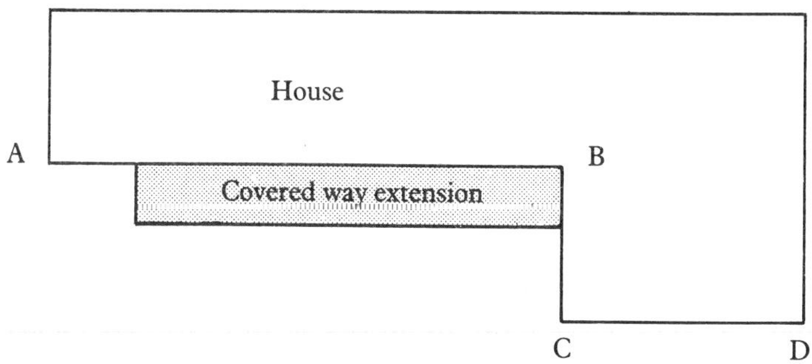

The planning authority had served an enforcement notice requiring the removal of the covered way the owner had built, on the ground that it projected beyond the original wall, A-B. It was held that for the purposes of the condition the whole of the road frontage, A-D, should be treated as a single wall and because the covered way did not project beyond the closest part of C–D, it satisfied the condition.

New dwellings

It will be remembered[95a] that in the case of new dwellings, building control supervision may have been carried out by N.H.B.C. Building Control Services Ltd. An "initial notice" served jointly by it and the builder or developer on the local

[95] (1983) 46 P. & C.R. 154.
[95a] See *ante* p.22.

authority will have taken the place of building regulation consent. The purchaser's solicitor should expect in reply to 9(c)(ii) confirmation by the local authority of its acceptance of the initial notice or confirmation from N.H.B.C. that the initial notice has been served jointly, with the date of service. Provided more than 10 days have elapsed since that date, the purchaser's solicitor can rely on this as evidence of building regulation consent.

Fire certificates

Current fire certificates? Those acting for purchasers proposing to buy properties for letting or conversion into flats should be aware of the fact that the environmental health department is currently pursuing an enforcement programme for houses in multiple occupation. In Bristol[96] the owners of two houses in Clifton were successfully prosecuted for failing to provide emergency fire measures for tenants. This was the first case of its kind in Bristol.

Occasionally it may be necessary for the purchaser's solicitor to request copies of other documents, a caravan site licence, established use certificate or industrial development certificate for instance.

10. Fixtures, fittings, etc (Unilaw, 6; Shaw & Sons Ltd., 11)

(A) Does the sale include all of the following items now on the property, and attached to or growing in it?

Trees, shrubs, plants, flowers and garden produce. Greenhouses, garden sheds and garden ornaments. Aerials. Fitted furniture and shelves. Electric switches, points and wall and ceiling fittings.

(B) What fixtures and fittings affixed to the property are not included in the sale?

(C) If the property has any fixed oil burning appliance, what arrangements are proposed for the sale to the purchaser on completion of any stock of oil?

Law relating to fixtures

The law relating to fixtures is vague and rarely litigated. Yet in practice the subject often generates a considerable amount of genuine aggravation. Its relevance to a vendor and purchaser of land is great. Articles that are not fixtures may be removed by the vendor at will and do not pass with the sale of the land without express agreement. The chattels may of course be bought separately by the purchaser, and when this occurs a schedule of chattels is usually annexed to the contract. Where however the article is a fixture (that is it has been so attached to the land as to become part of it[97]) then subject to an express reservation in the contract it is included in the purchase price and must be left for the purchaser.[98] The title to the fixture will pass on conveyance by virtue of section 62(1) of the Law of Property Act 1925, without the need for express mention. If the vendor wishes to remove or be paid separately for a fixture he must say so in the contract.

[96] August 1985.

[97] *Holland* v. *Hodgson* (1872) L.R. 7 C.P. 328, at 334; and on fixtures generally see (1985) 135 New L.J. 539–540; 588–589.

[98] *Phillips* v. *Lamdin* [1949] 2 K.B. 33.

The difficulty is that the classification of "fixture" or "chattel" in any particular case is far from straightforward. Most of the illustrative cases date from a more leisurely and gracious age when wood panelling,[99] tapestries[1] and stone statues[2] were all the rage. Even the more modern decisions are hardly relevant for your average suburban semi-detached—a marble statue and a sundial,[3] a stone ornament possibly of Chinese origin standing on a stone plinth in a goldfish pond?[4] A more recent case[5] is perhaps more illuminating. A large prefabricated greenhouse which was bolted to a concrete plinth which came with it and which was not affixed to the ground but lay on it under its own weight, was not a fixture but a chattel, and had not passed to the purchaser on conveyance.

Comparison of fixture enquiries

Enquiry 10 is designed to reduce problems of this nature to a minimum. The vendor is asked to confirm that "removeable" items commonly present on property like greenhouses, television aerials and power switches, are included in the sale. These items all lie on the fixture/chattel borderline. He is also asked to list any fixtures not included in the sale, and is given a clue as to what is meant by "fixtures" by the word "affixed." Unilaw simply ask: "Please list all items of fixtures and fittings which are being taken." They claim that concentrating on the items to be taken requires "the parties to think about the problem at as [*sic*] earlier stage as possible."[6] As one commentator[7] has remarked, given the difficulty of knowing exactly what is a fixture, "a fat lot of good thinking will do . . . . Will vendors provide a floor by floor inventory . . . or shall we get unhelpful, unrevealing formula responses?" Shaw & Sons Ltd. prefer: "Are all the items in the estate agent's particulars sheet included in the sale?" A good idea, but do estate agents usually list bird tables and garden gnomes in their particulars, and what if an agent is not used?

Hamp v. Bygrave

A case which shows the care that must be taken when answering enquiry 10 is *Hamp* v. *Bygrave*.[8] Included in the estate agent's particulars of sale of a house for £150,000 were eight outside light fittings, five stone flower urns, a stone statue, a pond ornament and a lead garden trough. During subsequent negotiations it was suggested by the vendor that the sale price could be lowered if the garden ornaments were excluded from the sale. This idea was rejected. Eventually, the parties agreed on a price of £147,500. The vendor's replies to preliminary enquiries (enquiry 11 on the 1980 version of Con 29) indicated that the ornaments were included in the sale,[9] but they were not mentioned in the contract itself. On taking possession following completion, the purchaser found that the ornaments had been removed and brought proceedings for their recovery. Boreham J. applying the twofold test for fixtures, namely the purpose and

[99] *Spyer* v. *Phillipson* [1931] 2 Ch. 183.
[1] *Leigh* v. *Taylor* [1902] A.C. 157.
[2] *D'Eyncourt* v. *Gregory* (1866) L.R. 3 Eq. 382.
[3] *Berkley* v. *Poulett* (1976) 241 E.G. 911; 242 E.G. 39.
[4] *Hamp* v. *Bygrave* (1983) 266 E.G. 720.
[5] *Dean* v. *Andrews* (1985) 135 New L.J. 728.
[6] Information leaflet.
[7] J. E. Adams (1985) 135 New L.J. 170, at p.173.
[8] (1983) 266 E.G. 720.
[9] They were not expressly excluded.

degree of annexation, found that the ornaments were chattels. However he said that it was clear from the sale particulars, the subsequent negotiations and replies to preliminary enquiries that the vendor regarded them as included in the sale and as part of the land and for this reason they were fixtures and passed to the purchaser. Alternatively he said that the vendor was estopped from denying that they were included in the sale.

11. Outgoings (Unilaw, 8; Shaw & Sons Ltd., 12)

(A)(i) What is the rateable value of the property?
(ii) Have any works been carried out at the property which might result in a revision of this?
(B) Does the hereditament, in which the property to be sold is included for rating purposes, also include any other property?
(C) What annual or periodic charges, other than general and water rates affect the property or its occupier?

How much will it cost me to live there?

This enquiry is in the main futuristic. The purchaser is trying to assess how much it will cost him to live in or otherwise occupy the property. Rates are not charged on the property but are payable by the occupier.[10] Therefore it is not usually necessary for the purchaser to ensure that they are paid up until completion. However this may be necessary where the property is tenanted and, either the rating authority has resolved to rate the owner[11] (generally small premises only), or the letting is a periodic tenancy and the owner has been rated because, although the tenant may be charged as occupier he has the right to recover from the owner,[12] who is defined for this purpose as the person entitled to receive the rack rent.[13] Occasionally it may also be necessary to ask if the property has been unused. Under section 17 of the General Rate Act 1967 rating authorities may resolve to bring Schedule 1 to the Act, which provides for the rating of unoccupied property into operation in their areas. Local searches will reveal the passing of such a resolution and the categories of property affected. When this happens, the rates so payable are the liability of the person entitled to possession and being a charge on the land can be collected from a purchaser if not paid before completion.[14] National condition 6 and Law Society condition 19(3) provide for the outgoings of the property to be apportioned on completion.[15] "Outgoings" has in practice been generally thought of as including general rate, water rate, sewerage charge, ground rent and rent charge. However under Law Society condition 19(2) where applicable, the vendor is not entitled to require apportionment of liabilities for which the purchaser is not accountable, *i.e.* rates.

Apportionment under the standard conditions

The point of asking 11A(ii) is that structural alterations can result in the increase in the rateable value of a property. Of

[10] General Rate Act 1967, s.16.
[11] *Ibid.*, s.55.
[12] *Ibid.*, s.56.
[13] *Ibid.*, s.115.
[14] *Westminster City Council* v. *Haymarket Publishing Ltd.* [1981] 1 W.L.R. 677.
[15] Note also the provisions as to service charges; National condition 6(5), Law Society condition 19(6).

importance here to residential conveyancers is the recent Court of Appeal's reserved judgment in three appeals[16] which concerned the construction and effect of section 21 of the Local Government Act 1974. According to section 21:

Local Government Act 1974, s.21

> "In the case of a hereditament which is a dwellinghouse . . . no proposal may be made under section 69 of [The General Rate Act 1967] for an increase in the gross value ascribed to the hereditament in the valuation list by reason of the making of structural alterations on or after April 1, 1974—
> (*a*) if and so far as the alterations are necessary for the purpose of installing a system for providing heating in two or more rooms in the hereditament or
> (*b*) if the proposal would be for an increase not exceeding such an amount as the secretary of state may by order specify. . . ."

By the Rating of Minor Structural Alterations to Dwellings (Specified Amount) Order 1974,[17] £30 was specified as the amount for the purposes of section 21(*b*).

In the first appeal, *Re Wright*, a house and garage were extended sometime after 1974. To take account of the alterations the valuation officer proposed an increase in rateable value of £67. But after he had taken into account other factors (namely a lorry park behind the house) he reduced the increase to £22. The local valuation court held that the proposed net increase, being less than £30, was precluded by section 21(*b*) and directed that no alteration should be made to the existing rateable value. The Lands Tribunal affirmed their decision. The Court of Appeal however disagreed. They said that the true purpose of section 21(*b*) was to prevent the making of minor increases in rateable values because of alterations. Consequently invalidated would be a valuation officer's proposal for an increase of less than £30 or one for more which the local valuation court deemed excessive. But where as in this case alterations to a house on the face of it justified an increase of more than £30 but other factors caused the net increase to be less than £30, then the increase would be allowed to go forward. This decision also applied to the third appeal, *Re Smith*, the facts being very similar.

In the second appeal, *Re Maudsley*, central heating was installed in a house before 1974 and its rateable value reflected this fact. After 1974 the house was extended, as was the central heating system. The valuation officer proposed an increase in rateable value from £354 to £510. The increase was disallowed by both the local valuation court and the Lands Tribunal because of section 21(*a*). The Court of Appeal, unable to reach a final decision through lack of evidence, gave the lower courts the following guideline: "Additions to an existing central heating system could be taken account of [in deciding whether to allow a proposed increase]: anything that amounted to the installation of such a system should not be taken into account."

Neither Unilaw nor Shaw & Sons Ltd. ask about alterations in their "Outgoings" questions, probably on the ground that alterations are adequately covered elsewhere on the forms and it

16 *Re Wright* [1985] R.A. 21.
17 S.I. 1974 No. 629.

Unilaw's question on outgoings

is up to the purchaser's solicitor to explain the significance of any to his client. Unilaw's question 8 is good and worth reproducing here:

"Please state whether the Vendor pays
(a) general rates—when due—and how much
(b) water rates—when due—and how much
(c) drainage rates—when due—and how much
(d) cesspit cleaning—how often—and how much
(e) licence fees for access
(f) licence fees for water abstraction—when due—and how much
(g) any other items. Please list."

Professor J. E. Adams[18] has suggested the addition of : "As to each of the above, will they be apportioned between the parties or dealt with direct and an undertaking for payment offered." Presumably he means "as to" the items not covered by the standard conditions[19]

Solicitors negligent in not checking rateable value

A case on rates and preliminary enquiries of general interest to practitioners is *Computastaff Ltd.* v. *Ingledew Brown Bennison and Garrett.*[20] Solicitors acting on behalf of a company proposing to take a lease asked the landlords in preliminary enquiries, what was the rateable value of the premises and were told £8,305. The company thought that figure wrong and would not have taken the lease if it was right. The solicitors then asked the company's estate agents who said that the rateable value was £3,305. The company took the lease and it turned out that the first figure, £8,305, was correct. The company's solicitors were held to be negligent in and here's the strange bit not checking the rateable value with the landlord's solicitors. Why not the local authority?

12. Completion (Unilaw, 10; Shaw & Sons Ltd., 1)

(A) How long after exchange of contracts will the Vendor be able to give vacant possession of the whole of the property?
(B) The Purchaser's solicitors wish to complete by adopting the Law Society's Code for Completion by Post (1984 edition). Do the Vendor's solicitors agree?

Sub-enquiry 12(B) was newly introduced in 1984 to take account of the Law Society's Code for Completion by Post (1984 edition). The new sub-enquiry in turn prompted the making of an exception to the vendor's solicitor's denial of responsibility for replies in the disclaimer, "in the case of any enquiry expressly requiring a reply from the Vendor's solicitors." The Law Society produced the new practice code for completion by post to ease concern felt amongst the profession following the decision of the Privy Council in *Edward Wong Finance Co. Ltd.* v. *Johnson Stokes and Master.*[21] The appeal from Hong Kong arose out of what their Lordships described as a "Hong Kong-style completion"; remitting the whole of the purchase money, advanced on mortgage to the purchaser, to the vendor's solicitor

Completion "Hong Kong-style"

[18] (1985) 135 New L.J. 173.
[19] Law Society condition 19, National condition 6.
[20] (1983) 133 New L.J. 598.
[21] [1984] A.C. 1296 and see M. Brahams (1984) 80 L.S. Gaz. 3135.

against the latter's undertaking to forward the documents of title, which would include discharge of the vendor's mortgage—very like our procedure on postal completions. Expert evidence was adduced to the court to show that this was the normal method of completing in Hong Kong. The vendor's solicitor ran off with the purchase money leaving the vendor in possession of the property and the vendor's mortgagees in possession of the deeds. The Privy Council held that the loss of the money must be borne by the purchaser's solicitors for failing to take the necessary steps to protect their client's interests. Their Lordships said that the purchaser's solicitors should have insisted on a normal "proper English-style completion" by which they meant the purchaser's solicitors handing over a banker's draft in exchange for *all* the necessary documents, including where appropriate a discharge of the vendor's mortgage. Their Lordships betrayed not only their ignorance of the common practice in this country of completing by post but also seemed unaware of the standard procedure (adopted on formal and postal completions) of accepting the vendor's solicitor's undertaking that the purchase money will be used to pay off any mortgage debt.

The Law Society's Code for Completion by Post (1984 ed.)

The Code (reproduced in Appendix N) provides a procedure for completion by post on an agency basis; the vendor's solicitor agrees to act as an unpaid agent for the purchaser's solicitor on completion. The purchaser's solicitor is protected from the implications of *Wong* because by virtue of clause 3 of the Code the vendor's solicitor undertakes that he has the express authority of the vendor and, if need be, the vendor's mortgagee, to receive the purchase moneys on their behalf. If the vendor's solicitor absconds with the money then they, not the purchaser's solicitor, bear the loss. Bearing in mind the high standards of our profession, it is probably of academic interest only to note that the Code does nothing to meet the suggestion that the *Wong* case also undermines the standard undertaking given by a vendor's solicitor at a formal completion regarding the discharge of a mortgage.

Vacant possession

The reader may find it helpful to link 12(A) with the contractual obligations of the parties. Under an open contract it is implied that vacant possession will be given on completion.[22] Both standard contracts require the vendor to state by special condition whether the sale will be with vacant possession or subject to tenancies.[23] Unilaw add to their normal completion question (as enquiry 11): "Please see that there is no rubbish left on the property at completion." If the vendor does leave excessive rubbish he will be in breach of his duty to give vacant possession. In *Cumberland Consolidated Holdings Ltd.* v. *Ireland*[24] a contract for the sale of a warehouse stated that vacant possession would be given on completion. The vendor left the cellars of the warehouse filled to about two-thirds of their height with hardened cement and empty drums. After completion the purchaser was able to compel the vendor to remove the rubbish. The Court of Appeal said that the term "vacant possession" included freedom from any physical "impediment which

No vacant possession if vendor leaves excessive rubbish, etc.

[22] *Cook* v. *Taylor* [1942] Ch. 349.
[23] National special condition C, Law Society special condition F.
[24] [1946] K.B. 264.

substantially prevents or interferes with the enjoyment of the right of possession of a substantial part of the property." It is further implied under an open contract that completion shall take place within a reasonable time, taking into account the legal business yet to be carried out.[25] Where one of the standard contracts is used the parties will usually fix a date for completion and insert it in the designated place on the contract form. If no date is agreed, by National condition 5(2) completion shall be on the twenty-sixth working day after the date of the contract or the delivery of the abstract, whichever is the later, and by Law Society condition 21(1) on the twenty-fifth working day after the date of the contract. To ease the banking arrangements of the parties Law Society condition 21(5)(a) and (b) provides that if completion does not take place before 2.30 p.m. (or such other time as is stated by special condition) then completion is deemed to have taken place on the next working day, for the purposes of claiming compensation for late completion. National condition 5(5)(i) less stringently states that if completion day falls on a Friday, the purchaser must complete before 2.15 p.m. Otherwise for the purpose of calculating apportionments and interest, completion is deemed to take place on the first working day thereafter.

Date and time for completion

13. New Properties

(A) Will the Vendor pay all charges for constructon and connection of the drainage system and the services?

(B) Are all the following included in the purchase price: fencing all the boundaries, laying all paths and drives, and levelling and clearing the garden area? If not, please give particulars.

This enquiry calls for no comment except to say that Unilaw and Shaw & Sons Ltd. omit such an enquiry.

Note on Development Land Tax (Unilaw, 9; Shaw & Sons Ltd., 13)

Development Land Tax was abolished with effect from March 19, 1985. Oyez have already revised Con 29 to reflect this and undoubtedly the other two publishers will soon follow suit. In the meantime users of their forms should delete the appropriate enquiry.

Leasehold[26]

"Leases constitute perhaps the most complex area of domestic conveyancing today." *Nationwide Building Society.*

Many owner-occupiers in England and Wales live in leasehold houses, flats and maisonettes. Houses are leasehold for mainly historical reasons. Therefore most house-owners were given the right to purchase their freeholds or extend their leases

[25] *Johnson* v. *Humphrey* [1946] 1 All E.R. 460.
[26] See generally, E. F. George and A. George *The Sale of Flats*, (5th ed., 1984).

by the Leasehold Reform Act 1967 (as amended). Flats and maisonettes present quite different problems. Owners of houses can in effect largely ignore their neighbours, owners of flats and maisonettes cannot. Even the simple case of two self-contained maisonettes with separate entrances involves questions of support, and insurance and repair of the main structure. Higher developments are complicated by such things as the maintenance of common parts and the provision of lifts and services. The burden of positive freehold covenants does not run with the land so as to bind successive owners,[27] so flats and maisonettes were and are sold on a leasehold basis, this being the only real alternative to ensure the enforceability of positive obligations. In addition building societies have resolutely set their faces against lending on freehold flats and upper maisonettes. Many flat and maisonette developments, especially the newer ones, with well-drafted leases, co-operative landlords and good managing agents function well—for the moment; others do not. For leaseholders of flats, etc., the main problems are twofold. First, what to do when the length of their leases falls below a certain number of years. Flats and maisonettes are not covered by the Leasehold Reform Act 1967 and lenders will not generally lend money on leasehold property where the lease has 40 years or less to run. The lease becomes unmarketable, a "depreciating asset." Mrs. Anne Grubb, a London solicitor, told the Farrand Committee[28]:

Problems with flats

> "At the present time, once a lease has 70 [*sic*] years or less to run, complicated and expensive negotiations are often necessary to protect the purchaser and his mortgagee and this of course is also a serious problem for the vendor, and the delays can hold up a long chain of conveyancing transactions.
>
> In addition to the question of delay, the present position appears to be a Landlord's charter for exploitation, and excessive premiums are sometimes requested by Landlords for the granting of a longer lease. The Landlord can refuse to extend the lease if the lessee does not accept his terms."

The second major problem is, quite simply, maintenance. Other practical problems facing purchasers of leaseholds will emerge as we discuss the enquiries themselves and some suggested additional enquiries. It is quite apparent that leaseholds are in need of reform. In the past decade the Law Commission have produced four reports of relevance—"Obligations of Landlords and Tenants" (1975 Law Com.No. 67), "The Law of Positive and Restrictive Covenants" (1984 Law Com.No. 127), "Covenants Restricting Dispositions, Alterations and Change of User" (1985 Law Com.No. 141), and "Forfeiture of Tenancies" (1985 Law Com.No. 142). The Building Societies Association published their report "Leaseholds—Time for a Change?" in July 1984 and the Farrand Committee acknowledged the need but made no suggestions for reform.[29] A committee of inquiry under the chairmanship of Mr. Edward Nugee, Q.C. set up by

[27] *Austerberry* v. *Corporation of Oldham* (1885) 29 Ch.D. 750.
[28] The Second Report of the Conveyancing Committee, 1985, para. 8.12.
[29] *Ibid.*, paras. 8.1–8.26.

the Minister of Housing and Construction, with terms of reference: "To collect and examine evidence of the nature, scale and incidence of problems for landlords and tenants arising from the management of privately owned blocks of flats; to assess the difficulties caused by management problems and to make recommendations on how they might be resolved" reported in October 1985.[29a] Amongst its recommendations are the introduction of a procedure for appointing a receiver or manager if the landlord neglects his duties, a new small claims procedure for dealing with disputes between landlord and tenant, and a review of the tax treatment of payments by way of service charge which can at present cause problems where a service charge is expressed to be payable as rent or if a reserve fund is established.

Overall long term suggestions for reform indicate the introduction of a system of Strata Title in England and Wales for flats and maisonettes. In the meantime enactment of the law commissions proposals for the creation of "land obligations" is urged.

Oyez's Con 29 (Long) contains five leasehold enquiries:

I. General (Unilaw, 12(a)-(e); Shaw & Sons Ltd, 1, 3, 4, 5, 6, 7)

(A) Is the lease under which the property is held a head lease or an underlease?

(B) Please state the names and addresses of the lessor, any superior lessors, their respective solicitors and the receivers of the rent.

(C) Please supply copies of all licences granted by the lessor, other than licences to assign.

(D) What steps have been taken to obtain the lessor's consent to the proposed assignment? Please supply a copy of any licence granted.

Headlease or underlease

The answer to enquiry I(A) should be read in conjunction with the answer to enquiry (V), below. The amount of title a purchaser of leasehold property is entitled to call for differs depending on whether the lease is a headlease or underlease. Underleasehold property carries with it the risk of forfeiture for acts committed by the underlessor; property held under a headlease does not. The underlease should contain a covenant by the underlessor to observe the lessee's covenants in the headlease. In the case of flats relief from forfeiture can present difficulties unless the total of the rents payable under the flat-underleases well exceeds the rent payable under the headlease. Then it is worthwhile for someone to take over the forfeited headlease. The problem is of course overcome where the headlease is assigned to a flat-owners' management company. Unilaw 12(a)(i) usefully adds a request for a copy of the lease or underlease if this has not already been supplied.

Identity of landlord

The evidence presented to the Nugee committee shows that difficulty is often experienced in discovering the identity of landlords (I(B)), even though failure to provide any residential tenant with the landlord's name and address on request or to notify him on a change of ownership within two months is an

[29a] A summary of the Nugee recommendations can be found in (1985) 129 S.J. 823.

offence.[30] One suggestion[31] (not recommended the Committee) is that breach of the obligation should be bolstered by suspension of the tenant's obligations under the lease. Here Unilaw's question 12(b)(i) is helpful: "Please confirm that the Lessor mentioned in the Lease[32] is the present Lessor and please confirm his present address."

Alteration and user covenants

Most leases contain covenants against the making of alterations to or changing the use of the property let. At present such covenants may be absolute, qualified (not to do the thing in question without the landlord's consent) or fully qualified (as for qualified, with the addition that consent is not to be unreasonably withheld). Section 19(2) of the Landlord and Tenant Act 1927 subjects qualified alteration (but not user) covenants to the "reasonableness" test. The Law Commission have recommended[33] that all qualified user or alteration covenants should be fully qualified. Question I(C) will tell the purchaser whether any consents to alterations or change of user have been given but not whether any such unauthorised behaviour has taken place. Shaw & Sons Ltd. ask (7): "Have any alterations been carried out which require the landlord's consent under the lease?" and Unilaw require confirmation that the lessor has given consent to any improvements to the property. A better enquiry would be: "Please supply details of all alterations additions or changes of use, with copy consents where appropriate, since the date of the Lease."

Consent to assign

The issue raised by I(D) is vital. Contracts should not normally be exchanged unless it is known that any requisite licence to assign is likely to be forthcoming. Readers might like to note that the Law Commission recommend[33] full qualification for covenants against disposition; any absolute covenant against disposition or surrender provision contained in any future lease to be transferred into fully qualified covenants. Unilaw's assumption (12(d)(ii)) that consent to the sale will be obtained before exchange of contracts is often unfounded, as recognised by Law Society condition 8(4) and National condition 11(5). Both conditions oblige the vendor to use his best endeavours to obtain any requisite licence to assign at his own expense before completion. Hence Shaw & Sons Ltd.'s enquiry (4(2)): "Please confirm it [the licence to assign] will be procured by the vendor at his own expense and a stamped original handed over on completion" is unnecessary where either standard contract form is used. However theirs is the only form that recognises that many leases require an assignee-purchaser to enter into fresh covenants with the lessor. Their enquiry 5: "If the lease requires any direct covenant between assignee and landlord, please supply the form of draft required by the landlord" could be added as an additional enquiry where one of the other two forms are used.

Shaw & Sons Ltd. include the following questions as to rent:

"9. (1) Is the current rent as stated in the Lease?
(2) If not, please explain the difference.

[30] Landlord and Tenant Act 1985, ss.1–3.
[31] Report of the Royal Institute of Chartered Surveyors on the Management of Blocks of Flats, 1983.
[32] "Lease" is defined to include "underlease."
[33] Law Com.No. 141, 1985.

10. Has any rent review under the Lease occurred and is there any memorandum of same?
11. Regardless of the lease provisions, is the rent actually paid in advance or in arrear at present?
12. (1) For what rent period does the vendor have the latest rent receipt for production on completion?
    (2) Is this a clear receipt?
    (3) If the landlord does not issue rent receipts, please confirm you will procure and hand over on completion a letter from the landlord or his agents confirming there is no outstanding claim against the tenant."

Rent

At one time it was possible to say that the rent should be sufficient to ensure that the lessor had an incentive to perform his covenants, but inflation has caused this to no longer be true of many rents payable under long leases of flats granted at a premium. Unless the reversion is vested in a flat-owners' management committee the purchaser takes the risk that the lessor's covenants may not be performed.

It has become increasingly popular for service charges to be reserved as rent. The main consequences of this are that the lessor can distrain for it and if he wishes to proceed for forfeiture he does not have to comply with the provisions of section 146 of the Law of Property Act 1925.

Rent Act 1977

Exceptionally the conveyancer may have to consider the Rent Act 1977. The more important results of property being within the Rent Act are:

(1) the lessee is given security of tenure and the lessor can only regain possession by obtaining a court order which will only be forthcoming if he proves one or more stated grounds;
(2) the amount of rent that can be charged is restricted if either party applies for the registration of a fair rent;
(3) generally *no premium can be required or received on the grant or assignment of the lease.*

The Rent Act applies to any dwelling-house (including a flat) which is let as a separate dwelling, provided its rateable value falls within prescribed limits[34] and the rent is not less than two-thirds of the rateable value.[35] Where a lease is granted for a term of 21 years or more (*i.e.* a long lease) section 5(4) of the Act provides that in computing the rent for the purpose of the latter requirement payments (however expressed) for rates, services, maintenance, or insurance should be disregarded. A trap for the unwary might be a provision for progressive rents or rent review or an item of service charge, for example the lessor's costs of

[34] See Rent Act 1977, s.4. Broadly speaking a property will be within the rateable value limits if its present rateable value is £1,500 or less in Greater London or £750 or less elsewhere. If the present rateable value of property is higher than this, it may still come within the rateable value limits if its rateable value on the valuation list which expired on March 31, 1973 was £600 or less in Greater London or £300 or less elsewhere.

[35] On the "appropriate day," that is, either March 23, 1965 if the property was rated at that time or if not, the date on which it became rated.

management,[36] which must be counted as rent, which might bring the property within the Act.

The Leasehold Reform Act 1967

The chief reason for knowing the rent is to see whether the Leasehold Reform Act 1967 (as amended by the Housing Act 1980 applies). Basically to qualify for the benefits bestowed by this Act, namely to purchase the reversion or claim an extended lease, the lessee must satisfy five conditions:

(1) he must have a lease of a house;
(2) the lease must be for a term exceeding 21 years;
(3) he must have occupied the house as his only or main residence for the whole of the last three years, or for a total of three out of the last 10 years;
(4) during this period of qualifying residence the rent must have been less than two-thirds of the rateable value;
(5) the rateable value[37] must be within prescribed limits.

The local authority's valuation officer will help with enquiries relating to rateable values but the purchaser of long leases of houses should ask by way of additional enquiry, how long the vendor has been resident in the house and whether he has served any notice on the landlord purporting to exercise his rights under the Leasehold Reform Act and if so whether he will assign the benefit of the notice to the purchaser.

The practice of asking for clear rent receipts has no legal basis[38] but is based on the concept that when buying leasehold property the purchaser's solicitor must see such a receipt to satisfy himself that there has been no breach of covenant under the lease, that is, so that either the receipt is withheld or qualified.

II. Covenants (Unilaw 12(i); Shaw & Sons Ltd., 8)

(A) Has the lessor complained of any breach of covenant?
(B) Has any obligation in the lease to paint or do any other work by or at a particular time been strictly fulfilled? If not please give details.
(C) Has the Vendor had cause to complain of any breach of the lessor's covenants?

Standard conditions of sale

If the contract incorporates either the Law Society's or National conditions of sale the purchaser is deemed to purchase with full knowledge of the actual state and condition of the property and will have to take it as it stands. (Law Society condition 5(2)(a), National condition 13(3)). The effect of the statutory[39] implied covenants for title is modified so as to preclude the purchaser from recovering damages from the vendor for breach of the vendor's repairing covenant in the lease (Law Society condition 8(5), National condition 11(7)). If any breach

[36] "Management" cannot be treated as part of "services" or "maintenance," for in Landlord and Tenant Act 1985, ss.18–25 (dealing with reasonableness of a service charge) one of the items specifically mentioned as well as "services" and "maintenance" is "the landlord's costs of management."
[37] See the Housing Act 1974, s.118. Generally speaking the limits are £1,500 in Greater London and £750 elsewhere.
[38] See the Law of Property Act 1925, s.45(2).
[39] See the Law of Property 1925, s.76(1)(*a*) and (*b*) and Parts I and II of the 2nd Sched., and the Land Registration Act 1925, s.24.

of covenant is revealed by enquiry II (A) or (B) the vendor should be required to remedy the breach before completion or prove that the breach has been formally waived by the landlord. No purchaser wishes to saddle himself with the responsibility of remedying a breach, if indeed it is capable of remedy. Many solicitors prefer to ask more specific questions as to the vendor's painting obligations under the lease. Here is one such:

> "If the Lease requires the exterior and/or interior of the property to be decorated this year, please state whether the Vendor will have carried this out by completion."

The simplicity of enquiry II(C) masks a matter of great importance to the purchaser of a flat or maisonette. Repairs especially are a frequent source of irritation to flat etc. owners. The Organisation of Private Tenants[40] complained to the Nugee committee of landlords failing to carry out repairs and allowing blocks of flats to deteriorate, or repairs done badly by "cowboy" workmen. The Building Societies Association[41] in its recent report drew attention to growing public concern over the decay of some blocks of flats. The Farrand Committee included this comment by Mrs. Anne Grubb in their report:

> "From time to time a Landlord Company will go into liquidation or a private landlord or landlord company will virtually disappear and be untraceable for all practical purposes. This means that it is impossible to enforce the Landlord's covenants. . . ."[42]

She suggests that some body on the lines of the Motor Insurers Bureau should be set up to provide the necessary services.

Defective schemes

Purchaser's solicitors are becoming more and more insistent in advising their clients not to accept defective schemes. Here they are concerned to see that there are effective and enforceable "lessor's" covenants. It should be noted that there is some doubt surrounding the proposition that if the lessee covenants in the lease to pay for or contribute towards repairs done or services provided by the lessor, the lessor is under an obligation to do or provide them, even through the lease is silent on this matter.[43] Some solicitors will reject a scheme where there is no covenant by the lessor to enforce covenants on the part of flat-owners of the other leases in the block so far as they affect the lessee.[44] The particular importance of this covenant to the purchaser is that the threat of forfeiture proceedings being brought ensures that all the flat owners pay their service charges. Another point of importance is the effect on the lessor's covenants of a disposal of the reversion. Although a disposal of the reversion by the original lessor does not affect his contractual liability, unless the lease

[40] A London based organisation.
[41] *Leaseholds—Time for a change?* 1983.
[42] The Second Report of the Conveyancing Committee, 1985, para. 8.24.
[43] *Barnes* v. *City of London Real Property Co. Ltd.* [1918] 2 Ch. 18. and *Edmonton Corporation* v. *W. M. Knowles Ltd.* (1961) 60 L.G.R. 124 suggests he is; *Duke of Westminster* v. *Guild* (1983) 267 E.G. 762 suggests he is not. But see *Liverpool Corporation* v. *Irwin* [1977] A.C. 239.
[44] Enforceability by the lessor is required because as a general rule the burden of positive covenants does not run with the land so as to bind successive flat owners *inter se*, even if the covenants are contained in a lease.

states otherwise, it does mean that the lessee cannot enforce personal covenants against (to supply hot water or provide central heating for instance) the current lessor—and then of course there is Mrs. Anne Grubb's problem.[45] Even where the purchaser's solicitor is entirely satisfied as to the lease provisions, there remains the fact that enforcement of covenants (against the lessor or a flat-owner) through the courts can be difficult and expensive. Accordingly II(C) tries to find out in advance whether there has been any breach of the lessor's covenants. Conveyancers may find it useful to add the question: "Is there any dispute between the Tenants and the Lessor, or between the Vendor and any other Tenant?" Shaw & Sons Ltd. include a similar enquiry—8. Complaints—in their form.

Management companies Enquiry II(C) ignores the fact that most modern flat developments involve management companies and/or managing agents. Most attractive to the purchaser is a flat-owners' management company which owns the freehold. Then many of the problems already and to be mentioned disappear. But others arise from personal squabbles, lack of interest and expertise. A flat-owners' management company with a concurrent or reversionary lease is almost as good except that it cannot cure the "depreciating asset" problem by extending the term of the lease. Sometimes a management company, owned by the flat-owners, the lessor or someone else, has no interest in the land. The covenants given by such a company should be backed up by covenants given by the reversioner in case the management company defaults. Furthermore since the link between the company and the flat-owners is contractual, assignees should be required to become members of the company or enter into a mutual deed of covenant (to ensure that lessee covenants are enforceable against them). No mention of management companies is made on Con 29. It is suggested that enquiry should be made as to the existence of a management company, and a request made for copies of the memorandum and articles. It should also be asked whether the purchaser will be required to become a member of the company and if so whether the consideration for the share transfer is included in the purchase price.

Tenants' associations Where the lessor remains responsible for maintenance and services, flat-owners will often form residents' associations, prompted either by dissatisfaction with the state of the building and/or defects in their leases which render them unmortgageable. Provision for "recognition" of these associations is made in section 29 of the Landlord and Tenant Act 1985. Again Con 29 does not cover residents' associations. It should be asked if there is one and if so how many flat-owners are members and who are the chairman and secretary.

Management company, residents' association or none, managing agents are often employed. Dissatisfaction with agents was another complaint voiced to the Nugee committee. The vendor should be asked for the name of managing agents where appropriate.

[45] See above, n.42.

III. Service charges (Unilaw 12(g)-(h); Shaw & Sons Ltd. 13–19)

(A) Please give details of service charge payments for the last three years, with any supporting accounts or vouchers that the Vendor has.

(B) Has the Vendor, or to his knowledge any predecessor in title, exercised a statutory right to obtain information? If so, with what result?

Statutory provisions

A service charge notionally represents the complete indemnity a landlord expects to get from his tenant for the performance of his obligations under the lease. However the Landlord and Tenant Act 1985,[46] imposes certain restrictions on service charges for flats. Section 18 of to the Act defines a service charge as an amount payable (however expressed) for services, repairs, maintenance, or insurance or the landlord's costs of management. The landlord can only recover the costs he incurs to the extent that they are reasonable and if the costs relate to services or works, these must be to a reasonable standard. If the charges are payable in advance they too must be reasonable. The county court has power to declare that an amount is or is not reasonable and as to the standard of work. In the event that the cost exceeds £25 times the number of flats in the building or £500 whichever is the greater then the landlord must obtain a minimum of two estimates for the works, at least one from a person wholly unconnected with the landlord, and a notice accompanied by a copy of the estimates must be given to each of the tenants inviting observations. The landlord must consider any tenant's observations. At least one month must elapse in any event from the service of the works notice before the landlord proceeds with the work, unless it is urgent. In addition a tenant of a flat has a statutory right to information, namely to obtain a written summary of the expenditure to which his service charge relates for the period in question. That period is either 12 months ending with the request, or as the case may be, the last full 12 monthly accounting period. The summary must then be provided within six months of the period in question having ended or one month of the request whichever is the later, and it must set out in detail the various costs and be certified by an independent qualified acountant as fair and sufficient. If service charge accounts are annually prepared, then the tenant must exercise his right to information by means of a written request served on the landlord not later than 12 months after the end of that year. If this is not done then the time limit is on costs relating to the 12 months preceding the request.

Calculation of service charge

The amount of service charge each flat owner has to pay is usually expressed in the lease as being a proportion of the landlord's total expenditure. The proportion normally depends on the number of the flats in the building but can be calculated according to floor-space. The actual amount of the charge will naturally vary from year to year and may be considerable if major repairs are carried out in any one year. Question III(A) is asked to give the purchaser an idea of how much it is likely to cost him to live in the flat. Conscientious conveyancers should also ask

[46] Ss.18–25.

Sinking funds

whether any unusual expenditure is anticipated (see Shaw & Sons Ltd. 17) and whether there is a sinking fund to cover major items of expenditure and if so what is its balance and where is it invested. If the lease is silent as to the ownership of a sinking fund (as many leases are) prima facie the fund belongs to the landlord—with the attendant danger of it disappearing on a change of ownership of the reversion or bankruptcy of the landlord. But, "if the terms upon which the person receives the money are that he is bound to keep it separate, either in a bank or elsewhere, and to hand that money so kept as a separate fund to the person entitled to it, then he is trustee of that money and must hand it over to the person who is his cestui que trust." In other words, in the absence of any express trust in the lease, if the fund is kept in a separate bank, etc., account then it belongs to the flat-owners. Only Unilaw ask about sinking funds.

Question III(B) refers to a tenant's right to information under the Landlord and Tenant Act 1985, mentioned above. Since it is in the purchaser's interest to discover as much as he can about the service charge it might be useful to ask for any estimates obtained for work not yet charged and evidence of any consultations with tenants or any tenants' association.

Nugee recommendations

The Nugee Committee[47] makes several recommendations regarding the payment of service charges. These include, the payment of all collected but unexpended service charges into a trust account with appropriate safeguards, a greater roll for tenants' associations in the consultation procedures for major works and a return to the system of major and minor works for the purposes of consultation.

National condition 6 and Law Society condition 19 provide for the apportionment of service charges on completion. Where the exact amount of the charge is not known at the time of completion, a provisional apportionment is to be made on the best estimate available and a final apportionment when the exact amount of the charge is known. (National condition 6(5); Law Society condition 19(6)).

IV. Insurance (Unilaw 12(f); Shaw & Sons Ltd. 20–24).

(A) Who effected the insurance policy currently covering the property?

(B) Please give particulars: insurers' and any insurance brokers' name and address, policy number, insured's name(s), risks covered, for what amount, premium, and date to which the property is insured.

"The insurance of leasehold property is a further problem which sometimes causes delays, particularly where the original insurance has been changed without notice. On occasion, it has even been found that a Landlord has allowed insurance to lapse and the lessee is not aware of the fact until he comes to sell the flat." Mrs. Anne Grubb's submission to the Conveyancing Committee, 1985.[48]

Enquiry IV(A) is asked because it can be, that even though the lease obliges the tenant to insure, the insurance policy is in

[47] Management of Privately owned Blocks of Flats, 1985, paras. 8.16–8.29.
[48] The Second Report of the Conveyancing Committee, 1985, para. 8.24.

fact taken out by the landlord. In this situation the tenant cannot compel the landlord to maintain the policy. In *Argy Trading Development Co. Ltd.* v. *Lapid Developments Ltd.*[49] the tenant covenanted to insure. Nevertheless the landlord took out a block policy covering other property as well and the tenant paid part of the premium instead of insuring himself. The block policy was later cancelled without notification to the tenant and the premises were partially destroyed by fire. The court held that the landlord was not liable to the tenant in negligence.

Where the vendor is obliged to insure under the terms of his lease, he must carry out his obligation down to completion (see Law Society condition 11(4), National condition 21(1)). Flat leases sometimes contain a covenant requiring the tenant to insure with a company specified, or some other office approved by the landlord. The landlord has the absolute right to withhold his approval without giving a reason.[50] This can cause problems where the purchaser's mortgagee also requires insurance through a specified, different agency. Accordingly Shaw & Sons Ltd. ask (23): "If the lease provides for insurance by the tenant with a nominated or approved insurance company please specify what company has been nominated or approved." Since the purchaser acquires an equitable interest in the property as soon as the contract is entered into, his interest should be noted on the vendor's policy.

Insurance with approved company

In the case of block insurance effected by the landlord (common with flats) the purchaser should ensure that the policy is on foot because the vendor does not warrant in the contract that the landlord's covenants have been complied with, or that they will be complied with until completion. Other points to check are, is the cover adequate?—this can be difficult in the case of flats because block policies do not often stipulate separate values for the various flats—and, are the terms of the policy acceptable to the purchaser's mortgagee? On this latter point it may be helpful to set out the Building Societies Association's preferences regarding the insurance of flats[51]:

Building societies and flat insurance

"(a) one policy covering the block (including common parts) with an acceptable insurer;

(b) the terms of the policy being as full as possible (*e.g.* to include subsidence especially) with the insured value being adequate and maintained at full reinstatement value, preferably on an index-linked basis.

(c) a clear and unambiguous arrangement whereby the society's interest in the property is known to the insurer (either by its being a joint insured or having its interest noted), it is kept informed of any alterations in the terms or amount of cover, it is told immediately of any failure to pay premiums (with perhaps a time-limited 'held covered' undertaking) and it is notified in the event of any substantial claim."

It should be remembered that a tenant of a flat has the right to challenge the reasonableness of his landlord's cost of

[49] [1977] 1 W.L.R. 444.
[50] *Viscount Tredegar* v. *Harwood* [1929] A.C. 72.
[51] *Leaseholds—Time for a Change?*, 1984, App. C.

insurannce under sections 18–25 of the Landlord and Tenant Act 1985.

V. Reversionary title (Unilaw 12(a)(ii); Shaw & Sons Ltd. 2)

Is there with the title deeds a marked abstract or office copy of the freehold title and of any superior lease?

Grant of headlease

Under an open contract for the grant of a head-lease the grantee has no right to call for the freehold title.[52] The standard conditions do not amend the open contract position and because it is unsatisfactory where the grantee is taking a long lease or paying a premium, he should reserve himself this right in the contract. Apart from the obvious reason of checking that the landlord has power to grant the lease the wisdom of contracting to investigate the freehold title is illustrated by the case of *White v. Bijou Mansions Ltd.*[53] There a proprietor registered with a freehold absolute title subject to a restrictive covenant, notice of which was given on the register, granted a lease without disclosing the restrictive covenant. The lease was subsequently registered. On an action being brought to enforce the covenant against the lessee, Simmonds J. rejected the argument that section 44(5)[54] of the Law of Property Act 1925 protected the lessee and held that he was bound by the covenant, because by section 20 of the Land Registration Act 1925 a disposition, including a lease of registered land, takes effect subject to the entries on the register. Had the lessor's land been unregistered the lessee would have been bound by the covenant if registered as a land charge under the Land Charges Act 1972 and the lessee would not have been entitled to claim compensation under section 25 of the Law of Property Act 1925. Furthermore a building society or other mortgagee who is assisting the purchase will wish to see the freehold title.

Grant of underlease

On the grant of an underlease the grantee is entitled to see the underlessor's title[55] (that is the lease out of which the underlease is to be carved), but not the freehold or any superior title. Again the standard conditions follow the common law. For the same reasons as on the grant of a headlease the grantee should contract to see the reversionary title, except where the underlessor is registered with absolute leasehold title in which case this will already have been done by the Land Registry. This may of course be impossible if the underlessor himself did not contract for more than his minimum entitlement to title.

[52] The Law of Property Act 1925, s.44 governs the title the purchaser is entitled to call for on the grant or assignment of a lease or underlease. And see *Gosling v. Woolf* [1893] 1 Q.B. 39.

[53] [1938] Ch. 351.

[54] "Where . . . an intending lessee or assignee is not entitled to call for the title to the freehold or leasehold reversion, as the case may be, he shall not . . . be deemed to be affected with notice of any matter or thing of which, if he had contracted that such title should be furnished, he might have had notice."

[55] There is some doubt as to whether a grantee of an underlease of registered land is entitled to see the underlessor's title. Title to registered land is deduced in accordance with s.110 of the Land Registration Act 1925 but that section expressly excludes a "lessee" and "lease" is defined to include "underlease." On the other hand s.110 applies to a "disposition" which otherwise includes "underlease." Since the position is unclear the title to be shown should be expressly mentioned in the contract.

Purchase of headlease or underlease

The open contract position is exactly the same on the purchase of an existing headlease or underlease: the purchaser is denied access to any superior title. The dangers to the purchaser of an existing headlease or underlease are the same as to a grantee of headlease or underlease. Therefore unless the vendor is registered with an absolute leasehold title the superior title should be expressly contracted for. Where however the contract is governed by the Law Society conditions of sale, the lease being sold is not registered with title absolute and is dated not more than 15 years prior to the date of the contract, this may not be necessary—the freehold and all other titles superior to the lease must be deduced for a period of not less than 15 years prior to the date of the grant of the lease (condition 8(2)). The National conditions contain no equivalent provision.

There is one more important reason why the grantee or purchaser should secure the right to call for the reversionary title. If his lease requires registration under the Land Registration Acts 1925–1971 and he cannot produce the reversionary title to the Registrar he will only be registered with good leasehold title[56]

Buying property subject to tenancies and licences

Background

The standard contract forms require the vendor to state by special condition, whether the property is sold with vacant possession or subject to tenancies (Law Society special condition F, National special condition C). If there is no express provision it is usually implied that vacant possession will be given on completion.[57] In any event occupation by a tenant may be notice to the purchaser of the tenant's rights in the case of unregistered land[58] or in the case of land with registered title an overriding interest. Furthermore certain licences may be binding on a subsequent purchaser.[59]

Disclosure obligations under the standard conditions

National condition 18(1) provides that: "Abstracts or copies of the leases or agreements (if in writing) . . . having been made available, the purchaser (whether he has inspected the same or not) shall be deemed to have notice of and shall take subject to the terms of all existing tenancies and the rights of the tenants . . . and such notice shall not be affected by any partial or incomplete statement in the Special Conditions with reference to the tenancies. . . . " Law Society condition 6(2) is in similar terms: "Copies or full particulars of all leases or tenancies not vested in the purchaser having been furnished to him, he shall be deemed to purchase with full knowledge thereof and shall take

[56] There is one exception. On the grant of a lease out of registered land (which itself requires registration) production of the superior land certificate is unnecessary where no premium was paid for the grant of the lease. This change of Land Registry practice came as a direct result of the decision in *Strand Securities Ltd.* v. *Caswell* [1965] Ch. 958. However in the type of leasehold conveyancing under discussion the practitioner is unlikely to come across a lease granted at a rack rent.

[57] *Cook* v. *Taylor* [1942] Ch. 349.

[58] *Hunt* v. *Luck* [1902] 1 Ch. 428. But subject to the provisions of the Land Charges Act 1972.

[59] See above, pp. 32 to 38.

the property subject to the rights of the tenants thereunder or by reason thereof." It will be noted that National condition 18(1) does not cover oral tenancies. A purchaser's solicitor who fails to inspect a lease having been afforded the opportunity so to do will be guilty of negligence.[60]

Once the purchaser has been supplied with the requisite information he is deemed to have full knowledge of the tenant's rights under the lease, for example the right to a statutory tenancy under the Rent Act 1977 or compensation for improvements made during the currency of the term. This is reinforced by Law Society condition 6(3) which states that: "The vendor gives no warranty as to the amount of rent lawfully recoverable from any tenant, as to the effect of any legislation in relation to any lease or tenancy or as to the compliance with any legislation affecting the same." However in relation to written communications received by a vendor landlord, it will be remembered that a wide ranging duty of disclosure is placed on the vendor by Law Society condition 3. Matters such as applications by a tenant for registration of his rent which are notified to a landlord should come to the purchaser's attention by this route. The National conditions have no equivalent to either Law Society condition 6(3) or 3.

Neither National condition 18(1), Law Society condition 6(2) nor Law Society condition 6(3) are likely to protect a vendor from liability for any statements amounting to misrepresentations. They are provisions excluding or restricting liability and therefore fall within section 3 of the Misrepresentation Act 1967.

Oyez provide two forms of supplementary enquiries for use alongside Con 29 (Long or Short) where the purchaser is buying property subject to a tenancy: Con 291 for business and residential tenancies and Con 292 for agricultural tenancies.

Con 291 The headnote to Con 291 asks the vendor to reply separately to each enquiry for each part of the property to be sold which is separately let and to provide information regarding licences. The form is then divided into three sections: the first contains general enquiries relevant to business and residential tenancies, the second questions relating to business tenancies only and the third questions on residential tenancies. In the case of residential tenancies the purchaser is warned that he may have to raise additional enquiries where the tenancy has been granted by a housing association, housing trust or the Crown Estate Commissioners. Additional enquiries would also be necessary if the property is let on a protected shorthold or assured tenancy, since neither are referred to specifically in the residential enquiries.

Con 292 Con 292 is for use where all or part of the property is let as an agricultural holding or an agricultural tied cottage and is similar in format to Con 291. Thus its three sections comprise first general enquiries, then tied cottage enquiries and last agricultural holdings enquiries. The vendor is again requested to answer each enquiry separately for each part of the property to be sold and told that in the case of an agricultural tied cottage, the enquiries are intended to extend to a licence to occupy.

[60] *Becker* v. *Partridge* [1966] 2 Q.B. 155.

Oyez's Con 291 and 292 are reproduced in Appendices E and F. Neither Unilaw nor Shaw & Sons Ltd. have as yet produced standard forms of tenancy enquiries. Shaw & Sons Ltd. have published a "Sublettings" form (?).

Standard additional enquiries

Oyez's Con 29 (Supplementary)

Oyez now provide a set of extra questions to accompany their basic enquiries. Their justification for this capitalising on what is now a growth industry is: "many conveyancing practitioners feel that to give a full service to the increasing number of first-time buyers and inexperienced people becoming owner/occupiers, they need to raise wider-ranging preliminary enquiries to provide more information." Con 29 (Supplementary) is the end product of Oyez's research into those additional enquiries most frequently made in practice. Where there is a need for additional enquiries (and Oyez warn that in many transactions raising them is a waste of time and money) the new form can be attached to either their Long or Short form of basic enquiries. No extra filling in is required. We understand that Con 29 (Supplementary) has been greeted with enthusiasm—one is sold for every ten basic Con 29s. Here it is—

Property

(a) Please give details of any of the following which have at any time affected the property:
  (i) Structural defects;
  (ii) Drainage defects;
  (iii) Defective foundations;
  (iv) Rising damp, dry or wet rot;
  (v) Infestation by wood boring insects.

(b) Has the property or the site been subject to:
  (i) Flooding?
  (ii) Landslip?
  (iii) Subsidence or heave?

(c) Is the property situated in an area where mining or underground extraction is carried on?

Services

(d) When was the electrical system:
  (i) Last tested and approved by the local electricity board?
  (ii) Comprehensively rewired?

(e) Please give details of the service provided by the local authority for emptying any private drainage system.

(f) When the central heating system was last in use, did it function completely satisfactorily?

(g) Will the Vendor give the Purchaser details of any burglar alarm?

(h) Please supply copies of any contracts for regular maintenance or servicing of fixed appliances, which the Purchaser could take over.

Vehicles

(i) Was the garage on the property erected at the same time as the dwelling, or, if later, when?
(j) Do parking restrictions apply to the road in front of the property, or have the police objected to vehicles being parked there?

Chattels and fixtures

(k) A copy of the estate agents' sale particulars is attached. Is any item mentioned there not included in the sale?
(l) Please confirm that no moveable or detachable item included in the sale is subject to any lease, hire, hire purchase or loan agreement or lien or any other claim by a third party.
(m) Do the telephone instruments on the property belong to British Telecommunications?

Financial

(n) What is the current annual amount payable in respect of the property for:
   (i) General rate?
   (ii) Water charges (including drainage and environmental charges)?
(o) Does this sale depend on the Vendor contracting to purchase another property?
(p) Please confirm that the Vendor will arrange for the appropriate authorities to read the electric, gas, water, and telephone meters on the day of actual completion.

Commentary

The questions grouped under the heading "Property" are reminiscent of those which used to appear in the first part of enquiry 9 on Con 29 (Long), criticised on the ground that they were more properly the concern of the purchaser's surveyor and dropped in the 1973 revision of that form. Although not suitable for inclusion in a basic enquiry these questions may be perfectly proper ones to ask in connection with property in certain areas. For example, five years ago the sea burst its walls in Clevedon, near Bristol, and flooded many homes, The beginnings of resultant structural problems might not be revealed in a survey. However, even where the questions are justifiably raised it is probable that vendors will be advised not to answer them. The rest of the questions call for no comment. They are clear and workmanlike and entirely suited to their stated purpose.

Shaw & Sons Ltd.'s "Information Memo"

Shaw & Sons Ltd. have also produced an extra set of questions, only they call theirs an "Information Memo." Some of the questions are perhaps a little too basic and not ones which the parties are happy to employ a solicitor as a medium to ask or answer. The vendor is asked, *inter alia*: "Do you have your milk delivered? If so, what is the name and local district address of the dairy company?"—and—"could you recommend any of the following? babysitters; plumber; carpenter; builder; central heating engineer."

Bristol Law Society recently[61] published guidelines to its

[61] November 1985.

members for the conduct by them of domestic conveyancing. Contained in these guidelines are recommended general additional enquiries and flat purchase enquiries. The interested reader will find them reproduced in Appendices J and K.

Other additional enquiries

Further additional enquiries raised will depend on the particular transaction. One which is quite often asked, and surprisingly not included in Con 29 (Supp.) as it is often of importance to the purchaser, is whether the vendor knows of any proposals for future development on neighbouring property. Two more could usefully be added here. On the rare occasion of a purchaser proposing to buy a caravan site, his solicitor will of course ask to see the site licence and planning permissions. Copies of any written statements or agreements given by the vendor (or his predecessor) under the Mobile Homes Act 1983 should also be requested. However the security of tenure given by the 1983 Act to mobile home "occupiers" does not depend on their possession of a written statement or agreement nor on their continuous occupation of the site. Therefore the vendor should be asked for a list of those currently entitled to park their vehicles on the site. And to finish—of wide import—the Potato Marketing Board have changed their procedure (with effect from January 1, 1985) for the transfer between registered potato producers of the basic area on which their potato quota is based. This means that solicitors acting for purchasers of potato growing land who wish to acquire any basic area the vendor has enjoyed in respect of it, have to enquire as to the amount of basic area associated with the land and the date on which the Board notified the vendor of his basic area, and seek confirmation that no basic area has been transferred since that date. Further information is obtainable on request from the Potato Marketing Board, Broadfield House, 4 Between Towns Road, Cowley, Oxford 4 3NA.

3 ENQUIRIES OF LOCAL AUTHORITIES

Introduction

In carrying out the wide variety of functions entrusted to them by statute local authorities are able to gather information about properties in their areas which is extremely useful to a potential purchaser of property. In order to enable a purchaser to tap into this huge reservoir of knowledge the Law Society in conjunction with various local authority organisations has from time to time approved a form of Enquiries of Local Authorities.

Forms There are two forms. Con 29A "Enquiries of District Councils" is for use in the whole of England and Wales excluding London. Form Con 29D "Enquiries of Local Authority" is for use in respect of properties situate in the area of London borough councils or the Corporation of London. See Appendices L and M.

Although it is the almost universal practice to submit either form Con 29A or Con 29D as appropriate there are two shortened form of enquiries Con 29AX and Con 29DX. The shorter forms incorporate the questions which appear on the full concertina type forms Con 29A and D by reference. In view of the fact that the possibility of overlooking the significance of a reply must be increased by the use of these shorter forms it is recommended that those advising purchasers use the full forms whenever possible.

The majority of the enquiries on forms Con 29A and D are aimed at eliciting information as to the impact of planning legislation on the property. An outline of the various statutory provisions appearing on the forms is given below. It is hoped that this will provide the reader with enough information to evaluate the local authority's replies and if necessary alert him to the fact that further research may be needed. Obviously, in particular cases further enquiries and recourse to detailed texts on planning law will be required.

Before dealing with the enquiries themselves it will be helpful to make some general comments about submitting the form and the value of the replies given by a local authority.

When to make the enquiries

Practice The form should be submitted along with the request for a search of the Register of Local Land Charges.[1] The usual practice is to make a local land charges search and submit the enquiries of the local authorities prior to exchange of contracts. This gives a potential purchaser the opportunity to pull out of the transaction if he finds some adverse matter on the local land charges register or in the replies to the enquiries given by the local authority—for

[1] See E.O. Bourne, *Handbook of Conveyancing Searches* (2nd ed., 1986) for the procedure for making such a search.

instance if the local authority tells him that it is about to build a motorway at the bottom of the garden of the property! The forms should be submitted as early as possible in the majority of cases because local authorities take on average four weeks to deal with the enquiries. In the case of some London borough councils the search and enquiries may take up to 12 weeks to be dealt with due to pressure of work within the council.[2] The address of the relevant local authority can be obtained from the *Oyez Guide to Local Authorities.* Remember to use form Con 29D when searching in respect of properties within the London area.

Fees

The form is divided into two parts. Part I contains the standard enquiries which will be answered as a matter of course by the local authority. The fee for obtaining replies to all the enquiries in Part I of the form is currently £10.60 in respect of each parcel of land. A fee of £2.65 must be paid for each additional parcel. If the fee calculated on this basis would exceed £100 arrangements can be made direct with the local authority to fix the amount of the fee. Part II contains various optional enquiries. Replies will only be given to those enquiries against which the applicant places his initials. A fee of £0.80 is charged for each optional enquiry which is answered whether the enquiry relates to one parcel of land or more. In addition to the enquiries which are printed on the form the purchasers' adviser may ask additional enquiries. A fee of £2.00 is payable in respect of each additional enquiry. A local authority has an absolute discretion as to whether it will answer such additional enquiries or not. In practice most local authorities try to be as helpful as possible.

Describing the property

There is a panel on the front of the form headed "Description of the Property" in which the postal address of the property should be inserted. Some of the enquiries deal with information relating to roads and paths in the immediate vicinity of the property. Consequently, the form requires the purchaser to specify roadways, footpaths and footways in addition to those given in the address on which information is sought in the enquiries. For example, any roads giving access to the rear of the property should be specified. A plan of the property should accompany the form whenever its boundaries are not clearly defined. In some cases the local authority may call for a plan to be submitted. Where a plan is sent with the request for a search of the local land charges register no further plan is required to accompany the form of enquiries. If a plan is to be submitted it should be on a scale large enough to adequately identify the boundaries of the property.

[2] Readers of *The Law Society Gazette* will be aware of the names of the local authorities which take the longest period to deal with the forms. The procedure for making a local land charges search is discussed in some detail in Bourne, *Handbook of Conveyancing Searches* (2nd ed., 1986).

Value of the local authority's replies

Making the enquiries of a local authority does not confer any priority period upon a purchaser. As the form makes clear in the headnotes[3] insofar as the replies relate to proposals of the local authority these may change. In this respect the value of any replies is limited. However, the replies will furnish the purchaser with a host of information about the property which his vendor is under no duty to disclose[4] (even if he knew it) and which the purchaser's survey might not reveal.

Local authority's liability for negligent replies

Disclaimer Headnote (3) on the front of form Con 29A reads as follows:

> "The Replies below are furnished after appropriate enquiries and in the belief that they are in accordance with the information at present available to the officers of the respective Councils, but on the distinct understanding that neither the District Council nor the County Council or any officer of either Council, is legally responsible therefor except for negligence. Any such liability for negligence shall extend not only to the person by or on whose behalf these Enquiries are made but also to a person (being a purchaser for the purposes of Section 10(3) of the Local Land Charges Act 1975) who or whose agent had knowledge, before the relevant time as defined by the said section of the Replies to these Enquiries."

Liability in tort This disclaimer was introduced after the case of *Coats Patons (Retail) Ltd.* v. *Birmingham Corporation.*[5] In this case the defendant corporation had approved the construction of a subway for pedestrians opposite a shop, which the plaintiff company proposed to purchase. In the course of their pre-contractual enquiries the plaintiffs submitted a form of enquiry to the corporation. One question on the form asked whether any proposals had been approved by the corporation for the construction of a subway or underpass within the highway immediately opposite the property. A clerk answered this enquiry incorrectly without making appropriate enquiries within the corporation, and the plaintiffs suffered loss as a result. The disclaimer on the form read as above without the words "except for negligence." It was held that the defendants were liable in tort for negligently failing to take reasonable care in answering the enquiry. The disclaimer failed to protect them because they did not make the appropriate enquiries within the highway department of the corporation. In the aftermath of this case many local authorities tried to disclaim any legal responsibility whatsoever for the replies furnished in response to the enquiries. The position was alleviated when after negotiations between the

[3] Headnote (4).
[4] See above, p. 5.
[5] (1971) 115 S.J. 757.

Law Society and various local authority organisations the present form of the disclaimer was agreed upon.

Liability in contract

It is possible that a local authority would be liable not only in tort but also in contract because a fee is payable for the replies. This could make a difference to the limitation period governing any cause of action which may accrue against a local authority. In respect of an action for breach of contract the time limit is six years from the date of the breach.[6] This would be the date upon which the incorrect replies are given. However, if an action was framed as a claim in the tort of negligence the relevant date for calculating the limitation period would be the date upon which damage occurred.[7] It is conceivable that this date could be materially later than the date upon which the replies were given. For example, in a case like *Coats*, the date upon which damage would be suffered is the date building operations to construct the underpass or subway commenced.

Effectiveness of disclaimer

Headnote (3) is an exclusion clause and as such its operation would be subject to section 3 of the Misrepresentation Act 1967 as amended by section 8 of the Unfair Contract Terms Act 1977. This provision introduces a test of reasonableness[8] to determine whether or not the exclusion clause is capable of being enforced.

It is not only the person who actually submits the form who may rely upon the replies as giving him a cause of action. If, for example, the vendors' solicitors submit a form and obtain replies which are relied upon subsequently by the purchaser in the event that the replies proved to have been made negligently the purchaser can sue the local authority in negligence. Obviously, in this case the contractual relationship is between the local authority and the vendor unless it is possible to argue that the vendors' solicitor made the search as agent for the purchaser. For these purposes a "purchaser" includes a lessee or a mortgagee.

Compulsory acquisition

Enquiry 14 asks whether the council has made any order (whether or not confirmed by the appropriate Secretary of State) or passed any resolution which is capable of being implemented for the compulsory acquisition[9] of the property. Needless to say, a positive reply to this enquiry will usually mean that the purchaser will withdraw from the transaction altogether. A negative reply to this enquiry does not necessarily mean that the land is not the subject of a compulsory purchase order. Numerous statutory bodies have the power to compulsorily acquire land in order to fulfil their functions. Consideration should be given to making enquiries of other bodies such as British Telecom, the local Electricity Board and the local water authority to name but a few!

The form for use in the London area will also reveal whether or not the Greater London Council made an order or passed any

[6] Limitation Act 1980, s.5.
[7] *Ibid.*, s.2 and see ss.11 and 14.
[8] See Unfair Contract Terms Act 1977, s.11.
[9] See Davies, *Law of Compulsory Purchase and Compensation* (4th ed., 1984) for a review of the law and procedure relating to compulsory acquisition of property.

resolution which would involve the acquisition of the property; form Con 29D, enquiry 20.

Public highways

A prospective purchaser of a property will want to be assured that he has adequate access to the property. If access to the property is via a private road he will want to know who is responsible for its maintenance. Furthermore, if he is to be responsible in whole or in part for the maintenance of access roads he will want to know the approximate extent of his liability.

As mentioned above, when completing the front of the form, the applicant is asked to give details in the panel dealing with the description of the property of roadways, footpaths and footways in respect of which information is required from the local authority.

Enquiries 1 and 2 in Part I of the form relate exclusively to existing and proposed roads on or near the property.

Roads maintained at the public's expense

The county council which is normally the highway authority for its area[10] is obliged to keep a register of highways maintainable at the public's expense pursuant to section 36 of the Highways Act 1980. A local authority will be able to tell a purchaser from this register whether all the roadways, footpaths and footways referred to on the front of the form are maintainable at the public expense. If the replies indicate that any of the roads and paths giving access to the property are privately maintained the purchaser's advisors will need to make enquiries of the vendor to establish first, that the purchaser will have all necessary rights of way and secondly, that the expense of maintaining the roads and so on will not be inordinately burdensome. The purchaser's advisors may be able to establish from the title documents that the purchaser has the necessary rights of way. For example, any rights of way benefiting the land may be shown on the office copy entries obtained by the purchaser's advisors. With unregistered land there may be an express grant of a right of way by deed. (In the absence of documentary evidence it may be possible to establish a right of way by prescription). Note also that the form of preliminary enquiries of the vendor will give information regarding rights of way and the cost of maintaining private roads.[11]

Charges

A purchaser's advisor should bear in mind the possibility that a county council may resolve pursuant to section 205 of the Highways Act 1980 to make up to a satisfactory standard, any road not "sewered, levelled, paved, metalled, flagged, chanelled or made good and lighted" properly. If a county council carry out any such work, a purchaser may find himself having to contribute towards the cost which will be apportioned between the owners of the premises fronting the street. Such costs become a charge on the property which binds any subsequent owner. Enquiry 1(B) will reveal whether any resolution to make up the roads

[10] Highways Act 1980, s.1.

[11] See p. 27, above.

fronting the property at the cost of the frontagers has been passed by the highway authority.[12]

Under section 37 of the Highways Act 1980 it is possible that a local authority will resolve to adopt a road or path as maintainable at the public expense, without cost to the frontagers. This will normally only happen where the road or path has been constructed to a satisfactory standard; has been dedicated as a public highway; and has been maintained in reasonable order, for a period of at least one year. Again, enquiry 1(B) will reveal whether the council has exercised its powers under section 37. Note also that a highway authority has power to adopt highways as maintainable at the public's expense by agreement.

Future development of roads

Enquiry 2 in Part I deals with the highway authority's future proposals for road construction or improvement. The reply to this enquiry should reveal the following information:

(1) Whether the local authority have been notified by the Secretary of State of an order or scheme for the construction or improvement of a trunk road or motorway, the centre line of which is within 200 metres of the property in question.
(2) Whether the local authority have approved any proposals themselves for the construction of a new road or the alteration or improvement of an existing road, the limits of construction of which fall within 200 metres of the property.
(3) Whether there are any proposals for reconstruction of any subways, underpasses, flyovers, footbridges, elevated roads or dual carriageways within 200 metres of the property.
(4) Whether the local authority has approved or been notified by the Secretary of State of any proposals for construction work on an adjacent highway which would necessitate the property being compulsorily acquired by the local highway authority.
(5) Whether the Secretary of State or the local authority has published proposals for the construction of a new road, the proposed route of which would be within 200 metres of the property.

The purchaser will obviously have formed his own ideas when viewing the property on the adequacy of access to it. The above information will indicate whether the present situation is to change within the forseeable future. If so, the purchaser will have to decide for himself whether the future proposals will adversely effect his enjoyment of the property. The prospective purchaser of a country cottage is unlikely to proceed if he discovers that the local highway authority is proposing to build a bypass at the bottom of the cottage's garden.

[12] See the Highways Act 1980, s.228 for the frontager's rights to object to such proceedings.

New housing developments

When a purchaser is buying a property which forms part of a newly constructed housing estate his advisors must be sure to investigate the position as to the construction and maintenance of the estate roads. A builder may be contractually bound to the purchaser to make up the roads and maintain them until they are adopted by the local authority without cost to the owners of the premises fronting the roads. In the case of the more well known quoted building companies, such a covenant may be considered sufficient although not ideal. However, in the case of smaller firms of builders the purchaser should not rely upon such a covenant alone. For example, if a builder subsequently becomes bankrupt or goes into insolvent liquidation the purchaser could not compel his builder to make up and maintain the roads to the required standards. He would be left with an unsecured claim for breach of contract in the bankruptcy or liquidation of the builder which in practical terms would prove useless. He would be left to find another construction company to carry out the necessary work. Failing this, the local authority would make up the roads themselves and charge the cost to the frontagers. The purchaser would be out of pocket!

Performance bonds

Ideally, a builder should have made an agreement with the local authority pursuant to section 38 of the Highways Act 1980. A builder will agree to construct estate roads in accordance with the local authority's usual requirements and maintain these until such time as the local authority is in a position to adopt them as public highways without cost to the frontagers. The builder will then obtain a performance bond, normally from a bank or insurance company, which supports the agreement. If the builder defaults and the local authority has to carry out works and recover the expense from the frontagers, the purchaser would be able to recover his loss from the bondsmen. The council may not be able to look direct to the bondsmen. This will depend upon the terms of the performance bond itself.[13] The council may, therefore, require payment from the frontagers leaving the frontagers to seek an indemnity from the bondsmen.

The reply to enquiry 1(C) will reveal whether the local authority has entered into any agreement relating to the adoption of any roadway, footpath or footway and if so whether the agreement is supported by a performance bond. A note on the form reminds the applicant, it is for the purchaser to satisfy himself as to the adequacy of the bond. For example, a bond under which the bondsman's liability is not to exceed a specified sum may well have become inadequate because of the effects of inflation. In most cases it will be difficult for a purchaser to establish whether a bond is adequate in the absence of advice from experts in highway construction. Nevertheless, the purchaser's advisors should try to obtain such details as are available.

[13] *i.e.* it is a question of construing the terms of the bond.

Diversion and closure of roads and footpaths

Enquiry II in Part II of the form asks whether the local authority has approved any proposals for the stopping up or diversion of any roads or footpaths referred to on the front of the form.

There are various provisions which allow a local authority, a magistrates' court or the Secretary of State to close or divert a road or path. The two most widely used provisions are those contained in the Highways Act 1980[14] and the Town and Country Planning Act 1971.[15] Broadly speaking the procedure for stopping up or diversion consists of an order being made, notice of the order being publicised, and the order being confirmed in the absence of any objections being received. Should objections be received it is possible that an enquiry would be held at which the desirability of making the order would be discussed. The situation which is commonly encountered in practice is that where planning permission for a development has been granted which would affect the enjoyment of an existing public right of way. The permission does not constitute authority to close or divert the right of way and it is possible that the completion of the development would lead to an offence of obstructing a highway being committed. The developer must seek an order pursuant to section 209 or 210 of the Town and Country Planning Act 1971 for the closure or diversion of any road or footpath interfering with completion of the development. Ideally, the application for planning permission and the application for authorisation to stop up or divert a road or path should be made concurrently. This will lead to a saving of time, although the stopping up or diversion order cannot be confirmed until such time as the related planning permission has been granted. In *Ashby* v. *Secretary of State for the Environment*[16] a builder sought a diversion order after all development along the line of the footpath in question had been completed. The Court of Appeal held that section 209 of the 1971 Act could only be used when some development still had to be carried out along the line of the public highway and that the section could not be used to retrospectively validate an unauthorised stopping up or diversion. It may be a condition of a planning permission that an alternative route be provided for use by the public.

Obviously, the existence of any proposals for a stopping up or diversion of any of the roads or footpaths described on the front of the form is of vital importance to a purchaser. Such proposals may affect access to the property on a permanent or temporary basis and the purchaser's advisor should consult him immediately. Note, however, that an order pursuant to the above provisions will not affect any private right of way which may have been expressly granted to a previous owner of the property before the road or path being stopped up or diverted was dedicated to the public.

[14] ss.116 to 118.

[15] ss.209 and 210, and see the Extinguishment of Public Right of Way Orders Regulations 1983 (S.I. 1983 No. 23).

[16] [1980] 1 W.L.R. 673.

Public footpaths

Enquiry I asks whether any public path or road used as a public path or byway which runs across the property has been shown in a draft or provisional definitive map pursuant to the Wildlife and Countryside Act 1981 or the National Parks and Access to the Countryside Act 1949.[17] If a public footpath appears on a "definitive map" and "statement" prepared by a local authority pursuant to either of the two statutes mentioned above, it is conclusive proof of the public's right to use the path. This does not mean that the absence of a path on such a map is conclusive proof that no public right of way exists over the land in question.[18] The right of the public to use such a path may be proved by other means such as long user.

A purchaser of property over which a public path runs must be careful not to interfere with the public's enjoyment of the path in any way. For example, it is a criminal offence to permanently plough up the surface of such a path or place a sign on or near such a path which contains a false or misleading statement likely to deter the public from using the path.[19] The purchaser must consider whether or not he is prepared to buy a property over which the public has an unfettered right of way.

Noise abatement

Enquiry X in Part II of the form asks the local authority whether it has resolved to make a noise abatement zone order pursuant to section 63 of the Control of Pollution Act 1974. Such an order may designate all or any part of the area of a local authority as a noise abatement zone. Similarly, it may apply to all premises within the zone or specific types of premises. For example, it may apply only to places of entertainment such as theatres and discotheques or to commercial premises such as offices, shops and warehouses. The order will require the owners of the specified buildings to keep the noise emanating from those buildings below a certain level. A register of the required levels is kept by a local authority and may be inspected free of charge.[20] The replies will indicate where the register can be inspected and whether or not there is an entry in that register which relates to the property being searched.

Effect of order

The fact that the property being purchased is within a noise abatement zone, may affect its value. For example, a local authority which wishes to keep noise below a certain level may not look favourably on future application for planning permission to change the use of the property from say use as a storage facility to use as an industrial building when the latter is bound to create more noise.

[17] Ss.27 to 38 of the 1949 Act have now been repealed by Sched.17 to and Pt. II of the 1981 Act.

[18] See *Andover Corporation* v. *Mundy* [1955] J.P.L. 518 where a footpath had been deliberately deleted from a map and yet this was not regarded as conclusive proof that no public rights were exercisable; see also *Suffolk County Council* v. *Mason* [1979] A.C. 705.

[19] Wildlife and Countryside Act 1981, s.61.

[20] Control of Pollution Act 1974, s.67.

If the noise emanating from the premises specified in the order is in excess of the noise level detailed in the register, a criminal offence is committed. In addition, the local authority may require the owner to carry out such works as are necessary to ensure that the noise eminating from the building is kept within the permitted levels. This could prove costly for the owner of the building.

Consents

Under section 65 of the Control of Pollution Act 1974, it is possible for a person to apply to the local authority for a written consent to exceed the noise levels recorded in the register. Such a consent may be general or limited to a specific occasion.

Smokeless zones

Enquiry 16 asks whether the property is included in an area in respect of which the local authority have passed a resolution to make a smoke control order pursuant to section 11 of the Clean Air Act 1956. Any existing order creating a smokeless zone should appear on the local land charges search.

In a smokeless zone it is an offence to emit smoke from a chimney.

The order may specify certain buildings which are exempt from its provisions. For example, certain public utilities may be exempt. It is essential that a purchaser of property within a smokeless zone should ensure that the existing heating appliances on the property he is buying are such as to allow him to comply with the provisions of the order. The preliminary enquiries of the vendor will indicate whether there is any central heating and it may be appropriate to add an additional enquiry expressly asking the vendor to confirm that all heating appliances allow compliance with the order.

Housing

Enquiries 15 and IX relate to housing matters.

Houses in multiple occupation

Houses in multiple occupation may be required to register with the local authority for the area.[21] The local authority may refuse to register such a house on the grounds that it is not in a fit state or the person having control of the house is not a fit and proper person.[22]

A house is in multiple occupation when it is lived in by the members of more than one family. It is usually lodging houses and hostels which are required to register.[23] The basic amenities in such houses (water supply, drainage, gas and electricity, light and heating) must conform to a minimum standard. The local authority may also require the person in control of the house to provide adequate fire escapes, proper storage for refuse and to keep the common parts of the house clean and free from

[21] Housing Act 1985, s.346.
[22] Housing Act 1985, s.347.
[23] See the Registered Homes Act 1984 for special provisions relating to homes for the care of the elderly, etc.

obstruction. Grants may be made to bring the property up to standard and this may be of interest to a purchaser who proposes to use the property as a lodging house.

The replies will indicate whether the property is registered under these provisions. If a purchaser intends to use the property in future for multiple occupation he should enquire further of the local authority whether registration will be necessary.

Slum clearance

Enquiry 15 asks the local authority if the property is a slum clearance area or a general improvement area. If the property is in a slum clearance area this may put an end to the transaction altogether as the local authority will compulsorily acquire the property in the future. It must do this before it decides to demolish the property and redevelop the site. A purchaser may also find it difficult to obtain finance from building societies and banks to aid the purchase of such a property.

General improvement areas

A general improvement area is declared under section 253 of the Housing Act 1985. These are areas of poor housing where the council has shown a commitment to rejuvenate the neighbourhood. Various powers allow the local authority to make grants to encourage owners of houses in such an area to improve their property. A homeowner may obtain a grant to enable him to install a bath, shower or toilet in his house for example. Compulsory purchase powers may also be used by the local authority in such areas to acquire property which is in such a serious state of disrepair that it is a danger to health.

Sewers

Enquiry 5 in Part I of the form attempts to elicit from the local authority information relating to the sewers and drains serving the property.

The importance of making adequate enquiry as to ownership of and liability to repair sewers and drains should not be underestimated.[24] A heavy financial burden may be cast upon the purchaser who is obliged to contribute towards the repair and maintenance of private sewers and drains. Furthermore, the fact that a sewer or drain is defective may amount to a nuisance (either public or private). A local authority or neighbour may then be in a position to compel the owner of the drain or sewer to carry out remedial works.

A "drain" is an underground pipe or open channel for carrying of water, soil and so on from one building or premises within the same curtilage into the cesspool or sewer. A sewer is any trench channel or pipe through which water or sewage flow.[25] A public sewer is a sewer vested in the water authority[26] or occasionally in the highway authority. A private sewer is one owned by one or more persons and serving their property which will usually lead to a public sewer. The replies will show how surface water and foul drainage is carried from the premises into a public sewer. If it is indicated that a private sewer serves the premises it will be necessary to make enquiry for the vendor to

[24] See (1980) 77 L.S.Gaz. 600.
[25] Jowitt, *Dictionary of English Law* (2nd ed.1977).
[26] Public Health Act 1936, s.20.

establish the costs of maintenance. The replies of the vendor to the preliminary enquiries may give the necessary information.

s.38 agreements

The reply would disclose any agreement pursuant to section 38 of the Public Health Act 1936. Under such an agreement the local authority may require that two buildings (presently not connected to main sewers) be drained in combination. A private sewer is constructed and the costs apportioned between the owners of the buildings. In some cases the local authority will contribute towards the cost of construction itself.[27] Once the drains have been constructed they will have to be maintained at the expense of the owners of the two properties which they serve.

s.18 agreements

The local authority is also asked whether it is aware of any agreement under section 18 of the 1936 Act for the adoption of a private sewer or drain. Such an agreement will be made between a water authority and a builder of a new housing estate. The procedure is similar to that described above[28] in relation to roads on new housing developments in that a bond may have been obtained by the builder to support his obligation to construct the sewers and drains to an acceptable standard. If the local authority is not aware of any such agreement enquiry should be made direct of the water authority itself who may have details. Another point to watch in connection with the construction of new premises is the power given to local authorities to insist that premises be drained into an existing public sewer if there is one within 100 feet of the property, at a level which makes a connection possible.[29] The expense of carrying out such work (which would have to be borne by the purchaser) could be considerable.

Recovery of expenses

Under certain provisions of the 1936 Act and the Public Health Act 1961 a water authority may recover certain expenses from the owners of premises served by one of its sewers. Under section 24 of the 1936 Act the cost of maintaining renewing or improving public sewers may be recovered if the sewer was on October 1, 1937:

(1) vested in the local authority but lying under private premises;
(2) a combined drain (a drain serving several premises) which the local authority was not under a duty to maintain at that date.

Sections 12 and 13 of the 1961 Act allow a water authority to reclaim the expense of constructing a public sewer in a highway maintainable at the public expense (or when a street is laid out on land under which there runs a public sewer). The presence of the public sewer must have increased the value of the property fronting the highway before any apportionment of the costs is made. The power to recover expenditure under sections 12 and 13 of the 1961 Act is now exercised by water authorities for the area in which the property is situate. Should a negative reply to the question dealing with this matter be received from the local

27 This is usually the case where the nearest public sewer to which a connection can be made is more than 100 feet from the property.
28 See p.77 above.
29 Public Health Act 1936, s.37 (as amended). This power is not available to local authorities in the Inner London area.

authority it may be necessary to confirm the position with the relevant water authority direct.

Registered land

Enquiry 18 asks whether the land which is being searched against is situate in an area where registration of title under the Land Registration Acts is compulsory on sale. Details of the relevant district land registry and the date compulsory registration was introduced in the area will also be specified.

This enquiry does not obviate the need to make a search of the Public Index Map which may reveal other information of interest to a purchaser such as whether the land is subject to a caution against first registration. Such a search can be made by completing Form 96 and sending it to the appropriate district land registry. The fee for such a search is £2.00.

Long term planning policy

Enquiry 7 attempts to elicit from a local authority information relating to the long term planning policy for the region in which the property is situate.

Types of plans

The large scale development plans of a local authority are set out in the structure plan and the local plan. The function of these plans is to provide the necessary framework for development control and co-ordinate the direction of development.

Structure plans give a general indication of where development should be located and its scale. Local plans provide detailed locations for the future supply of land for housing and industry, define the boundaries of areas of restraint and co-ordinate development programmes in more detail.

The county planning authority will be responsible for drawing up a structure plan. Normally, the district planning authority will draw up the local plan. However, it is possible that the county planning authority will draw up both these plans in some special cases.

In the London area the provisions relating to long term planning policy are slightly different. The Greater London Council was responsible for drawing up the Greater London Development Plan (formerly the Initial Development Plan for Greater London). The London borough councils are primarily responsible for drawing up the local plans. Under the Local Government Act 1985[30] the functions of the Greater London Council in this respect were transferred to the London borough councils, metropolitan districts and other existing authorities as from April 1, 1986. This means that the provisions for the preparation of structure and local plans within the London area will gradually fall into line with the rest of the country.

The structure plan A structure plan consists of a written statement containing the broad principles for planning control

[30] See Sched. 1.

within an area usually covered by a single county council although two county councils may make a joint structure plan covering the whole of their respective areas. The written statement will be accompanied by a "key diagram" and an "explanatory memorandum." The key diagram will be illustrative of the policy contained in the written statement. The explanatory memorandum will summarise the reasons justifying the various policies and general proposals formulated in the written statement.

Content The structure plan will contain sections on the principal physical and economic characteristics of the area. Population size and distribution will also be dealt with. The plan will indicate the county planning authority's proposals for the scale, diversity and pattern of industry and commerce. For example, the written statement may contain proposals designed to encourage a particular type of industrial development within the area. The structure plan would also describe land use policies relating to the transport infrastructure, the provision of housing in the area and other matters such as pollution control, conservation and the provision of recreational facilities. The county planning authority's broad policies and proposals for all types of development would be set out at some length in the structure plan.

Procedure The procedure for the preparation of a structure plan is as follows:

(1) A county planning authority carries out a survey to collate the necessary demographic, land utilisation and other economic data necessary to enable it to formulate a general planning policy for the area.
(2) Preliminary drafts of the various documents which make up the structure plan are prepared.
(3) The tentative proposals contained in the preliminary draft of the structure plan are publicised within the area. The general public is given the opportunity to make representations to the county planning authority. The county planning authority is under a duty to consider such representations. The publicity requirements are an integral part of the procedure for drawing up a definitive structure plan. Strict rules have to be followed by the county planning authority to ensure that the consultative stage is meaningful.
(4) The final draft of the structure plan is sent to the Secretary of State for his consideration together with a statement by the county planning authority that they have complied with the publicity requirements.
(5) If the Secretary of State is satisfied that in addition to the documents submitted to him further information or investigation is needed in order to enable him to reach a decision as to whether or not the structure plan should be approved, modified or refused he can order that an examination in public should take place. This gives the general public another opportunity to make representations on the contents of the structure plan to a government appointed inspector who will conduct the necessary investigations and hold such meetings as may be appropriate.

(6) The Secretary of State modifies, approves or refuses to approve the structure plan.
(7) The structure plan is printed in its final form and made available for members of the public.

The local plan A local plan is an elaboration of the broad policies contained in a structure plan. From this plan a purchaser will be able to learn in some detail what the local planning authority proposes for the future both in relation to himself and to the property he proposes to acquire.

A district council does not have to draw up a local plan. As Department of Environment Circular 22 of 1984 suggests, "Local plans are likely to be needed where the strategic policies in the Structure plan need to be developed in more detail, the Structure Plan provision for development and other use of land needs to be related to particular sites and local planning issues need to be brought before the public."

A local plan consists of a written statement similar in style to that contained in a structure plan together with a proposals map which will define specific areas of land and designate them for a particular type of use such as residential or commercial. The map might also show particular sites upon which say shopping centres are to be built.

Procedure

The procedure for the preparation of a local plan is not unlike that for a structure plan. However, a local plan does not need to be approved by the Secretary of State although he does have a residual power to call in local plans which are particularly contraversial or have otherwise been drawn to his attention. If anything the publicity and consultative stages involved in drawing up a local plan are more extensive than with a structure plan. Local enquiries and meetings will be held at which the provisions of a local plan will be discussed in detail. Once in a final form the district council will pass a resolution to adopt the local plan as a definitive statement of detailed planning policy for the area covered by the plan.

Purpose of structure and local plans

The objective in drawing up the structure and local plans is to achieve a clear and concise statement of policies and proposals for development in the area which strikes a satisfactory balance between the preservation of amenity and the economic welfare of the area. Both structure and local plans will be constantly reviewed as the needs of the area change and necessitate a reassessment of planning policy. The Town and Country Planning Act 1971 as amended by the Local Government, Planning and Land Act 1980 sets out detailed procedures for the review and modification of structure and local plans.

Enquiry 7 will provide a prospective purchaser of a property with the following information:

(1) the stage which has been reached in the preparation of the structure plan for the area including the property;
(2) the existence of any proposals for the alteration of the structure plan or in London the Greater London Development Plan;
(3) the existence of any proposals for the alteration of an adopted local plan;
(4) what the designated primary use is for the area including the property and whether any specific provisions affecting the property have been set out in the structure plan, the

local plan or any non-statutory plan which has been drawn up by the local authority;

(5) whether or not the property is situated in an area where there is an old style development plan (in the London area the Initial Development Plan for Greater London) still in force.

Commercial clients

The long term planning policies for an area are unlikely to be of great interest to the purchaser of a dwelling house. They may, however, be of interest to property developers or other commercial clients who wish to have some indication of the planning authorities' proposals for the future of the area before carrying out large scale building operations. For example, a residential property developer who purchases a site which is considered to have a high development value attributed to it may find his plans frustrated if the property is zoned for industrial use only.

Challenging a structure or local plan

Section 244(1) of the Town and Country Planning Act 1971 contains provisions which allow any person aggrieved by the contents of a structure or local plan to apply to have it set aside as invalid on the basis that the authority which drew it up acted outside of the powers conferred on it by the 1971 Act. Generally speaking, such an application must be made within six weeks of the structure or local plan having been adopted. For example, in *Great Portland Estates plc* v. *Westminster City Council*[31] a substantial landowner in the council's area attacked the council's local plan on the basis *inter alia* it had regard to an irrelevant factor, namely the interests of individual occupiers. The council had stated that it proposed to use its planning powers in such a manner as to ensure the survival of certain old established light industrial activities which added to the diverse character of the area and proposed to issue non-statutory guidelines with that objective in mind restricting new office developments (which would bring higher rents for the plaintiff). The Court of Appeal accepted the plaintiff's argument and quashed the local plan insofar as it restricted new office development. The decision on this aspect was upheld in the House of Lords insofar as the non-statutory guidelines on when new office development would be allowed were concerned. The House of Lords considered any such guidelines should have been contained in the local plan itself.

Building Regulations

Enquiry 4 asks the local authority if they have authorised any proceedings in respect of an infringement of the Building Regulations. The form used for properties in the London area contains a note to the effect that this particular enquiry is not applicable to Inner London boroughs. This is because there is a special system of control based on by-laws and the London Building Acts 1930 to 1939 in the Inner London area. Otherwise the Building Regulations apply to the whole of England and Wales.

[31] [1984] 3 W.L.R. 1035.

The purpose of the Building Regulations is to secure the health, safety, welfare and convenience of people. The regulations lay down minimum standards to be complied with when constructing a new building or making any alteration or improvement to an old one. A full discussion of the provisions contained in the regulations is outside the scope of this book. However, standards are laid down for such matters as thermal insulation, safety in the event of fire, ventilation, damp proofing, and control of space and water heating systems.

Need to obtain consent

Any person who wishes to construct a new building or in any way alter an existing one to which the regulations apply, should give notice of his intention to carry out such works to the local authority. It is possible to commence works before notice is given to the local authority, although in this case the builder runs the risk of the requisite consent not being granted. He would then be liable for the removal or alteration of any works which infringe the regulations.

Contravention of the regulations is a criminal offence punishable by a fine. Furthermore, the local authority or any person may apply for an injunction requiring the removal or alteration of the works which contravene the regulations.

If the building owner does not comply with any notice which is served on him by the local authority, the local authority has residual powers to enter upon the land and carry out the necessary works itself.

It is in a purchaser's interest to find out if proceedings for breach of the Building Regulations have been started in respect of the property before contracts for its purchase are exchanged. This would enable him to seek a reduction in the purchase price to take account of the cost of the works necessary to remedy the breach. If a purchaser completes the purchase, he will have to remedy any breach of the regulations if this vendor has not done so, and his may prove time consuming and expensive.

Local authority's duty of care

Any breach of the duties imposed by the Building Regulations is capable of founding an action at civil law. In the case of *Dutton* v. *Bognor Regis U.D.C.*,[32] a building inspector employed by the local authority negligently made an inspection of the foundations of a house. The building began to collapse due to the defective condition of the foundations. It was held that the local authority acting by the building inspector owed a duty of care not only to the original purchaser of the house but also to subsequent purchasers. This duty of care had been broken and the purchasers could recover damages in the tort of negligence from the local authority.

The local authority will supply copies of all Building Regulation consents, if asked to do so in an additional enquiry.

Planning permission

We have already seen[33] in discussing the preliminary enquiries of the vendor that a purchaser will be interested in the planning history of the property he proposes to buy and in particular in

[32] [1972] 1 Q.B. 373.

[33] See above, pp.42 *et seq.*

ensuring the necessary planning permissions have been or can be obtained. He will obtain some information from the vendor. However, the purchaser's enquiries of the local authority will reveal most if not all of the details of the property's planning history.

Development

To recap it is necessary to obtain planning permission from the local authority before any"development" can take place. Section 22(1) of the Town and Country Planning Act 1971, defines development as "the carrying out of building, engineering, mining or other operations in, on, over or under land, or the making of any material change in the use of any building or other land." Normally, the district council will be the local planning authority to whom all applications for planning permission should be sent. Certain activities which would otherwise constitute "development" within section 22 are deemed to have been granted permission. However, the scope of these automatic permissions is fairly restrictive.

Outline or detailed permission

A planning application may be for either outline or detailed planning permission. An outline planning permission will be granted on the basis that further details of the development will be submitted to the local authority at a future date in connection with all the "reserved matters" detailed in the permission. For example, outline planning permission may be granted for the construction of a shopping centre, but require details of the provision of parking spaces to be submitted before detailed planning permission is granted. A detailed planning permission is one which the local planning authority has all the information it requires to consider the desirability of the development.

Public register

Pursuant to section 34 of the Town and Country Planning Act 1971, every local planning authority must keep a register of planning applications and decisions. The information contained in the Register will be of interest to prospective purchasers for two reasons. First, it will reveal the local planning authorities attitude towards the development and use of the property the purchaser is proposing to buy. Secondly, in the case of land being acquired for development, it will allow the developer to assess the potential of the site more realistically. Part I of "the Register of Planning Applications" contains details of all pending applications for planning permission, together with any plans and drawings which may have been submitted. Part II gives details of planning applications[34] which have already been considered by local planning authorities. In addition, any relevant plans and drawings, the date of the decision to grant or refuse permission and details of any conditions imposed will be given. The Register is open to public inspection and the replies will indicate where the Register can be inspected.

In appropriate cases, it may be worthwhile obtaining copies of all planning permissions relating to the property from the local authority. Indeed, some local authorities send such copies as a matter of course. An additional enquiry can be added asking for such copies and undertaking to pay the reasonable and proper photocopying charges of the local authority. The purchaser can

[34] Part II will give details of applications for a determination under the Town and Country Planning Act 1971, s.53.

then ask the vendor to confirm that any conditions attached to the planning permissions have been complied with.

The information contained in the Register of Planning Applications is useful because it will relate to neighbouring properties as well as the property being purchased. Any prospective purchaser may be interested to know what development is going to be carried out in the immediate vicinity of the property he is buying and whether this would have an adverse affect upon his enjoyment of the property. The Register will enable him to ascertain such information at an early stage and allow him to make such follow-up enquiries as he may deem to be appropriate.

Failure to obtain a planning permission prior to the commencement of works which amount to development although not advisable is not of itself a criminal offence. However, it is open for the local planning authority to serve an enforcement notice[35] requiring the removal of such works. Failure to comply with such a notice is a criminal offence. Enforcement notices are discussed in more detail below.[36]

The General Development Order The Town and Country Planning General Development Order 1977[37] obviates the need to make an express application for planning permission in certain cases. The General Development Order contains 23 classes of "permitted development." Perhaps the most important type of "permitted development" for present purposes is that contained in Class I of the General Development Order. This permits the enlargement, improvement or other alteration of a dwelling-house so long as the external cubic content of the original dwelling-house is not exceeded by more than 70 cubic metres or 15 per cent. (in the case of a terraced house the limits are respectively 50 cubic metres and 10 per cent.). Furthermore, the height of the enlargement or alteration must not exceed the highest part of the roof of the original house and must not extend beyond the forward most part of any wall of the house fronting the highway. In *North-West Leicester District Council* v. *Secretary of State for the Environment*[38] the court considered the question relating to projection beyond the forward most part of any wall of the original dwelling-house. The house in question was "L shaped" as shown in the diagram on page 47.

Permitted development

The local planning authority objected to the new extension on the grounds it projected beyond the original wall A to B. It was held that, for the purposes of the condition imposed by the General Development Order, the whole of the road frontage A to D should be treated as a single wall with parts at different distances from the road. The extension did not project beyond the closest part which ran from C to D. The condition set out in the General Development Order had therefore been complied with.

[35] Under the Town and Country Planning Act 1971, s.87.
[36] See below, p.93.
[37] S.I. 1977 No. 289 (as amended).
[38] (1984) 4 P.L.B. 59 and see discussion at p.47, above.

Permitted development

The other 22 Classes of "permitted development" will repay careful examination. The following are some examples of "permitted development."

Class II

> the erection or construction of gates, fences, walls or other means of enclosure not exceeding one metre in height or two metres subject to certain conditions being complied with.

Class III

> development consisting of a change of use to use as a light industrial building (as defined in the Town and Country Planning (Use Classes) Order 1972) from use as a general industrial building (as so defined).

Class IV

> the erection of buildings or plant and machinery on land which has the benefit of planning permission for the carrying out of building operations provided such buildings or plant and machinery are removed when the building work is complete.

Class IX

> the carrying out of works required for the maintenance or improvement of an unadopted street or private way being works carried out on land within the boundaries of the street or way.

Reference should be made to the terms of the General Development Order itself for the limitations and conditions imposed upon "permitted development" in any particular case.

Withdrawal of "deemed" permissions

In certain areas the benefit of the provisions contained in the General Development Order dealing with "permitted development" will have been withdrawn. Under article 4 of the General Development Order the Secretary of State or local planning authority may direct that the provisions of the order shall not apply either to a specified area, for example, a conservation area, or to a particular type of development. These directions are commonly referred to as "article 4 directions." The effect of an article 4 direction is to withdraw the deemed planning permission granted by the Order and make it necessary for anyone proposing to carry out development which would otherwise be within the scope of the Order to make an express application for planning permission to the local authority. So, the purchaser who proposes to build an extention to his newly acquired property will need to obtain express planning permission if an article 4 direction is in force in respect of the area in which his new property is situate. The reply to Enquiry 8 will show whether the local authority has resolved to make a direction under article 4 relating to the restriction of permitted development.

Revocation and modification of planning permissions The benefit of a planning permission, including a "deemed permission" pursuant to the General Development Order,[39]

[39] See above, p.89.

attaches to the land—it is usually not personal to the individual or company who applied for it (although it is not unknown for a condition to be attached to a planning permission, making it personal). The benefit of any planning permission enures for the benefit of everybody interested in the land subject only to the conditions in the permission itself and the local planning authority's right to revoke or modify it.[40]

Revocation Under section 45 of the Town and Country Planning Act 1971 a local planning authority may revoke or modify a planning permission before:

(1) building operations to which the permission relates have been completed; or
(2) any change of use authorised by the permission has occurred.

Any order revoking or modifying a planning permission will normally have to be confirmed by the Secretary of State prior to implementation.[41]

Compensation Compensation is payable to the owner or occupier of land for loss or damage which is the result of any order under section 45. Such compensation may include a sum in respect of wasted expenditure, for example, the costs of having a site cleared prior to commencing construction.[42] A claim for compensation must be made to the local planning authority within six months of the order revoking or modifying the permission being made.

Under section 51 of the 1971 Act a local planning authority may require the owner or occupier of land to remove a building which was erected *with* planning permission. Similarly, an order under this section may require the discontinuance of any lawful use of the property. Compensation is payable[43] in respect of the depreciation in the value of the owner's or occupier's interest in the land, disturbance and any expenditure incurred in complying with the order. Again, any claim for compensation must be made to the local planning authority within six months of the order being made.

Appeals against orders made pursuant to sections 45 and 51 lie to the High Court provided they are lodged within six weeks of the making of the order.[44]

Enquiry 9 will reveal whether the local authority has resolved to make any order under the above provisions.

Purchase notices The owner[45] of land which has been subject to some adverse planning decision—whether that be the refusal of consent or its grant subject to onerous conditions—may in certain circumstances require the local authority to purchase his interest in the land. The owner must serve a purchase notice on the local authority[46] within a year of the planning decision which

[40] Town and Country Planning Act 1971, s.45.
[41] See *ibid.*, s.46. The owner or occupier will be given the opportunity to make representations.
[42] *Holmes* v. *Bradfield R.D.C.* [1949] 2 K.B.1.
[43] Town and Country Planning Act 1971, s.178.
[44] *Ibid.*, ss.242 and 245.
[45] As defined by *ibid.*, s.290.
[46] *Ibid.*, s.180.

"blighted" his property. In some cases[47] the purchase notice will require confirmation by the Secretary of State.

A purchase notice may be served by the owner of land falling within one of the categories specified in section 71 of the Land Compensation Act 1973. This is land which has been earmarked by either the local authority or the Secretary of State as possibly required for the purposes of any government department local authority or statutory undertaker.

Enquiry 7(E) asks whether the property is included in any of the categories of land specified in section 71 of the Land Compensation Act 1973. A positive reply will warn the purchaser that he may be buying "blighted" land which would be difficult to sell in the future. Indeed, it could well be that in the near future the land would be subject to compulsory purchase proceedings. The purchaser's advisers will have to make additional enquiries of the appropriate governmental or local authority to establish the authority's plans for the future use of the property.

Completion, enforcement and stop notices

Enquiry VI asks whether the local authority have resolved to terminate any planning permissions in force in respect of the property by means of completion notice pursuant to section 44 of the Town and Country Planning Act 1971.

A person may obtain planning permission to carry out a development and begin the works necessary to implement the permission. However, it is possible that such works may not be completed within the time limit specified in the conditions attached to the permission. If a developer having commenced work was allowed to sit back and do nothing an eyesore might be created.

Where a development has been started but remains uncompleted at the expiry of time limits laid down in a planning permission and the local planning authority is of the opinion that the work necessary to complete the development will not be executed within a reasonable period, they may serve a "completion notice" on the developer requiring him to finish the project he has started or lose the benefit of the planning permission altogether.

Completion notice A completion notice must be served on the owner and occupier of the property to which it relates and on any other person likely to be affected by its service.[48] Falling within the latter category of persons would be a building contractor employed by an owner of land to carry out works of construction.

A completion notice will specify that the planning permission to which it relates will cease to have effect upon a specified date. This date will be not less than 12 months from the date of the notice itself.[49] The notice will show which works are necessary to complete the development in accordance with the

[47] *Ibid.*, s.181.
[48] Town and Country Planning Act 1971, s.44(3)(*a*).
[49] *Ibid.*, s.44(2).

planning permission and describe those which have at the time of the notice's service not been carried out by the developer. If these works remain uncompleted by the date specified in the notice the planning permission ceases to have effect in respect of all development except that already carried out in pursuance of the planning permission.

A completion notice must be confirmed by the Secretary of State before the date upon which it takes effect.[50] The Secretary of State has a discretion to substitute a longer period for completion of the works if he feels this appropriate.

Obviously, if a purchaser is relying upon an existing planning permission which is subject to termination pursuant to this procedure, he will need to ensure that he can comply with the completion notice or satisfy the local planning authority that the notice should be withdrawn. The purchaser may wish to ask the local planning authority to extend the time limit imposed by the completion notice pending completion of his purchase.

Enforcement notice Where there has been a breach of planning control, the local planning authority may issue an "enforcement notice" pursuant to section 87 of the 1971 Act. A breach may take the form of non-compliance with a condition attached to the planning permission or simply the failure to obtain planning permission at all. If the breach involves a material change of use of the property an enforcement notice may be issued at any time after the breach has taken place. However, where the breach consists of unauthorised building or other operations an enforcement notice may only be issued during the four years immediately after the breach.[51] Exceptionally, the four-year rule also applies in the case of an unauthorised change of use of a building to use as a single dwelling house.

A copy of the notice must be served on the owner or occupier of the land affected together with any other person having an interest in the land who would be materially affected.[52]

The notice must specify:[53]

(1) the alleged breach of planning control;
(2) the steps to be taken to remedy the breach;
(3) the date on which that notice is to take effect;
(4) the period (beginning with the date on which the notice is to take effect) for complying with the steps required to be taken to remedy the breach.[54]

Failure to comply

Failure to comply with an enforcement notice is a criminal offence.[55] In default of compliance the local planning authority have powers to enter into the land and carry out the work specified in the notice itself. The local planning authority may

[50] *Ibid.*, s.44(3)(*b*).
[51] *Ibid.*, s.87(5).
[52] See *Burn* v. *Secretary of State for the Environment* (1971) 219 E.G. 586 for the position where the breach consists of both unauthorised building or other operations and an unauthorised material change of use.
[53] Town and Country Planning Act 1971, s.87(6).
[54] The local authority may extend this period: s.89(6) of the 1971 Act. See also *Joyner* v. *Guildford Corporation* (1954) 5 P. & C.R. 30. 1971 Act, s.90: see (1983) 80 L.S.Gaz. 1471.
[55] Town and Country Planning Act 1971, s.89.

recover the expense of such works from the current owner of the land, whether he is responsible for the unauthorised development or not.

Register of enforcement and stop notices

Enforcement notices were formerly registrable as local land charges. Where such notices have been served on or after November 27, 1981, they are more likely to appear in the Register of Enforcement and Stop Notices kept by the local planning authority under section 92A of the 1971 Act. The register contains the information contained in the notice itself and additionally the date on which the local planning authority was satisfied that the notice had been complied with (if this is appropriate). The reply to enquiry 6 will reveal whether there are any entries in respect of the property being searched in the register. Details of where the register can be inspected will also be given.

It is important that potential purchasers are made aware of any enforcement notice affecting land they propose to buy. It is possible that if they complete the purchase and their vendor has failed to comply with an enforcement notice served prior to completion that they may be named as a party in any criminal proceeding taken against the vendor by the local planning authority.[56] Similarly, they may be guilty of criminal offence if they use the land or permit it to be used in contravention of an enforcement notice prohibiting an unauthorised change of use. If the local authority indicates that an enforcement notice has been served it is essential for the purchaser to obtain details from the vendor. The vendor may have already given details of any enforcement notice in his replies to the preliminary enquiries submitted to him by the purchaser.[57] Of course, in the last resort a purchaser may go ahead and complete the transaction in the knowledge that he may be liable to take the steps required to comply with the enforcement notice. This could prove expensive!

Appeal

Provided that the enforcement notice has not yet come into effect, there is another option open to the purchaser. He may appeal against the enforcement notice, or procure that his vendor appeals against it for him. An appeal against an enforcement notice may be made by any person on whom the notice has been served or any other person having an interest in the land.[58]

The grounds upon which an appeal may be based are as follows:[59]

(1) Planning permission should be granted for the development to which the notice relates. Where the alleged breach of planning control consists of non-compliance with a condition, the applicant may allege that the condition should be discharged for example on the basis that it fulfils no useful planning purpose.

(2) There has not been any breach of planning control in that the matters referred to in the enforcement notice do not constitute a breach of planning law. For example, that the

[56] *Ibid.*
[57] See above, p.44.
[58] See Town and Country Planning Act 1971, ss.88,88A and 88B.
[59] *Ibid.*, s.88(1).

development complained of is permitted development within the scope of the Town and Country Planning (General Development) Order.

(3) Where the alleged breach consists of building or other operations that the four year period referred to above had expired before the notice had been served. This ground is also available in respect of a change of use to use as a single dwelling-house.

(4) That there was some irregularity in the service of the notice.

(5) That the steps required by the notice are excessively onerous and not reasonably necessary to remedy the breach of planning control.

(6) That the time allowed for compliance with the steps detailed in the notice is unreasonably short.

Appeal lies in the first instance to the Secretary of State who has wide powers to vary the terms of the notice or grant planning permission for the development specified in it. The procedure may prove to be time consuming, and expensive and in most cases it will not be attractive to a purchaser.

Stop notice Stop notices are used in conjunction with enforcement notices. When an appeal is made against an enforcement notice, the enforcement notice is of no effect pending the outcome of the appeal. It is possible that during the period between lodging of the appeal and the final decision by the Secretary of State works would be carried out on the land which is subject to the notice which would later be declared unlawful. It may not be possible for remedial steps to be taken to alleviate the effects of such works should the enforcement notice later be upheld by the Secretary of State. If the local planning authority is of the opinion that there may be an attempt to carry out such works pending the outcome of any appeal against an enforcement notice, it may serve a "stop notice" pursuant to section 90 of the 1971 Act to preserve the status quo.

A stop notice may be served upon any person who appears to the local authority to have an interest in the land or to be engaged in any activity prohibited by the notice. For example, it would be possible for the local planning authority to serve a contractor about to start building operations on the land. The effect of the stop notice is to prohibit all persons served from carrying out any activity which may be specified in the notice and which is alleged in the enforcement notice (a copy of which is annexed to the stop notice) to be a breach of planning control. Non-compliance with a stop notice is punishable by a fine or imprisonment.

A stop notice will cease to have effect if:

(1) The enforcement notice proceedings are resolved by either compliance or successful appeal or the notice is withdrawn.

(2) The period for compliance in the enforcement notice expires. Obviously, this period cannot expire until the appeal has been settled, because the effect of the notice is suspended pending the outcome of the appeal.

(3) The stop notice is withdrawn by the local planning authority.

If the enforcement notice upon which the stop notice is based is set aside on appeal or withdrawn the local planning authority may be liable to pay compensation to the owners or occupiers of the land for any loss they have incurred which is directly attributable to the service of the stop notice.[60] For example, an owner of land might obtain compensation for any damages paid to a firm of builders he employed who were forced to delay starting work, because a stop notice had been served.

The reply to enquiry 6(A) will show whether any stop notice has been served. If a positive response is received, it will be necessary for the purchaser to make appropriate enquiries of his vendor and the local planning authority to obtain the fullest possible details to ensure the notice is being complied with. If a purchaser is himself engaged in some activity on the property pending completion of the sale, he should consult with the local planning authority to ensure he is not committing a criminal offence.

Tree preservation orders

Enquiry 9 asks whether the local authority has resolved to make an order under section 60 of the Town and Country Planning Act 1971.[61] Where it considers it expedient in the interests of preserving amenity a local authority may make a tree preservation order. Such an order, which may be made in respect of an individual or group of trees, makes it an offence to cut down, top, lop, uproot or otherwise wilfully damage the trees unless the consent of the local authority is first obtained. Where a tree which is subject to a preservation order is dying or in a dangerous state it may be cut down without obtaining the consent of the local authority.

Once a tree preservation order has been made it will be registered as a local land charge and should appear on the official certificate of search.

Section 169 of the Town and Country Planning Act 1971

Enquiry 10 asks "Has compensation been paid by the Council under s.169 of the T&CP Act 1971?"

Refusal of planning permission

Under section 169 of the Town and Country Planning Act 1971 compensation is payable whenever the Secretary of State, either on appeal from the local planning authority or on the reference of an application to him for determination, refuses planning permission, or grants it subject to conditions, for certain types of development which are specified in Part II of Schedule 8 to the 1971 Act. Broadly speaking, the types of development which fall within Part II of Schedule 8 may be described as development which is incidental to the existing use

60 Town and Country Planning Act 1971, s.177.

61 As amended by the Local Government, Planning and Land Act 1980 and the Local Government and Planning (Amendment) Act 1981.

of land. For example, the enlargement of premises or their improvement or division into units without any material change of use taking place is development falling within Part II of Schedule 8.

In practice it was unusual for an application for planning permission to be refused if the development was of the type specified in Part II of Schedule 8 to the 1971 Act. Local planning authorities were loath to make themselves liable to pay substantial claims for compensation under the section. One particular type of development caused great concern amongst many local planning authorities. This was the enlargement of existing blocks of flats within the tolerances laid down by Schedules 8 and 18 to the 1971 Act. These lay down certain limits as to the size of the enlargement. In *Peaktop Properties (Hampstead) Ltd.* v. *Camden London Borough Council*[62] the claimant company owned two blocks of flats in Belsize Grove London NW3. It applied for planning permission to enlarge the blocks by building another eleven flats on the top of each block. Permission was refused and the company asked for £142,500 compensation for refusal of planning permission under section 169 of the 1971 Act being the difference between the value of its interest in the two blocks of flats with permission to build the additional flats and the value of its interest without such permission. The company's claim for compensation failed on a technicality.[63] However, the Court of Appeal held that in principle, development of this nature if refused by the Secretary of State could lead to a local planning authority becoming liable to pay the unsuccessful applicant compensation. Local planning authorities, especially those within inner city areas, were placed in an extremely difficult position. If they refused planning permission for enlargements to blocks of flats they risked having to pay large sums of compensation they could ill afford. However, granting permission for such development might have an undesirable effect on local amenity. For example, it might lead to an increase in traffic congestion in the area.

The Town and Country Planning (Compensation) Act 1985 was passed to alleviate the pressure placed upon local planning authorities by the decision in *Peaktop*.

The provisions of the 1985 Act have effect in relation to the refusal or conditional grant of planning permission on any application made after September 23, 1985.[64] Section 1(2) of the 1985 Act effectively excludes from Part II of Schedule 8 development which consists of the enlargement of blocks of flats by the addition of a number of new flats. Other types of development which fall within Part II of Schedule 8 are not affected by the new Act.

Amount of compensation

As already mentioned the amount of compensation payable under section 169 is the difference between the value of the applicant's interest in the land would have with the unconditional permission (which has in fact been refused or granted subject to conditions) and the value of his interest without such permission or with the conditional permission as the case may be.

[62] (1982) 262 E.G. 239.

[63] In relation to the area of the extensions which fell outside of the permitted tolerances.

[64] 1985 Act, s.3.

Once compensation has been paid under section 169 in respect of a particular type of development a subsequent applicant for a similar planning permission cannot make a claim for compensation should his application also be refused or granted subject to conditions.

Subsequent owners of land who successfully apply for planning permission for development which had previously been refused and in respect of which compensation has been paid by the local planning authority do not have to repay any compensation paid to their predecessors in title by the council.

The reply to enquiry 10 should give details of any payment of compensation which has been made. Apart from putting the prospective purchaser on notice that planning permission for a certain type of development has been turned down and so cannot form the basis of a claim for compensation in the future it should also be borne in mind that any compensation paid under section 169 would reduce the amount of compensation payable in the future should the land be compulsorily acquired.[65]

Control of advertising

Enquiry III in Part II of the form will give a purchaser the following information:

Register of contents

1. Whether there are any entries relating to the property in the register of applications for consent to display an advertisement kept by the local authority.[66] The consent of the local authority is required for the display of any outdoor advertisement.[67] The form refers to the Town and Country Planning (Control of Advertisements)Regulations 1969.[68] These have now been replaced by the Town and Country Planning (Control of Advertisements) Regulations 1984[69] which contain the relevant law. References to the new regulations are given in brackets if they differ.

"Advertisement" is defined in section 290 of the Town and Country Planning Act 1971 in extremely wide terms. It would include not only a trade name painted over a shop but also posters and doorplates. Advertisements on enclosed land which are not readily visible to the public are exempt from control along with certain other forms of advertising.[70] It is an offence to display an advertisement without first obtaining any consent which may be required.[71]

2. The place where the register referred to above can be inspected. If there are entries relating to the property it may be appropriate to inspect the register to ascertain the details of any consent which may have been granted. A purchaser who intends

[65] Land Compensation Act 1961, s.15.
[66] Reg. 31.
[67] Reg. 6.
[68] S.I. 1969 No. 1532.
[69] S.I. 1984 No. 421 which is in substantially the same form as the earlier regulations.
[70] Reg. 3.
[71] Reg. 8.

to run a business from the property he is buying will want to be sure he can advertise his services.

3. Whether the Secretary of State has given notice under regulation 15 withdrawing the deemed consent given to certain forms of advertising by regulation 14. Certain advertisements such as professional nameplates, church notice boards and temporary advertisements may be displayed without consent subject to the local authority's right to challenge their display. A notice under regulation 15 is similar in effect to an "article 4" direction described earlier.[72]

Discontinuance notice

4. Whether the local authority has resolved to serve a discontinuance notice under regulation 16. If the local authority consider it expedient in the interests of amenity or public safety they may serve a notice requiring the removal of an advertisement displayed by virtue of a deemed consent under the Regulations. If such a notice has already been served the replies will indicate whether its provisions have been complied with to the satisfaction of the local authority.

5. Whether the local authority has resolved to make an order defining the area in which the property is situate as an area of special control pursuant to regulation 26. Within such areas there will be tighter control over the display of advertisements. Indeed the local authority can only grant consent for the display of certain types of advertising such as notices relating to local activities, advertisements promoting public safety and so on.

Listed buildings

Several questions on the form relate to listed buildings. These are as follows:

(1) Enquiry 13 asks whether the local authority has authorised the service of a building preservation notice under section 58 of the Town and Country Planning Act 1971.
(2) Enquiry IV asks whether any listed building consents have been granted or refused and whether any listed building enforcement notice has been served in respect of the property.
(3) Enquiry V asks whether the local authority has served any repairs notices under section 115 of the 1971 Act. The local authority is also asked whether it has authorised any compulsory purchase order in relation to the property pursuant to section 114 of the 1971 Act and if so whether a "minimum compensation" provision was included in such order.

Section 54(1) of the 1971 Act provides:

> "For the purpose of this Act and with a view to the guidance of local planning authorities in the performance of their functions under this Act in relation to buildings of special architectural or historic interest, the Secretary of State shall compile lists of such buildings, or approve, with or without

[72] See above, p.89.

> modifications such lists compiled by the Historic Buildings and Monuments Commission for England . . . or by other persons or bodies of persons, and may amend any lists so compiled or approved . . . "

The Department of the Environment is charged with the preservation of our building heritage. The Department constantly surveys areas of the country seeking buildings which are of special architectural or historic interest and which are considered worthy of preservation. In addition to this general procedure for listing a building maybe "spot listed" if it is considered to be in imminent danger of demolition.

Procedure

The Department of the Environment submits a list of buildings to the Secretary of State for his approval. Once the Secretary of State approves the list the building becomes a "listed building" and the special provisions as to development control apply in relation to it.

In addition to inclusion in a list the building may be graded. Grade I listed buildings are buildings of outstanding national interest. Grade II listed buildings are buildings of special architectural or historic interest which warrant every effort being made to save them. The significance of grading lies in the availability of financial grants for the preservation of buildings.

Once a list has been approved by the Secretary of State he will send a copy of it to all local authorities concerned and it will be registered in the register of local land charges. At the same time as registering the list in the local land charges register each local authority will notify the owners and occupiers of the buildings which appear in the list that special planning rules will apply to the building in the future.

Effect of listing

Once a building has been listed any work (whether or not such work would constitute development within the meaning of the 1971 Act) which affects the special character of the building can only be carried out if a "listed building consent" is first obtained. To carry out such works without obtaining listed building consent is a criminal offence punishable on summary conviction by imprisonment not exceeding three months or a fine of £1,000 or both and on conviction on indictment by imprisonment not exceeding 12 months or an unlimited fine. Note that internal works of decoration or alteration may require a listed building consent if they would change the character of the building.

Listing can have a drastic effect on the value of a property. In *Amalgamated Investment & Property Co. Ltd.* v. *John Walker & Sons Ltd.*[73] a group of companies contracted to buy a warehouse in Commercial Road, London, for £1.7 million with a view to its redevelopment. The day after exchange of contracts the warehouse was listed. The group would have had to apply for listed building consent before they could develop the property. The evidence before the court showed that if consent was refused the value of the warehouse would have fallen by over £1.5 million. Perhaps in an attempt to try and avoid the *John Walker* type of case the Local Government, Planning and Land Act 1980 introduced a procedure whereby a person, who need not be the

[73] [1977] 1 W.L.R. 164.

Certificate of intention

owner of the building in question, may apply for a certificate from the Department of Environment stating that the Department does not intend to list the building during the next five years. If such a certificate is granted the Secretary of State is precluded from exercising his powers pursuant to sections 54 and 58 of the 1971 Act during that period.

Turning now to the specific statutory provisions dealt with on the form:

(i) Listed building consent If a person intends to execute works for the demolition of a listed building or for its alteration or extension in any manner which would affect its character as a building of special architectural or historic interest he must first apply for a listed building consent.[74] This must be distinguished from the grant of any planning permission which may also be required. In areas outside London the application for listed building consent should normally be made to the district council. In the London area there used to be a two-tier system. Initially, the application used to be made to the London borough council who could refer it to the Greater London Council. Now, of course, the Greater London Council has been abolished. Listed building consent may be granted subject to such conditions as may be deemed necessary to preserve the character of the building. In particular section 56(5) of the 1971 Act provides that consent for the demolition of a listed building may be granted subject to a condition that the building shall not be demolished before a contract for the carrying out of works of redevelopment of the site has been made, and planning permission granted for those works. This provision is designed to avoid a situation whereby a listed building is demolished in the absence of any clear cut plans as to what is to replace it. An insight into the attitude taken by planning authorities for listed building consents to demolish may be gleaned from the following passage in the Department of Environment's circular 12/81:

Conditions attached to consent

> "the Secretary of State has made it plain that the Government are determined to implement current policies to preserve the best of our heritage. He will not be prepared to grant Listed Building Consent for the demolition of a listed building unless he is satisfied that every possible effort has been made to continue the present use or to find a suitable alternative use for the building."

The availability of finance for conversion of the building or for providing an alternative use for the building is a factor which the district council or London borough council will take into account when considering any application for listed building consent.

Compensation for refusal of consent

If the Secretary of State refuses listed building consent or grants it subject to conditions compensation may be payable to the applicant under section 171 of the 1971 Act. The refusal must be by the Secretary of State either on appeal or referral to him. In addition the proposed works must not amount to development within section 22 of the 1971 Act or if they would they must fall

[74] Town and Country Planning Act 1971, Sched. 11 (as amended by Sched. 15 to the Local Government, Planning and Land Act 1980).

within the development permitted by the General Development Order. The applicant will have to show that the value of his interest in the land is less than it would have been had listed building consent been granted or the condition not attached to the consent as appropriate. The measure of compensation payable is, broadly speaking, the amount by which the Secretary of State's decision adversely affects the value of the applicant's interest in the land.

Where listed building consent is refused or granted subject to conditions it is also possible for the owner of the building to serve a purchase notice on the local planning authority. If the owner can show that the land is not capable of beneficial use either without listed building consent or subject to the conditions which have been imposed and that there are no other works which could reasonably be carried out to make the land capable of beneficial use the local planning authority may be required to purchase the building.[75]

Enquiry IV(a) will reveal whether the local authority or the Secretary of State has granted or refused any listed building consent pursuant to section 55 of the 1971 Act.

Listed building enforcement notice

Where the local planning authority finds that works are being carried out to a listed building in contravention of section 55(1) or (4) they may serve a listed building enforcement notice under section 96 of the 1971 Act specifying the alleged contravention and requiring steps to be taken to restore the building to its former state. If it is not reasonably practicable to restore the building the notice may require further works to be carried out to alleviate the effect of the works which were carried out without listed building consent. If the contravention consists of non-compliance with conditions attached to a listed building consent the notice will specify such works as are necessary to bring the building to the state in which it would have been had the conditions of the listed building consent been complied with. A listed building enforcement notice must be served not later than 28 days after the date of its issue and not less than 28 days before the date specified in the notice as the date on which it is to take effect. The persons to be served are the owner and occupier of the building together with any other person having an interest in the building which would be materially affected.[76] Failure to comply with a listed building enforcement notice is an offence punishable by fine or imprisonment. Owners who purchase a property after a listed building enforcement notice has been served may be brought before a court and even become liable for non-compliance with the notice in certain circumstances.[77]

The reply to enquiry IV will show whether the local authority have resolved to serve a listed building enforcement notice. If one has been served the local authority will indicate whether it has been satisfactorily complied with.

Repairs notice

It may well be that an owner of a listed building will deliberately allow his property to fall into a state of disrepair in an attempt to force the local planning authority to grant him listed building consent for development of the property in order to rid

[75] Town and Country Planning Act 1971, s.190.
[76] *Ibid.*, s.96(3).
[77] *Ibid.*, s.98.

themselves of an eyesore. Under section 115 of the 1971 Act the local planning authority may serve upon such an owner a "repairs notice." The notice will set out the works considered necessary by a local planning authority to put the building into a reasonable state of preservation. Enquiry V(A) will reveal whether the local authority have served a repairs notice. If such a notice has been served it is likely that the local authority plans to take steps to compulsorily acquire the property. The repairs notices must be served at least two months prior to the initiation of compulsory purchase proceedings in respect of a listed building.

Compulsory acquisition

Under section 114 of the 1971 Act the Secretary of State or the local authority might compulsorily acquire a listed building which has not been kept in a reasonable state of preservation provided that a repairs notice has been served at least two months before the initiation of the procedure to acquire. The reply to enquiry V(B) will indicate whether the local authority have authorised the making of an order for compulsory acquisition of the property.

There are two bases of compensation for calculating the amount to be paid to an owner of a listed building which is to be compulsorily acquired. Normally the compensation will be either the site value of the property as it stands or the value of the site on the assumption that listed building consent would be granted for demolition or any other works, except where such development has been the subject of an application in the past and has been refused or was granted subject to conditions.[78] However, where the owner of a listed building has deliberately let it fall into disrepair in order to justify its demolition so that he can develop the site or an adjoining piece of property the local authority may include a direction for "minimum compensation" provided this has been authorised by the Secretary of State. Where such a direction is included in the compulsory purchase order the amount of compensation payable will be the value of the bare site of the property as it stands. It is assumed that the site has no development potential and that the only listed building consents which would be granted would be those for works to restore the building to a reasonable state of repair. The amount of compensation will not be as high as under the normal basis where, broadly speaking, the depressive effects of the listing of a building on its value is disregarded.[79]

(ii) Building preservation notice The listing procedure is quite cumbersome and it can take some time for the details of a building to be submitted by the Department of Environment to the Secretary of State and finally included in the list under section 54 of the 1971 Act. Occasionally, it is necessary to take emergency action to preserve a building whilst consideration is given to its inclusion in a list. Section 58(1) of the 1971 Act provides that a district planning authority in the case of a building in their area which is not a listed building but which is

[78] In practice it would usually be assumed that planning permission would be granted only for development within the terms of Sched. 8 to the Town and Country Planning Act 1971.

[79] An appeal against the amount of compensation awarded lies to the magistrates' court; s.117 of the 1971 Act.

of special architectural or historic interest and which is in danger of demolition or alteration in such a way as to affect its character may serve on the owner or occupier of the building a notice stating that the building appears to them to be of special architectural or historic interest and that they have requested the Secretary of State to consider including it in a list compiled under section 54. This is the building preservation notice procedure.

Effect of notice

Once a building preservation notice has been served on the owner or occupier of a building[80] the building is treated as if it were a listed building. A building preservation notice remains in force for 6 months after the date upon which it is served or until the Secretary of State includes the building in a list prepared by him pursuant to section 54 whichever is the earlier. If the notice lapses or if it is decided not to list the building the local planning authority may be liable to pay compensation to the owner for loss suffered as a result of the building preservation notice being served.[81] Such compensation may consist, for example, of damages for breach of contract paid by the owner of a building to a developer who had to discontinue work whilst the notice was in force. The reply to enquiry 13 will indicate whether the local planning authority has authorised service of a building preservation notice. If such a notice has been served it is possible that the building will be listed in the future and the purchaser might wish to withdraw from the transaction.

Conservation areas

We have seen that listing a building under section 54 of the Town and Country Planning Act 1971 will provide adequate protection for individual buildings of special architectural or historic interest. By designating an area as a conservation area under section 277 of the 1971 Act[82] a local authority can provide similar protection for *areas* of special architectural or historic interest where it is desirable to preserve or enhance the character and appearance of such areas.

Conservation areas vary in size from groups of buildings to whole town centres or villages.

Within conservation areas special attention is paid by a local authority to all forms of development.[83]

When the local planning authority receives an application for planning permission it must give details of the application in the local press and on the site of the proposed development. The local planning authority has a duty to consider representations made by members of the public in respect of the proposed development.

Before demolishing a building within a conservation area listed building consent must first be obtained.[84] Indeed, many

[80] In cases of extreme urgency the notice may be "served" by affixing it to the building in question itself.

[81] Town and Country Planning Act 1971, s.173.

[82] As substituted by the Town and Country (Amenities) Act 1974.

[83] In this context "development" is used in a wider sense than its strict statutory meaning within s.22 of the 1971 Act: see above, p.88.

[84] With certain exemptions; see DOE Circular 23/1977.

local planning authorities within conservation areas will require anybody seeking permission to demolish a building to enter into a binding agreement[85] for the re-development of the site in accordance with approved plans. This prevents an applicant from demolishing a building and leaving the site vacant or replacing it with a building which would deleteriously affect the appearance and character of the conservation area.

The local planning authority is also given special powers to protect trees within the area[86] and to carry out urgent repairs to vacant buildings without the consent (but at the expense!) of the owners.[87]

By way of an example of the detailed control which may be exercised by a local planning authority within a conservation area reference can be made to *Re Royal Crescent*[88] in which it was held that in principle a local planning authority could serve an enforcement notice to stop an owner of a house from painting his front door yellow!

Enquiry XII will reveal whether or not the property is within a conservation area designated prior to August 31, 1974. Details of conservation areas designated on or after that date are registerable as local land charges and should appear on the official certificate of search of the local land charges register.

Areas of outstanding natural beauty

Enquiry VII asks whether any order has been made under section 87 of the National Parks and Access to the Countryside Act 1949 affecting the property.

The Countryside Commission is charged with the preservation of natural beauty within England and Wales. Under section 87 of the 1949 Act the Commission may designate an area as one of outstanding natural beauty. Many such areas varying in size from Chichester Harbour to the whole of Cornwall have been designated as areas of outstanding natural beauty.

The main affects of designation are as follows:

(1) The range of permitted development under the Town and Country Planning (General Development) Order 1977 is restricted.

(2) Any local planning authority whose area consists of or includes the whole or any part of an area of outstanding natural beauty has power to take all such action as appears expedient in order to preserve and enhance the natural beauty of the area and its promotion for the enjoyment of the public. A local planning authority may provide special financial assistance for people who wish to build within the area in order to enable them to use materials which will preserve the character of the locality.

[85] Possibly with the council under s.52 of the 1971 Act but not necessarily. The agreement could be with a builder.

[86] Which are broadly speaking treated as though they were subject to a tree preservation order.

[87] s.101 of the 1971 Act; see also s.115 for buildings which have been listed.

[88] [1973] J.P.L. 27.

(3) A local planning authority may consult the Commission in respect of any application for planning permission which they receive and must consult with Commission when drawing up structure and local plans encompassing the area.
(4) The Commission must be consulted over any development which affects access to the area.

As with conservation areas the importance of a positive reply to this enquiry is that a stricter regime of development control will apply. The purchaser should be informed of this as it may affect his plans for the property.

Urban development areas

Enquiry XI asks whether the property is situated in an urban development area.

Under section 134 of the Local Government, Planning and Land Act 1980 the Secretary of State may designate an area as an urban development area. The area of land designated must be within or have a common boundary with a metropolitan district or Inner London borough.

The primary purposes of designating an area as an urban development area are to:

(1) bring land into effective use;
(2) encourage new industrial and commercial development;
(3) enhance amenity within the area;
(4) encourage people to live within the area by providing adequate social facilities.

Once an urban development area has been designated by the Secretary of State[89] he will create an urban development corporation. The urban development corporation will consult with the local authorities who have an interest in the area's rejuvenation and decide upon the best policies for securing the above objectives.

An urban development corporation is given wide ranging powers in order to enable it to carry out its functions. It can acquire land by agreement or compulsory purchase and it may dispose of land upon such terms as it deems appropriate.

When an urban development corporation has been constituted it will establish a set of development proposals for the area. Once such development proposals have been adopted the Secretary of State may make a special development order[90] to the effect that all development in accordance with the published proposals shall not require an express grant of planning permission. In effect this removes a local planning authority's power to regulate development which is in accordance with a scheme published by an urban development corporation. In respect of all other development which is outside the stated objectives the local planning authority will retain control unless the Secretary of State makes an order stating that the urban

[89] Parliament must approve such designation.
[90] ss.142 to 144 of the 1971 Act.

development corporation is to take over all aspects of planning control within the urban development area.

An urban development corporation is supposed to be a transient creature. Once an area has been renewed it can transfer the whole of its functions to the various local authorities over which the urban development area was superimposed.

If the reply to enquiry XI reveals that the property being purchased is within an urban development area it will give the address of the urban development corporation's principal office. It is important that the purchaser's legal advisers should find out exactly what functions have been transferred from the local authority to the urban development corporation. For example, if the urban development corporation is charged with the enforcement of planning control they will be able to provide information as to service of enforcement notices and compulsory purchase notices amongst other useful information.

Enterprise zones

Enquiry XII in Part II will indicate whether the property is within an enterprise zone.

An enterprise zone may be designated by the Secretary of State.[91] A scheme to encourage industrial growth within the area will be drawn up by the district council in whose area the enterprise zone lies.[92]

Within an enterprise zone there is a relaxation of many laws which discourage industrial growth. Furthermore, certain financial benefits are available so that these areas become attractive to industry. The benefits which include the following are usually available throughout the life of an enterprise zone which is normally 10 years:

Benefits available

(i) **Simplified planning** The scheme of development published by the district council will specify certain types of development for which express planning permission will not be necessary. It will also specify types of development which under no circumstances will be allowed within the area, for example, the storage and manufacture of hazardous substances or the construction of buildings over a certain height. Other development may be exempted from the usual planning regime subject to consultation on an informal basis. This may be the case,for example, in connection with provision of roads providing access to the enterprise zone.

The usual procedure will have to be followed to obtain planning permission for development which does not fall within the terms of the scheme drawn up by the district council. However, such applications will be dealt with more expeditiously than would normally be the case.

(ii) **Taxation** Within an enterprise zone increased capital allowances may be available in respect of expenditure on

[91] Local Government, Planning and Land Act 1980, ss.165 and 166.
[92] *Ibid.*, s.179 and Sched. 32.

industrial buildings. This will be extremely attractive to commercial clients.

(iii) **General rates** Within an enterprise zone general rates are not levied on industrial or commercial property.

(iv) **Other advantages** These include exemption from industrial training levies and relaxation of numerous other regulations which tend to discourage industrial growth.

As with urban development areas it is possible that a separate enterprise zone authority will be set up to administer planning control. If the reply to this enquiry indicates that the property is within an enterprise zone the purchaser's advisers must make appropriate enquiries to see whether or not any functions have been transferred from the local authority to the enterprise zone authority necessitating direct enquiry of the latter authority.

Improvement areas

Under section 4 of the Inner Urban Areas Act 1978 a district council may resolve to designate an area as one which is in need of improvement. The council may then make provision for loans and grants towards the improvement of buildings used for industrial and commercial purposes within that area. Obviously, this will be a relevant consideration for a commericial purchaser proposing to move into such an area.

Rates

Section 17 of and Schedule 1 to the General Rate Act 1967 provide that owners of unoccupied properties may be charged a proportion of the rates which would be payable if their properties were occupied.

In order to be able to levy rates on unoccupied property a local council must adopt the provisions of section 17 by passing a resolution to that effect. The resolution will specify the proportion of the full rate to be levied on unoccupied property and the date from which the provisions of the 1967 Act are to apply. The resolution may also specify the types of property upon which so called "empty rates" will be charged. The local authority may differentiate between particular areas of land and types of buildings within their district by charging empty rates at differing levels or not at all. For example, if a particular area suffered from planning blight which made it difficult to sell unoccupied commercial premises such an area could be specifically exempted from the provisions of section 17.

The maximum proportion of unoccupied rates which may be levied on buildings other than dwelling-houses is 50 per cent. of the full rate.

For the first three months (or six months in the case of a newly built dwelling-house) of a period during which a building is unoccupied no empty rates are chargeable. However, a change of ownership within the three (or six) month period will not result in an extension of the time during which the property may remain unoccupied free from the possibility of empty rates being levied. For example, if a purchaser buys a property which has been empty for two months he will become liable to have empty rates levied against the property should he not move in immediately one month after completion of the sale to him. The period of grace may be extended beyond three months by the local council should they so resolve.

There are certain exemptions from the provisions of section 17. Most importantly, where an owner is prohibited by law from occupying a building or allowing it to be occupied he will not have to pay empty rates no matter how long it remains unoccupied.

Special provisions apply in respect of properties in the City of London.

The reply to enquiry 17 in Part I of the form will specify the categories of properties upon which empty rates are being levied, the date the provisions of the 1967 Act were brought into force and the proportion of the full rate payable in respect of the different areas and categories of property affected.

Informal notices

Enquiry 3 asks for details of any "outstanding statutory or informal notices" issued by the council in respect of the property under the Public Health Acts, Housing Acts or Highway Acts. If the purchaser requires information in respect of other enactments he should ask an appropriate additional enquiry.

The information revealed in reply to this enquiry may be extremely helpful. For example, the authors recall an occasion where the local authority disclosed that an informal notice had been served upon the owner of certain vacant hotel premises stating that extensive remedial work would have to be carried out before part of the premises could be used as a restaurant. In the light of this information the purchaser successfully negotiated a reduction in the purchase price for the property to take into account the cost of such works. Other matters disclosed by a local authority may include informal notices served indicating that the highways adjacent to the property are to be widened or other development carried out on or near the property.

For properties within Inner London boroughs the reply to enquiry 3 will also reveal whether or not there are any outstanding statutory or informal notices served by the council pursuant to the London Building Acts. These Acts function as a set of Building Regulations for the Inner London area. The council may, for example, have served a notice upon an owner requiring him to carry out repairs to a party wall.

Pipelines

Enquiry VIII asks if any map has been deposited under section 35 of the Pipelines Act 1962 or section 32 of the Gas Act 1972 showing a pipeline within 100 feet of the property. Maps will be deposit pursuant to these provisions when it is proposed to construct or divert pipelines. The maps will give an indication, as to the route to be taken by the pipeline, they do not show their exact location on the property.

Before any construction work is commenced on surface land within 10 feet of a pipeline, the consent of the Secretary of State must be obtained. Any building erected in default may be required to be demolished if it is not possible to execute other works to safeguard the pipelines. The Secretary of State may also order that any such building be vacated beforehand.

Clearly if a positive reply is received to this enquiry steps need to be taken to ensure the purchaser is aware of the dangers. He may have to reshuffle his plans to build on or near the property which he proposes to buy. The authority which owns the pipeline will have to be contacted if the exact location of the pipeline is to be ascertained and may need to be consulted regarding the building works to be carried out.

If this question is to be asked of the local authority it is essential that a plan is sent with the form of enquiries to enable them to give as accurate a reply as possible.

4 OTHER SOURCES OF INFORMATION

Personal Inspections

A. At the property

CHECK	WHY
1. *Residential property*	
(a) Rights of non-owning occupiers. Members of vendor's family, mistresses, tenants, squatters, contractual licensees	Unregistered land—rights may bind purchaser with actual, constructive or imputed notice Registered land—rights may be binding on purchaser as overriding interests within section 70(1)(*g*), (*f*) or (*k*) of the Land Registration Act 1925.
(b) Rights of way or other informal arrangements	Unregistered land—rights may bind purchaser with actual, constructive or imputed notice Registered land—rights may constitute overriding interests within section 70(1)(*a*) of the Land Registration Act 1925.
(c) Property and boundaries correspond with contractual description and plan	To avoid disputes and possible rescission of the contract.
(d) Improvements to the property	Planning and building consents. Possible increase in rateable value. Leasehold property—was landlord's consent obtained (if necessary)?
(e) Extensions	Planning and building consents. Has extension used up permitted increase in cubic content? Rate increases. Leasehold property—landlord's consent?
(f) New properties and conversions, cracks, etc.	Claim against the builder or N.H.B.C.
(g) Cavity wall insulation	Building regulations. Danger to health.
(h) Fixtures and fittings	To avoid later arguement. Apportionment of purchase price.
(i) Routes of services	May affect plans for building work. Authority has powers to enter land and maintain equipment.
(j) Leasehold property; state and condition	Purchaser deemed to buy with full knowledge of actual state and condition. Liability for breach of repairing covenant. Deterioration of exterior and, or common parts of block of flats indicates inadequate management.
2. *Commercial property*	
(a) Rights of non-owning occupiers. Tenants, squatters, contractual licensees, service occupants	As for residential properties.
(b) Rights of way and other informal arrangements	As for residential properties.
(c) Routes of services	May affect plans for future development. Authorities have power to enter onto land to maintain equipment.

(d) Stock in trade	Apportionment of purchase price
(e) Building operations	Planning and building regulation consents. Rate increases Leaseholds—landlord's consents?
(f) Present user	Unauthorised development? Is planning permission required for purchaser's intended use?
(g) Advertisements	Are they permitted? Will the purchaser have to apply for permission to display his advertisements?
(h) Leasehold property—state and condition	Purchaser deemed to buy with full knowledge of actual state and condition. As for residential properties.

B. At the offices of the local authority

CHECK	WHY
1. *Residential property*	
(a) Register of planning applications and decisions	For details of those relating to this and neighbouring property. Planning authority's attitude to future development.
(b) Local plan	Shows long-term plans for development in immediately surrounding area.
(c) Register of enforcement and stop notices	Breach of planning control.
(d) Register of listed buildings	More stringent planning controls.
(e) Register of advertisements	Are any public signs or private advertisements attached to property permitted?
(f) Maps of pipelines	Shows intended route of pipelines if building work contemplated pipeline owner must be contracted for exact location. Consent of Secretary of State required to build within 10 feet of pipeline.
2. *Commercial property*	
(a) Register of planning applications and decisions	As for residential property.
(b) Structure plan	Long term policies for the area. Zoning in the future for different purposes and information about transport infrastructure, for instance.
(c) Local plan	As for residential property.
(d) Register of enforcement and stop notices	Breach of planning control.
(e) Register of listed buildings	Extra controls.
(f) Register of advertisements	Permitted advertising.

Subsidence

Nationalisation

(i) Coal[1] The nationalisation of coal began with the setting-up of a register of coal. The Coal (Registration of Ownership) Act 1937 required all those with interests in coal and coal mines voluntarily to register these interests. Coal the mineral was then nationalised by the Coal Acts 1938 and 1943 and the coal industry by the Coal Industry Nationalisation Act 1946. Most coal and coal mines now belong to the National Coal Board (N.C.B.). The rights of the N.C.B. to work coal and lower the surface of the land and the rights of surface owners to compensation for resulting damage depend on the distribution of ownership of the

[1] See P. Vincent, (1984) L.S. Gaz. 1589.

surface of the land and the minerals on January 1, 1939. If on that date the surface and the minerals were in different fee simple ownership or the surface and minerals were in the same fee simple ownership but subject to a minerals lease then the N.C.B. has the same rights as the "pre-takeover" mineral owner or lessee, hopefully recorded in the 1938 register. In the established coalfields problems have arisen because the old mining agreements rarely gave surface owners any rights of support. They therefore had to carry out repairs at their own expense. The Coal Mining (Subsidence) Acts 1950 and 1957 gave some relief to these people by requiring the N.C.B. to repair damaged property but did not give compensation for consequential loss. However further relief is given under the N.C.B.'s Code of Practice. The Waddilove Committee reported adversely on the situation in 1984 but at the time of writing it remains unchanged.

Where on January 1,1939 the land and minerals were simply in the same fee simple ownership, the N.C.B. have the right to work the coal and withdraw support but only on payment of proper compensation and subject to the following conditions.[2]

(1) the giving of three months' notice;
(2) the publication of a notice identifying the land;
(3) the publication of the notices in the London Gazette and local newspapers for two successive weeks.

Building works

Anyone wishing to erect a building on land in respect of which the N.C.B. has served a notice withdrawing rights of support must submit details of their proposals to the Board, who may specify work to the foundations or changes to the specifications at their expense. If the Board recommends precautions but they are not incorporated then the Board's liability for repair is limited to the cost which would have been incurred had the precaution been incorporated. Surface owners in the newer coal fields (Selby and Belvoir being the latest) generally have the benefit of these better rights, there having been no pre-nationalisation severance of the land and minerals. The same will of course be true for those living in the area of the future mines planned for Oxfordshire and Warwickshire. In the newer coalfields the danger to subsidence is less because of improved technology.

Subsidence

Coalfields new or old, it is important for the purchaser to know whether the property he is intending to buy is liable to subsidence, whether any compensation has been claimed and whether a notice to withdraw support has been published. Enquiries should be made with N.C.B. area office in the appropriate coalfield. A list of addresses is available from the Mining Research Development Establishment—Bretby, Stanhope, Bretby near Burton on Trent. The area office will reply in the form of a written report for which there is a basic charge of £13.70. For enquiries relating to sites outside coalfields the charge is £6.80.

If opencast mining affects or is likely to affect the property, further enquiries should be made with the Opencast Executive, 200 Lichfield Lane, Berry Hill, Mansfield, Notts. NG18 4RG.

[2] Coal Industry Act 1975, s.2.

(ii) Limestone Limestone mining was a major industry in the West Midlands for over 200 years. However the last mine to be worked there was closed in the mid 1930s. Following an incident of subsidence in 1978 on an industrial estate in Sandwell caused by the partial collapse of an old limestone working, the government empowered the Department of the Environment to carry out remedial works to former underground workings. Consequently the Department of the Environment commissioned an investigation by consultants into limestone workings in the West Midlands. They concluded that the risk of subsidence was low. Their report (published in 1983) can be inspected at the offices of each of the metropolitan boroughs concerned, namely Dudley, Walsall, Sandwell and Wolverhampton. In addition a summary of the report can be bought for £1.50 from the Department of the Environment, West Midlands Regional Office, Fine Ways Tower, Frederick Road, Birmingham 15 (post free). In Dudley and Wolverhampton only a few privately owned properties are affected by limestone workings. In Sandwell the properties affected are mainly council houses or large industrial estates. Dudley, Sandwell and Walsall recommend that limestone enquiries be made on the purchase of a council house. Each of the four metropolitan boroughs have different procedures for dealing with limestone enquiries.

Walsall Walsall automatically informs the purchaser whether the property is undermined by limestone workings when he submits his local search and enquiries, by means of a letter attached to the replies. No extra enquiry is necessary and no fee is payable. Any general legal questions on limestone workings should be forwarded to the Head of Legal Services, Civil Centre, Walsall WS1 1TP, technical enquiries to the Director of Engineering and Town Planning at the same address.

Sandwell Sandwell will only answer limestone enquiries as part of the purchaser's local searches. This question should be added to Part II of form Con 29A: "Is the property affected by limestone workings?" and the appropriate additional enquiry fee paid.

Dudley Enquiry may be made by letter or by way of additional enquiry on Part II of Con 29A. Legal questions should be addressed to the assistant borough solicitor, Council House, Dudley, West Midlands DY1 1HF, but technical enquiries should be made to the Public Works Department, Council House, Mary Stevens Park, Stourbridge, West Midlands DY8 2AA.

Wolverhampton Wolverhampton deal with enquiries in the same manner as Dudley but prefer them to be made in a separate letter to the Structural Department, Civic Centre, St. Peters Square, Wolverhampton WV1 1RG.

Sizeable deposits of limestone are found and presently quarried in Derbyshire and in the Bristol area. We suggest contacting the appropriate quarriers for further details. In Derbyshire the main limestone quarriers are: Mandell Mining Company at Sheldon near Bakewell, Lime Manufacturers and

Suppliers at Carsington, Hoveringsham Stone Company at Cromford, and Grangemill Quarry, Ben Junior Limited at Worksworth. In the Bristol area the main company is the Amey Roadstone Corporation Limited whose head office is in Frome.

(iii) Tin and Clay Tin and clay are mainly worked in Cornwall and Devon. Subsidence enquiries relating to tin mining should be sent to the Cornish Chamber of Mines, Mount Wellington, Ferrys Platt, Chacewater, Cornwall, accompanied by a large scale ordnance survey map identifying the property. A fee of £30.00 is payable where the enquiries relate to a single property, £60.00 for development land. There is no formal clay enquiry procedure. The companies concerned with producing the clay should be contacted direct. In Cornwall the chief company is China Clay plc at St. Austell, and in Devon, English Ball Clays at Newton Abbott.

Railway fences and tunnels

Fences British Rail are under an obligation to fence certain land they own. Generally speaking the obligation (which is not very wide) arose in this way. When the railways were first built, the land acquired to build them on was largely farmland. The railway companies were under a duty to fence the railway to prevent farm stock from straying onto the line and causing injury to passengers. Sometimes the companies contracted out of this obligation. It was then up to the farmer to fence his boundaries. The railways were amalgamated in 1923 and nationalised in 1948 and British Rail took over any responsibility for fencing from their predecessors in title. British Rail are like their predecessor in title under no general duty to stop people from trespassing on the railway, merely stock. In so far as the acquisition of new land is concerned, British Rail have maintained a policy of expressly contracting out of fencing responsibilities and on the sale of land owned by them extract a covenant from the purchaser to erect and maintain fences where appropriate.

British Rail will inform a purchaser who is buying land abutting an existing or disused railway whether they are responsible for fences or not. Enquiry should be made in writing to the appropriate regional office of British Railways Property Board. These are:

Southern: Dennison House 296/298 Vauxhall Bridge Road,London SW1V 1AG
South Western: Temple Gate House, Temple Gate, Bristol BS1 6PX
Midland: Stanier House, 10 Holliday Street, Birmingham BT1 1TG.
Eastern: Great Northern House, 79/81 Euston Road, London NW1 2RT
North Eastern: Headquarters Offices, York, YO1 1HP
North Western: 34 High Street,Manchester M4 QB
Scottish: Rail House 58 Port Dundas Road, Glasgow G4 0HG

In parts of London, the Midlands and the North responsibility for travel co–ordination has been taken over by the Passenger Executives and some railways are now owned by them. Such being the case enquiry should be addressed to the civil engineering department of the executive concerned:

London (Regional Transport) Transport Executive: 55 Broadway, Westminster, London SW1H 0BD
Greater Manchester: PO Box 429, County Hall, Piccadilly Gardens, Manchester M60 1HX
Merseyside: 24 Hatton Garden Liverpool L3 2AN
WestMidlands: 16 Summer Lane, Birmingham B19 3SD
Tyne and Wear: Cuthbert House, All Saints, Newcastle upon Tyne NE1 2DA
South Yorkshire: Exchange St., Sheffield S2 5SZ
West Yorkshire: Metro House, West Parade, Wakefield WF1 1NS

All the above mentioned offices charge a fee for answering enquiries according to the work involved. It is helpful to enclose a plan identifying the property with the enquiry.

Some railways have been sold to private organisations like railway preservation societies. In appropriate cases contact should be made direct with these organisations.

Tunnels If it is known or thought that a railway tunnel runs under the land which is the subject of the proposed sale the purchaser's solicitor should enquire as to its existence, location, ownership (in the absence of contrary agreement it probably belongs to the railway owner) and any rights of the tunnel owner to enter onto the land and maintain the tunnel. The tunnel may be part of an overground railway in which case enquiries should be addressed to the offices already listed. If part of an underground railway the people the write to are:

London Underground: London (Regional Transport) Transport Executive (address above)
Newcastle Underground: Tyne and Wear Passenger Transport Executive (address above)

Water

The Water Act 1973 set up 10 regional water authorities to be responsible for, *inter alia*, the supply of water, for sewerage and sewage disposal, for the prevention of pollution of rivers and coastal waters and for supervising land drainage, in England and Wales. Enquiry with the appropriate regional water authority may be necessary on the purchaser's behalf in the following circumstances:

(A) Where the land which is the subject of the proposed sale is bordered or crossed by a river or stream. Clarification as to responsibility for maintenance of the river banks should be sought. If it rests with the owner of the land the authority should be asked whether it has served a notice of disrepair[3] on the

[3] This should be revealed in answer to the purchaser's enquiries of the vendor.

vendor, so that an appropriate indemnity can be obtained from him. Where the authority is liable to maintain the river banks it may have rights to enter onto the land to carry out its obligations.

(B) Where the purchaser proposes to build or extend. Plans which are submitted for Building Regulation consent from the local authority may be rejected or conditionally approved if the building work is to be carried out over a sewer, drain or water pipe. Their exact routes must be discovered.

(C) A licence may be required to abstract water under the provisions of the Water Resources Act 1963.[4] The act prohibits the abstraction of water from any natural source except for domestic purposes, without the consent of the water authority in whose area the source lies. The benefit of an existing licence to abstract water is automatically transferred to the purchaser, but will lapse unless the authority is informed of the change of occupation within one month of the date of change of occupation.

(D) No-one may obstruct the flow of any watercourse such as by a dam or weir without the permission of the local water authority or alter any obstruction in the watercourse without permission.[5] This applies whether the creating of an obstruction is for domestic purposes, for example an ornamental pond or lake or for agricultural or industrial purposes. An impoundment licence is rarely granted because of the danger of flooding.

(E) It is an offence to discharge without licence trade effluent into a sewer, stream, coastal water or specified underground water.[6] The water authority should be asked whether a licence exists and if so on what terms, and the licence should ideally be transferred into the purchaser's name on completion.

No fixed fee is charged for answering enquiries, which should be made in writing and accompanied by a plan of the property.

Here are the addresses of the 10 regional water authorities:

Wessex: Wessex House, Passage Street, Bristol BS2 0JQ
South West: Peninsula House, Rydon Lane, Exeter EX2 7HR
Southern: Guildbourne House, Chatsworth Road, Worthing BN11 1LD
Thames: Nugent House, Vastem Road, Reading RG1 8DB
Anglian: Ambury Road, Huntingdon PE18 6NZ
Severn—Trent: Abetson House, 2297 Coventry Road,Sheldon, Birmingham B26 3PS
Yorkshire: West Riding House, 67 Albion Street, Leeds LS1 5AA
North-West: Dawson House, Great Sankey, Warrington WA5 3LW
Northumbrian: Northumbria House, Regent Centre, Gosforth, Newcastle-upon-Tyne NE3 3PX
Wales: Cambrian Way, Brecon, Powys LD3 7HP

In addition the National Water Council, 1 Queen Anne's Gate, London SW1H 9BT (01–222–8111) will answer any general enquiry.

[4] See above, p.52.
[5] Land Drainage Act 1976.
[6] Control of Pollution Act 1974.

Canals Where the property abuts a canal, enquiries should be made with the British Waterways Board whose national headquarters are at Melbury House, Melbury Terrace, London NW1 6JX. If the canal is also used as a drain it is the joint responsibility of the British Waterways Board and the regional water authority and both organisations will have to be contacted. A few canals belong to conservationists. Enquiries relating to ownership and maintenance should be made to them direct.

Electricity

Responsibility for the generation of electricity in England and Wales rests with the Central Electricity Generating Board. The Board is under a duty to supply electricity in bulk to the twelve area boards for distribution to consumers.[7] Lines providing supply can interfere with farming and cultivation, prevent the working of minerals and restrict development. Compensation is payable. A board may at any time, enter upon any land where an electricity line has lawfully been laid in order to maintain it, without obtaining the prior consent of the owner or occupier.

The Central Electricity Generating Board and the area boards will supply details of agreements relating to the placing of cables above or below ground and of approved future proposals. They also keep records of the location of all their existing cables and installations. These records are open to public inspection and copies can be taken away. A small fee is charged for this service.

Central Electricity Generating Board

Area Offices:

South West: Bedminster Down, Bridgewater Road, Bristol BS13 8AN
South East: Bankside House, Sumner Street, London SE1 9JU
Midlands: Haslucks Green Road, Shirley, Solihull, West Midlands, B90 4PD
North West: Europa House, Bird Hall Lane, Cheadle Heath, Stockport SK3 0XA
North East: Beckwith Knowle, Otley Road, Harrogate HG3 1PS

Area Boards:

South West: Electricity House, Colston House, Bristol BS1 4TS
South Wales: St Mellons, Cardiff CF3 9XW
Southern: Southern Electricity House, Littlewick Green, nr. Maidenhead, Berks. SL6 3QB
South East: Grand Avenue, Hove, Sussex BN3 2LS
London: Templar House, 81–87 High Holborn, London WC1V 6NU
Eastern: PO Box 40, Whearstead, Ipswich IP9 2Q

[7] Electricity Act 1957.

East Midlands: PO Box B4, North PDO 398, Coppice Road, Arnold, Notts. NG5 7HX
Midland: Mucklow Hill, Halesowen, Worcestershire B62 8BP
Merseyside and North Wales: Sealand Road, Chester CH1 4LR
North East: Carliol House, Newcastle-upon-Tyne NE99 15E
Yorkshire: Wetherby Road, Scarcroft, Leeds LS14 3HS
North Western: Cheetwood Road, Manchester M8 8BA.

Gas

Gas is the province of the British Gas Corporation.[8] It has powers, *inter alia*, to search and bore for and get natural gas and petroleum in the form of crude oil, to acquire, manufacture, transmit and distribute gas and to manufacture, treat and sell by-products obtained from manufacturing gas. It may also store gas underground provided it has an authorisation order from the Secretary of State.[9] Land within a storage area might undergo some depreciation in value.

Where gas pipes are lawfully laid in private land the Corporation may enter onto the land to repair, replace or alter the pipes, on giving prior notice to the owner or occupier. No notice need be given in the case of an emergency. It is an offence to damage any equipment of the Corporation. Purchasers wishing to develop must therefore ascertain its location on the property they intend buying.

Enquiry should be made by letter, enclosing a plan of the property to regional head office of the British Gas Corporation concerned. The location of any Corporation equipment will be marked on the plan and returned free of charge.

Regional head offices of the British Gas Corporation

British Gas Corporation: Rivermill House, 152 Grosvenor Road, London SW1V 3JL
South West: Riverside, Temple Street, Keynsham, Bristol BS18 1EQ
Southern: 80 St. Mary's Road, Southampton SO9 5AT
South East: Segas House, Catherine Street, Croydon, Surrey CR9 1JM
Eastern: Star House, Potters Bar, Herts. EN6 2PD
East Midlands: PO Box 145, De Montfort Road, Leicester LE1 9DB
West Midlands: Wharf Lane, Solihull, West Midlands B91 2JP
Northern: Nor Gas House, Killingworth, PO Box 1GB, Newcastle-upon-Tyne NE99 1GB
North Eastern: New York Road, Leeds LS2 7PE
North West: Welman House, Altringham, Cheshire WA15 8AE

[8] Gas Act 1972.
[9] Gas Act 1965.

North Thames: North Thames House, London Road, Staines, Middlesex TW18 4AE
Wales: 11 Helmont House, Churchill Way, Cardiff CS1 4NB

Telecommunications

1981 saw the creation[10] of British Telecommunications, a public company which took over from the Post Office the exclusive privilege and task of running telecommunication systems in the British Isles. The Corporation may (amongst other things) place and maintain a telegraph (wires, pipes,cables, etc., used for the purpose of transmitting telegraphic messages and ancillary equipment) on, over or under private land and may alter and remove such equipment. It may in addition lay deep telegraphic lines for defence purposes. British Telecom try to arrange a convenient date and time with the owner or occupier before they enter onto private property to construct or repair lines, except of course in an emergency. Generally speaking anyone who damages property belonging to the Corporation has to pay the cost of making it good.

Enquiries on behalf of a purchaser intending to develop the land the subject of the proposed sale should be directed to the relevant area office of British Telecom, which will inform the enquirer as to the whereabouts of its equipment free of charge.

British Telecom districts and areas

Anglian Coastal (Colchester, Norwich, Southend-on-Sea): St. Peters House, 22 St. Peters Street, Colchester CO1 1ET
Central Midlands (Birmingham, Coventry): Richmond House, 84 Newhall Street, Birmingham B3 1BA
Dundee: 21 Ward Road,Dundee DD1 1BA
East Midlands (Leicester, Northampton, Nottingham): 200 Charles Street, Leicester LE1 1BA
Edinburgh: Telephone House, 357 Gorgie Road, Edinburgh EH11 2RP
Lancs and Cumbria (Blackburn, Lancaster, Preston): Telephone House, 170–175 Moor Lane, Preston PR1 1BA
Liverpool (Liverpool, Isle of Man): Imperial Buildings, Exchange Street East, Liverpool L2 3XX
London Centre: Dial House, 151 Shaftesbury House, London WC2H 8BA
London City: Riverside House, 2a Southwark Bridge Road, London SE1 9BA
London East: Telephone House, 4–20 Woodgrange Road, Forest Gate, London E7 0BA
London North: Telephone House, Crouch End Hill, London N8 8BA
London North Central: Fleet Building, 40 Shoe Lane, London EC4A 3DD

[10] British Telecommunications Act 1981.

London North West: Telephone House, 1–15 Shoot-up-Hill, London NW2 3BA
London South: Impact House, 2 Edridge Road, Croydon CR9 1BT
London South Central: Emang House, St. George's Circus, London SE1 8BA
London South East: Telephone House, 24 Westmoreland Place, Masons Hill, Bromley BR1 1BA
London South West: Telephone House, 21–23 Worple Road, London SW19 4BA
London West: Westel House, 32–38 Uxbridge Road, London W5 2BA
Manchester (Manchester Central, North and South): Telecommunications House, 91 London Road, Manchester M60 1MQ
Mid Yorkshire (Bradford, Leeds, York): Telecom House, 35 Lisbon Street, Leeds LS1 1A
Mid Anglia (Cambridge, Peterborough): Clarendon House, Clarendon Road, Cambridge CB2 2BA
North and West Midlands (Stoke-on-Trent, West Midlands): Telecom House, Church Street, Wolverhampton WV2 4BA
North Downs and Weald (Canterbury, Tunbridge Wells): Telephone House, Rheims Way, Canterbury CT1 3BA
North East (Middlesbrough, Newcastle-upon-Tyne): Swan House, 157 Pilgrim Street, Newcastle-upon-Tyne NE 1BA
North of Scotland (Aberdeen, the North of Scotland): Caledonian House, 232 Union Street, Aberdeen AB9 2BB
North Wales and the Marches (Chester, Shrewsbury): Telephone House, Smithfield Road, Shrewsbury SY1 1BA
Northern Ireland (Belfast): Churchill House, 20 Victoria Square, Belfast BT1 4BA
Severnside (Bristol, Gloucester): Mercury House, Bond Street, Bristol BS1 3TD
Sheffield and Lincoln: Telephone House, Charter Square, Sheffield S1 1BA
Solent (Bournemouth, Southampton): Telephone House, 70–75 High Street, Southampton SO9 1BB
South Downs (Bristol, Portsmouth): Telephone House, 125 Preston Road, Brighton BN1 6BG
South Midlands and Chillterns (Bedford, Oxford): Telephone House, 25–27 St.Johns Street, Bedford MK42 0BA
South Wales (Cardiff, Swansea): 25 Pendwyallt Road, Coryton, Cardiff CF4 7YR
Thamesway (Guildford, Reading): Sunley House, 49 Friar Street, Reading RG1 1BA
West of Scotland (Glasgow, Scotland West): Marland House, George Street, Glasgow G1 1BA
Westward (Exeter, Plymouth, Taunton): Exbridge House, Commercial Road, Exeter EX2 4BB

Pipelines

By virtue of the Pipelines Act 1962 the Secretary of State may authorise the construction of cross-country pipelines. Expressly excluded from the Act are pipes of the British Gas Corporation, the Central Electricity Generating Board and area boards, and the United Kingdom Atomic Energy Authority. The importance of pipelines to some purchasers is that the permission of the Secretary of State is necessary to build on surface land within 10 feet of a pipeline. Any unauthorised building might have to be demolished. There is no provision for the registration of a pipeline or works, but a map showing its route must be deposited with the local authority before construction or deviation work is begun. The maps are open to public inspection. Optional enquiry VIII on the Enquiries of the Local Authority form asks whether any such map has been deposited showing a pipeline within 100 feet of the property.[11] However the maps only show the *intended* route of a pipeline — a deviation of not more than 100 feet laterally from the route shown on the deposited map is permitted. The owner of the pipeline should be asked to pinpoint its exact location where appropriate. A map of the property should accompany the enquiry.

Survey

We have already seen that a vendor is under no obligation to disclose to a purchaser any defects in the physical condition of the property.[12] This is part of the basic rule — *caveat emptor*. The purchaser must satisfy himself as to the condition of the property and its fitness for any particular purpose.[13]

There are conflicting views as to whether a purchaser's advisors should tell him of the need to have a survey of the property carried out. The Council of the Law Society in its written evidence to the Royal Commission on Legal Services expressed the view that normal conveyancing practice dictated that a solicitor should advise his client on the desirability of instructing a surveyor.[14] In the case of domestic conveyancing the purchaser will normally be buying with the aid of finance provided by a bank or building society. In such cases the bank or building society will insist on a survey of some sort being obtained for its own purposes at least.[15] After all, the mortgagee will need to satisfy itself as to the adequacy of its security!

Types of survey There are, broadly speaking, three types of survey — the full structural survey, the intermediate survey (sometimes called a "report on condition and valuation" by building societies) and the mortgage valuation.

[11] Pipe Lines (Limits of Deviation) Regulations 1962 (S.I. 1962 No. 2845). See above, p.109.
[12] *Hill* v. *Harris* [1965] 2 Q.B. 601; see *Hone* v. *Benson* (1978) 248 E.G. 1013 for the duty of care owed by original builders of D.I.Y. vendors in relation to the physical condition of the property.
[13] *Hill* v. *Harris*, above.
[14] Memorandum No. 3, Pt. I.
[15] Building Societies Act 1962, s.25.

A full structural survey is based on a thorough and detailed examination of the property. It will deal with every aspect of the property, it's structure and internal decorative state. The surveyor will carry out a detailed search for defects of any kind.

An intermediate survey will not be so detailed as a full structural survey and so will be obtained more cheaply. It will usually provide general information on the state of repair and the condition of the property. The surveyor will seek symptoms which will enable him to draw to the attention of the purchaser any matters which might cause him to withdraw from the sale or negotiate a reduction in the purchase price. Normally, a surveyor will not inspect parts of the property which are covered or unexposed when carrying out such a survey.

A mortgage valuation report will be prepared for the mortgagee. Its primary purpose is to assist the mortgagee in deciding whether or not the property is a suitable security for the proposed loan. The scope of such a report is limited and may not reveal defects which would be disclosed in either of the other types of survey referred to above.

Whatever type of survey it is decided to have carried out it should be commissioned prior to exchange of contracts. Obviously, once contracts have been exchanged the purchaser is bound to take the property and cannot withdraw or renegotiate the price.

Liability for negligent surveys A surveyor is like any other professional in that he owes a duty of care in proferring his advice and opinions on a property to take reasonable care in carrying out their work and preparing their reports. This duty of care is owed not only to a surveyors client but also to anybody else whose relationship with the surveyor is sufficiently proximate.[16] In *Yianni* v. *Edwin Evans & Sons*[17] a purchaser intended to buy a house with the aid of a building society mortgage. The building society instructed the defendants to prepare a mortgage valuation report. In their instructions to the defendants the society named the purchasers, gave details of the purchase price and the amount of the proposed loan. The defendants reported that the property was adequate security for the advance. In fact the house suffered from subsidence and distortion of the foundations. Having paid £15,000 for the house in January the purchasers found themselves with the prospect of paying £18,000 to repair the foundations in October of the same year! The purchasers brought an action against the surveyor for damages for negligence alleging that the defendants statement in their report to the building society that the house was adequate security for the advance was negligent. The purchasers further claimed that the surveyor should reasonably have contemplated that the society would pass on the contents of the report to them and that they would rely upon it (to their loss) in completing the purchase. The defendants admitted negligence but denied that they owed any duty of care to the purchasers. Furthermore, they argued that the purchasers were contributorily negligent in not obtaining an independent survey despite having received a warning to do so from the

[16] *Cann* v. *Willson* (1888) 39 Ch.D. 39.
[17] [1982] 1 Q.B. 438.

society. The court held that the purchasers could recover damages from the surveyor and that they had not been contributorily negligent in failing to have an independent survey of the property carried out. As Park J. stated:

> "[it is] said a decision in favour of the plaintiffs would encourage applicants for a mortgage to have no independent survey of the house they wished to buy. I can see nothing objectionable in a practice which would result in a house being surveyed once by one surveyor.[18]

In deciding whether or not a surveyor has been negligent it is important to establish that which he has agreed to do. The more limited the scope of the report or survey the more difficult it may be to prove negligence. No doubt where a full structural survey fails to disclose a defective roof a court will readily find against a surveyor.[19] However, what of the surveyor who fails to detect damp in a roof having agreed only to carry out an intermediate survey.[20] The principles upon which a court will proceed have still to be firmly established.

The measure of damages recoverable by a purchaser misled by a negligent survey was discussed in *Perry* v. *Sidney Phillips & Son*.[21] The Court of Appeal held that the correct measure of damages was the difference between the price actually paid for the property and the market value of it as at the date of purchase. A purchaser may also be able to recover a sum in respect of distress and discomfort suffered as a result of the survey until necessary repairs are completed.

[18] *Ibid.*, at p. 443.

[19] *Perry* v. *Sidney Phillips & Son* [1982] 1 W.L.R. 1297; see also *Philips* v. *Ward* [1956] 1 W.L.R. 471; *Bolton* v. *Puley* (1982) 267 E.G. 1160.

[20] *Fisher* v. *Knowles* (1982) 262 E.G. 1083.

[21] [1982] 1 W.L.R. 1297.

APPENDICES

APP.		PAGE
A	Con 29 (Long), Oyez, Enquiries Before Contract	127
B	Convey. 1, Unilaw, Enquiries Prior to Contract for Sale	131
C	(General) Form Q1, Shaw & Sons, Preliminary Enquiries	135
D	(Leasehold) Form Q2, Shaw & Sons, Preliminary Enquiries	139
E	Con 291, Oyez, General Tenancy Enquiries	143
F	Con 292, Oyez, Agricultural Tenancy Enquiries	147
G	Con 29, Oyez, Supplementary Enquiries Before Contract	151
H	Form Q7, Shaw & Sons, Information Memo	153
J	Additional Enquiries Before Contract, Bristol Law Society	157
K	Flat Purchase Enquiries, Bristol Law Society	159
L	Con 29A, Oyez, Enquiries of District Councils	161
M	Con 29D, Oyez, Enquiries of Local Authority	169
N	The Law Society's Code for Completion by Post	177
O	The Law Society's Contract for Sale (1984 Revision)	179
P	The National Contract of Sale Twentieth Edition	183

Enquiries before Contract Nos. Q1, Q2 and Q7 (Appendices C, D and H) are reproduced by permission of the publishers, Shaw & Sons Ltd., Shaway House, Bell Green Lane, Lower Sydenham, London, SE26 5AE, from whom copies may be obtained.

Con 29 (Long), Con 29 (Supp.), Con 291, Con 292, Con 29A and Con 29D (Appendices A, E, F, G, L, and M) are reproduced by kind permission of the Solicitors' Law Stationery Society plc, Oyez House, P.O. Box 55, 27 Crimscott St., London SE1 5TS.

Additional Enquiries Before Contract and Flat Purchase Enquiries (Appendices J and K) are reproduced by kind permission of Bristol Law Society.

Convey. 1 (Appendix B) is reproduced by kind permission of UNILAW, from whose members (see n. 6a on p. 6) copies may be obtained.

The Law Society's Contract for Sale (1984 Revision) and the Code for Completion by Post (Appendices O and N) are reproduced by kind permission of the Law Society and of the Solicitors' Law Stationery Society plc.

The National Contract of Sale (20th edition 1981) (Appendix P) is reproduced by kind permission of the Solicitors' Law Stationery Society plc.

oyez

ENQUIRIES

BEFORE CONTRACT

In cases of property subject to a tenancy, forms **Con 291** (general business and residential tenancies) *or* **Con 292** (agricultural tenancies) should also be used.

Short description of the property

re ....

Parties ....

to ....

Please strike out enquiries which are not applicable

Replies are requested to the following enquiries.

....

Proposed purchaser's solicitors.

Date .... 198 ....

The replies are as follows.

....

Proposed vendor's solicitors.

Date .... 198 ...

GENERAL ENQUIRIES

REPLIES

These replies, except in the case of any enquiry expressly requiring a reply from the Vendor's solicitors, are given on behalf of the proposed Vendor and without responsibility on the part of his solicitors their partners or employees. They are believed to be correct but the accuracy is not guaranteed and they do not obviate the need to make appropriate searches, enquiries and inspections.

1. Boundaries

(A) To whom do all the boundary walls, fences, hedges and ditches belong?

(B) If no definite indications exist, which has the Vendor maintained or regarded as his responsibility?

2. Disputes

(A) Is the Vendor aware of any past or current disputes regarding boundaries, easements, covenants or other matters relating to the property or its use?

(B) During the last three years, has the Vendor complained or had cause to complain about the state and condition, or the manner of use, of any adjoining or neighbouring property? If so, please give particulars.

3. Notices

Please give particulars of all notices relating to the property, or to matters likely to affect its use or enjoyment, that the Vendor (or to his knowledge, any predecessor in title) has given or received.

4. Guarantees etc.

(A) Please supply a copy of any of the following of which the Purchaser is to have the benefit:

agreement, covenant, guarantee, warranty, bond, certificate, indemnity and insurance policy,

relating to any of the following matters:

the construction of the property, or any part of it, or of any building of which it forms part;
any repair or replacement of, or treatment or improvement to the fabric of the property;
the maintenance of any accessway;
the construction costs of any road (including lighting, drainage and crossovers) to which the property fronts, and the charges for adopting any such road as maintainable at the public expense;
a defective title;
breach of any restrictive covenant.

(B) (i) What defects or other matters have become apparent, or adverse claims have been made by third parties, which might give rise to a claim under any document mentioned in (A)?

(ii) Has notice of such defect, matter or adverse claim been given? If so, please give particulars.

(iii) Please give particulars of all such claims already made, whether or not already settled.

5. Services

(A) Does the property have drainage, water, electricity and gas services? Which of them are connected to the mains?

(B) Is the water supply metered?

(C) Do any of the services (except where part of the mains) pass through or over property not included in the sale?

(D) If so, please give details of route and particulars of any easement, grant, exception, reservation, wayleave, licence or consent authorising this.

(E) Please supply a copy of any licence to abstract water and of any consent or licence relating to drainage, issued in respect of the property or the activities carried on there.

6. Facilities

(A) Except in the case of public rights or where particulars have already been given, what rights are there for the use of the following facilities, whether enjoyed by the owner or occupier of the property, or over the property for the benefit of other property:

- —Access for light and air;
- —Access for pedestrians and vehicles;
- —Emergency escape routes;
- —Pipes and wires for services not dealt with in Enquiry 5.
- —Access and facilities for repair, maintenance and replacement.

Please supply copies of any relevant documents.

(B) Has any person taken any action to stop (whether immediately or at some future time) the use of any facility? If so, please give particulars.

(C) In respect of maintenance, repair or replacement work on any land or fixtures affording any facility:

(i) What work has been done by the Vendor (or, to his knowledge, any predecessor in title), and when?

(ii) What work has the Vendor been called upon to do which has not yet been done?

(iii) What sums has the Vendor contributed to work done by others, and when? Is any demand for such sums still outstanding?

(iv) What sums has the Vendor called upon others to contribute, and when? Is any demand still outstanding?

7. Adverse Rights

(A) Is the Vendor aware of any rights or informal arrangements specifically affecting the property, other than any disclosed in the draft contract or immediately apparent on inspection, which are exercisable by virtue of an easement, grant, wayleave, licence, consent, agreement relating to an ancient monument or land near it, or otherwise or which are in the nature of public or common rights?

(B) (i) Please give the full names, and ages if under 18, of all persons in actual occupation of the property.

(ii) What legal or equitable interest in the property has each of those persons?

(C) Is the Vendor aware of any other overriding interests as defined by the Land Registration Act 1925, s. 70(1)?

8. Restrictions

(A) Have all restrictions affecting the property or its use been observed up to the date hereof? If not, please give details.

(B) Where such restrictions have in the past required any person's consent or approval of plans, does the Vendor have written evidence of that consent or approval?

9. Planning etc.

(A) (i) When did the present use of the property commence?

(ii) Has this use been continuous since it commenced?

(B) During the four years immediately prior to receipt of these enquiries:

(i) Were any of the buildings on the property erected, or have any been altered or added to?

(ii) Have any other building, engineering, mining or other operations been carried out in, on, over or under the property?

(iii) Has any condition or limitation on any planning permission not been complied with?

If so, please give details.

(C) Please supply a copy of:

(i) Any planning permission authorising or imposing conditions upon the present use of the property, and the erection or retention of the buildings now on it.

(ii) Any bye-law approval or building regulation consent relating to those buildings.

(iii) Any current fire certificate.

10. Fixtures, Fittings etc.

(A) Does the sale include all of the following items now on the property, and attached to or growing in it?

Trees, shrubs, plants, flowers, and garden produce. Greenhouses, garden sheds and garden ornaments. Aerials. Fitted furniture and shelves. Electric switches, points and wall and ceiling fittings.

(B) What fixtures and fittings affixed to the property are not included in the sale?

(C) If the property has any fixed oil burning appliance, what arrangements are proposed for the sale to the purchaser on completion of any stock of oil?

11. Outgoings

(A) (i) What is the rateable value of the property?

(ii) Have any works been carried out at the property which might result in a revision of this?

(B) Does the hereditament, in which the property to be sold is included for rating purposes, also include any other property?

(C) What annual or periodic charges, other than general and water rates, affect the property or its occupier?

12. Completion

(A) How long after exchange of contracts will the Vendor be able to give vacant possession of the whole of the property?

(B) The Purchaser's solicitors wish to complete by adopting the Law Society's Code for Completion by Post (1984 edition). Do the Vendor's solicitors agree?

13. New Properties

(A) Will the Vendor pay all charges for construction and connection of the drainage system and the services?

(B) Are all the following included in the purchase price: fencing all boundaries, laying all paths and drives, and levelling and clearing the garden area? If not, please give particulars.

ADDITIONAL ENQUIRIES

For Leasehold Enquiries and further Additional Enquiries see over

LEASEHOLD ENQUIRIES

1. General

(A) Is the lease under which the property is held a head lease or an underlease?

(B) Please state the names and addresses of the lessor, any superior lessors, their respective solicitors, and the receivers of the rent.

(C) Please supply copies of all licences granted by the lessor, other than licences to assign.

(D) What steps have been taken to obtain the lessor's consent to the proposed assignment? Please supply a copy of any licence granted.

II. Covenants

(A) Has the lessor complained of any breach of covenant?

(B) Has any obligation in the lease to paint or do any other work by or at a particular time been strictly fulfilled? If not, please give details.

(C) Has the Vendor had cause to complain of any breach of the lessor's covenants?

III. Service Charge

(A) Please give details of service charge payments for the last three years, with any supporting accounts or vouchers that the Vendor has.

(B) Has the Vendor, or to his knowledge any predecessor in title, exercised a statutory right to obtain information? If so, with what result?

IV. Insurance

(A) Who effected the insurance policy currently covering the property?

(B) Please give particulars: insurers' and any insurance brokers' name and address, policy number, insured's name(s), risks covered, for what amount, premium, and date to which the property is insured.

V. Reversionary Title

Is there with the title deeds a marked abstract or office copy of the freehold title and of any superior lease?

ADDITIONAL ENQUIRIES

★ ★ ★ ★

ENQUIRIES PRIOR TO CONTRACT FOR SALE

Property ....

....

Proposed Vendor ....

Proposed Purchaser ....

Please answer the following enquiries:

Solicitor for proposed purchaser

Date

The replies are as stated hereunder

Solicitor for proposed vendor

Date

ENQUIRIES

Please delete those questions not applicable to the transaction

1. Boundaries and disputes

(a) Please supply a plan showing the property indicating ownership, or if this is not known, the maintenance of the boundaries with "T" marks.

(b) Please show on the plan, with "H" marks, any party walls and indicate their length.

(c) When were the boundary fences last repaired?

(d) Has the Vendor erected a fence on a boundary which is in a neighbour's ownership? If so, has the Vendor carried out this work with the neighbour's consent?

(e) Has the property mooring rights attached to its river boundary?

(f) If the property is under construction, please confirm that the plot will be fenced by the Vendor before completion as part of the purchase price and please confirm the dimensions of the plot.

(g) Has any neighbour claimed ownership of any of the boundaries or that the Vendor has encroached on the neighbour's land?

If so give details and send us all the attendant correspondence.

(h) Has the Vendor or Vendors predecessor in title been in dispute with any neighbour or third party over any matter whatsoever within the last 12 years.

2. Notices

(a) Has the Vendor received any notice from the local authority about the property?

(b) Has the Vendor received any notices about the property or affecting the property from any neighbour, local or national body or group or any other person whatsoever?

(c) If the answer to (a) or (b) is yes, please give full details and let us have copies of the relevant correspondence.

3. Works carried out at the Property

(a) Please state which of the following improvements the Vendor has carried out to the Property within the last 5 years

(i) installation of central heating (ii) installation of fitted kitchen (iii) installation of new bathroom equipment (iv) re-wiring (v) extensions at ground level (vi) loft room built (vii) garage (viii) extensions above ground level (ix) additional rooms, outhouses

(b) Are there any other improvements which have been made. If so, please attach list.

(c) Please state whether the items mentioned in either (a) or (b) above required planning permission or bye-law consents or building

REPLIES

The replies hereunder are given by or on behalf of the proposed Vendor. To the best of the Vendor's knowledge and belief the replies are true but where replies can be verified by searches, inspection or survey the Purchaser is deemed to have made such searches, inspections and surveys and these replies shall not be used to form the basis of any claim the Purchaser may make against the Vendor.

regulation consent and supply copies thereof.

(d) Has the property the benefit of

(i) a NHBC agreement with or without any additional cover under whatever scheme has been available during the last ten years.

(ii) guarantee for work carried out for weatherproofing, damp proofing, dry rot, wet rot or any insect infestation.

(iii) guarantees for any building works or extensions or roof repairs or renewals

(iv) guarantees for any central heating or electrical wiring

(v) guarantees for any other works whatsoever

(e) Please confirm that the Vendor will assign the benefit of any of the above guarantees.

(f) Please state if the Vendor has any maintenance contracts for any central heating or other system needing overhauling periodically; with whom if the contract is assignable; and if the Vendor will assign the benefit of any contract.

4. Services to Property

(a) Is there mains water, electricity, gas, drainage?

(b) If so, please supply plan showing the running of these services if it is not already dealt with in the contract.

(c) Has the Vendor the legal capacity to grant or to convey easements for the above services over adjoining land? If so, please supply title to these if different from title to Property.

(d) Has the Vendor granted similar rights to any other person? If so, to whom?

(e) Do these others have to contribute to the cost? If so on what basis.

5. Adverse rights; restrictions etc.

(a) (i) Does the Vendor know of any person having rights over the property in opposition to his own and/or are there any persons exercising rights about which he ought to know?

(ii) If so, how are these rights exercised?

(b) (i) How many persons occupy the property? Please state the names and ages of those persons.

(ii) Has any person other than the Vendor any equitable or registrable right over the Property?

(iii) If so, please confirm that the persons having such rights will be parties to the contract and that they will vacate on completion.

(c) Please state which, if any, of the following affect the Property:

(i) Fishing and/or sporting rights

(ii) Restrictive covenants

(iii) Positive convenants

(iv) Rent Charges

(v) Chancel Repair liability or corn Rents

(vi) A right to hold a fair or gymkhana

(vii) Declarations

If so, please send full details.

(d) Is the Property being sold subject to

(i) any bridle paths?

(ii) foot paths?

(iii) foot paths or bridle paths in the course of being incorporated in the definitive maps?

(iv) rights of way?

(v) rights for timber extraction?

(vi) rights to extract water?

(vii) rights of common?

If so, please give all relevant details.

(e) Is the Property in

(i) a coal mining area?

(ii) a salt mining area?

(iii) a tin mining area?

(iv) a natural gas or oil exploration area?

If so, please confirm in each case that

(i) there are no outstanding leases

(ii) all compensation for damage is covered by the relevant authority

(iii) compensation has not been paid in respect of the property

(f) Is the Property sold with the benefit of

(i) rights of access

(ii) rights of air and light

(iii) rights of common over other land.

If so, please let us have details.

6. Fixtures and fittings

Please list all items of fixtures and fittings which are being *taken* and all items of fixtures and fittings which are to *remain*.

7. For semi-detached and terraced houses only

Does the Vendor know whether the adjoining owner has made any improvements to the adjoining house which could affect the property e.g. demolition of internal load bearing walls without replacing a corresponding support.

8. Outgoings

Please state whether the Vendor pays

(a) general rates – when due – and how much

(b) water rates – when due – and how much

(c) drainage rates – when due – and how much

(d) cesspit cleaning – how often – and how much

(e) licence fees for access

(f) licence fees for water abstraction – when due – and how much

(g) any other items. Please list.

Please state whether these items will be apportioned on completion or dealt with direct and the relevant undertaking supplied.

9. Residence

Is the Vendor resident outside UK?

10. Completion

(a) When does the Vendor require completion?

(b) Please confirm that the Vendor and all other occupiers will be out of house before 12 noon.

11. Please instruct the Vendor that no rubbish is to be left at the property at completion.

ADDITIONAL ENQUIRIES

Unilaw members: Services to Lawyers Limited; Stephen Cox & Co. Limited; Meredith Ray & Littler Limited; Dennis Welbourn Limited.

PRELIMINARY ENQUIRIES

*GENERAL – FORM Q1

Property

Purchaser	Vendor
Purchaser's Solicitors	Vendor's Solicitors
Signed:.. Date:..	Signed:.. Date:..
*(In the case of Leasehold property, Commercial property, Business Premises and Sublet Property, add forms Q2, Q3, Q4 and Q5 respectively to these enquiries.) [Additional enquiries are added on form Q6.]	Notes: The replies below, whilst believed to be correct, are not given by the Vendor to induce the Purchaser to enter into any Agreement and the Purchaser must verify all replies to the extent the same admit of independent verification by inspection, examination, survey, searches or otherwise. No responsibility will attach to the Vendor's Solicitors or their employees.

Possession

1. (1) Is the Vendor buying another property linked to this sale? If so:-
   (a) what stage has this reached?
   (b) How many vendors are there in any chain of sales above the Vendor?

   (2) Is the Vendor proposing any completion period or date other than 4 weeks after exchange?

   (3) Where a completion date will only be fixed by notice or certificate, please indicate approximately when this is likely to be.

Title

2. (1) If title is registered:-
   (a) who will hold the land/charge certificate after exchange?
   (b) Please confirm you will forward office copy entries before exchange

   (2) If title is unregistered
   (a) please supply an identification plan of the site location;
   (b) which is the applicable district Land Registry?
   (c) is the property in an area of compulsory registration?
   (d) who will hold the deeds after exchange for inspection purposes?

   (3) (a) Is the Vendor aware of any title imperfections (major or minor) which might cause problems? (It will help avoid delay after exchange if you warn us at this stage).

(b) (i) Is there in existence any restrictive covenant policy or other indemnity policy affecting the property?
(ii) If so, is it freely assignable to the Purchaser?
(iii) Please confirm it will be assigned to the Purchaser.

(4) Is any part of the property tenanted?

Mortgages

3. (a) Is there a second or third mortgage on the property? If so, please provide details.
(b) Please confirm the property is sold free of all mortgages.
(c) Will already-receipted or already-discharged documents be handed over on completion or merely undertakings for same?

Boundaries

4. If the deeds do not show to whom the property boundaries belong:-
(a) which ones has the Vendor in the past maintained and/or
(b) which has the Vendor regarded as his/her responsibility?

Access

5. (a) Is there a driveway/access road at the property from a public road?
(b) Does it pass over land belonging to any person other than the Vendor?
(c) Is any part of it shared with any other person, either in use or in ownership?
(d) If (b) and (c) above apply, please explain how the shared rights originated.
(e) Is there any footpath from the property which is not maintained by a local council? If so:-
(i) to whom does the footpath land belong?
(ii) has it been the subject of repair work in the past and by whom?
(iii) have the Vendor or previous owners been called upon to contribute to the upkeep of the path?
(iv) has there been any difficulty over the Vendor's use of the path?

Services

6. (a) Are any of the gas, electric, water, sewage and drainage *not* connected to mains services?
   (b) If not,
      (i) by what arrangement do they exist?
      (ii) are any charges payable for such use?
   (c) Does the Vendor know of any claim for works to be done or for payment in respect of such facilities (other than supply)?

Disputes

7. Does the Vendor know of
   (a) any disputes, claim or demand or
   (b) any notice received from any source or
   (c) any breach of any restriction affecting the property or its use or
   (d) any disagreement or argument with neighbours past or present about the property, its boundaries or use?

Guarantees and Indemnities

8. (1) Do any of the following exist in respect of the property and will the Vendor assign to the Purchaser the benefit of:-
      (a) Treatment guarantee;
      (b) NHBC certificate;
      (c) any maintenance agreement or indemnity deed or bond?
   (2) Has the Vendor claimed under any insurance policy or guarantee in respect of (i) flooding; (ii) subsidence; (iii) damp, rot or infestation or (iv) any structural or drainage problems?

Adverse Rights

9. (1) Other than disclosed in the draft contract or obvious from inspection, does the Vendor know of any rights in favour of any other person over any part of the property or its use?
   (2) If any persons, 18 years or over, also occupy the property, please supply their names and confirm they will counter-sign the contract together with the Vendor under the following added clause:- "In consideration of the purchaser entering into this Agreement I undertake not to seek to enforce any right to possession or occupation whether arising by statute or any equitable interest or otherwise in the property to which I may be or become entitled".

Planning

10. (1) During the last 4 years has the Vendor or his predecessors carried out any works at the property which would require planning consent or building regulation or bye-law consent?
    (2) Does the Vendor hold any consents from whatever period?
    (3) (a) If there is a garage at the property was it built more recently than the property?
    (b) If so, were all consents obtained for it?

Fixtures and fittings

11. (1) Are all the items in the estate agents particulars sheet included in the sale?
    (2) Please list any fixtures or fittings (other than free-standing items) which the Vendor proposes to remove.
    (3) If there is central heating installed
    (a) is it oil-fired?
    (b) is it the Vendor's unencumbered property?

Outgoings

12. (1) What is the rateable value of the property?
    (2) Aside from gas, electricity, general and water rates, telephone rent or service charge, are there any other sums regularly payable in respect of the property?

Additional Enquiries

13. Please also deal with any additional enquiries on Form Q6 annexed.-

Information Memo

14. To help you as well as the purchaser, we enclose Form Q7 in duplicate for you to forward to the Vendor. If Part II has been answered, please confirm you will hold it until exchange and then send it to us.

PRELIMINARY ENQUIRIES

(LEASEHOLD) — FORM Q2

Note: These are *additional* enquiries to the general questions on Form Q1 which should accompany this questionnaire.

Property

Estate Owners

1. Please supply
   (1) The name and address of the immediate current landlords
   (2) The name and address of their managing or rent-collecting agents (if any)
   (3) The name and address of their solicitors (if any) upon whom notice of assignment must be served.

2. Is the immediate landlord the freeholder? If not, please
   (1) list all superior landlords;
   (2) supply a copy of each superior lease and freehold title.
   (3) If copies of superior landlords' title are not being supplied, please confirm there are no additional covenants undisclosed which would affect the lease being sold or use of the property.

3. Please supply copies of all previous licences or deeds affecting the property (other than pure licences to assign).

4. (1) If landlord's consent to assignment or change of use is required, has this yet been applied for?
   (2) Please confirm it will be procured by the Vendor at his expense and a stamped original handed over on completion.

5. If the lease requires any direct covenant between assignee and landlord, please supply the form of draft required by the Landlord.

The Lease

6. (1) If the lease is an underlease or sublease, please supply evidence it has been registered with all superior reversioners.
   (2) If you have no such evidence, please confirm you will ask the Landlord's Solicitors if there is such evidence with their deeds.

SHAW & SONS LTD., Shaway House, London SE26 5AE

Alterations

7. Have any alterations been carried out which require landlord's consent under the lease?

Complaints

8. Has there been any dispute with or complaint by the Landlord about the lease provisions, the premises or their use?

Rent

9. (1) Is the current rent as stated in the Lease?
   (2) If not, please explain the difference.

10. Has any rent review under the Lease occurred and is there any memorandum of same?

11. Regardless of the lease provisions, is the rent actually paid in advance or in arrear at present?

12. (1) For what rent period does the Vendor have the latest rent receipt for production on completion?
   (2) Is this a clear receipt?
   (3) If the landlord does not issue rent receipts, please confirm you will procure and hand over on completion a letter from the landlord or his agents confirming there is no outstanding claim against the tenant.

Service Charge

13. Please give details of service charge demands during each of the last two years.

14. Please supply copies of all accounts in support of such demands.

15. Are there any demands still unpaid?

16. Does the service charge demand include any insurance premium for the property?

17. Does the Vendor know of any recent or anticipated expenditure which may unusually affect the service charge?

18. If the lease does not stipulate an exact proportion, please ascertain from the landlord on what ratio basis service expenditure is apportioned to the tenant.

19. If the current service charge is not yet known at the completion date, please confirm the contract will provide for the Vendor promptly to refund when known to the purchaser upon demand any arrear proportion prior to completion.

Insurance

20. Regardless of the lease provisions, who actually maintains the current insurance on the property?

21. If the landlord, please supply a copy or summary of the policy and up-to-date endorsements.

22. If a block policy, what amount of cover is allocated to the property being sold?

23. If the lease provides for insurance by the tenant with a nominated or approved insurance company, please specify what company has been nominated or approved

24. Has the Vendor had cause to claim under the policy?

Associations

25 (1) Is there relating to the property a management company or residents association? If so:-

(2) is the Vendor a member?

(3) Please supply copies of all documents relating to the association including memorandum and articles

(4) Please confirm that on completion the Vendor will hand over the membership certificate and a signed stock transfer form.

(5) What is the name and address of the Secretary of the association?

26. **Additional Enquiries**

Please also deal with any additional enquiries on form Q6 annexed.

–oyez–GENERAL

TENANCY ENQUIRIES

FOR USE WITH ENQUIRIES BEFORE CONTRACT WHERE ALL OR PART OF THE PROPERTY IS LET OR OCCUPIED ON LICENCE
(For Agricultural Holdings and Agricultural Tied Cottages, use Agricultural Tenancy Enquiries).

Short description of the property re ....

Parties ....

to ....

Please strike out enquiries which are not applicable

Replies are requested to the following additional enquiries.

Please reply separately for each part of the property to be sold which is separately let.

The words 'landlord' and 'tenant' should be construed to include predecessors in title wherever possible.

Licensees If all or any part of the property is occupied by a licensee, please reply to the appropriate enquires in respect of that occupation, making it clear that the agreement is a licence. In that case, read 'tenancy' and 'letting' as licence, 'tenant' as 'licensee', 'landlord' as licensor, and 'rent' as sum contracted to be paid under the licence.

....
Proposed purchaser's solicitor

Date .... 198 ....

The replies are as follows.

....
Proposed vendor's solicitor

Date .... 198 ....

REPLIES

These replies are given on behalf of the proposed vendor and without responsibility on the part of his solicitors their partners or employees. They are believed to be correct but the accuracy is not guaranteed and they do not obviate the need to make appropriate searches, enquiries and inspections.

GENERAL INQUIRIES

A. Tenant

What are the full names and address of the tenant?

B. Terms of letting

(1) Please supply a copy of the lease, tenancy agreement and any other document evidencing all or any of the terms of letting, and any variations thereof.

(2) Unless shown on any copy document supplied:

(i) What part of the property to be sold is let to the tenant, and what rights has the tenant over other parts of the property?

(ii) When was the tenancy originally granted?

(iii) What is the period of the letting?

(iv) How much is the rent, on what days or dates is it payable, in advance or in arrear?

(v) What express repairing and other obligations have been undertaken respectively by the landlord and the tenant?

(3) What licences or consents have been given by the landlord to the tenant?

C. Sub-letting

If the vendor is aware of any sub-letting of all or part of the demised premises, what are:

(i) the full names and address of the sub-tenant?

(ii) the terms of the sub-letting?

D. Insurance

If the tenant or a sub-tenant insures the demised premises, please give particulars of the existing cover, stating insurers' name and address, policy number, insureds' name(s), risks covered, for what amount, premium and date to which the property is insured.

E. Orders, etc.

Please supply copies of any of the following which relate to or affect the term of the letting or which affect the use of the property when let:

(i) orders of any court, tribunal or local authority;

(ii) notices served on or by the local authority, and any acknowledgement received from the local authority;

(iii) undertakings given by the landlord or the tenant.

F. Disputes

(1) Have the terms of the tenancy or any dispute between landlord and tenant been the subject of proceedings before any court, tribunal or arbitrator, or are any such proceedings pending? If so, please give particulars.
(2) Is the tenant now, or has he previously been, in arrear in paying the rent?
(3) Of what other breaches of covenant by the tenant, continuing or past, is the vendor aware?
(4) Has the tenant complained of any breach of the landlord's obligations?

G. Rent revision

(1) Please give particulars of the result of any rent review determined under the lease, including the award of any arbitrator or valuer.
(2) Have the landlord and the tenant concluded any agreement as to the rent payable for any future period? If so please give particulars.
(3) Has the tenant or any sub-tenant made any improvement to the demised premises which is to be ignored in agreeing or determining any future rent?

BUSINESS TENANCY ENQUIRIES

Please reply to enquiries in this section if the letting may be affected by the Landlord and Tenant Act 1954, Pt. II.

H. Duration of business

Since what date have the demised premises been occupied for the purposes of the business now carried on by the tenant?

I. Improvements

(1) Is the tenant entitled on quitting the demised premises at the termination of the tenancy to any compensation for improvements?
(2) Has the tenant made any improvement which is to be ignored in determining a new rent, under the Landlord and Tenant Act 1954, s. 34 (1) (*c*) as amended by the Law of Property Act 1969?

J. New tenancy

Have terms been agreed for any new tenancy to be granted to the tenant? If so, please supply a copy of any written agreement or particulars of any oral agreement.

RESIDENTIAL TENANCY ENQUIRIES

Please reply to enquiries in this section if any part of the property is used for residential purposes. It may be necessary to raise additional enquiries in respect of tenancies granted by housing associations, housing trusts and the Crown Estate Commissioners.

K. Application of statutory rules

(1) Is the tenancy:
 (i) regulated?
 (ii) a restricted contract?
 (iii) treated as a restricted contract, becasue there is a resident landlord?
(2) What was the rateable value of the demised premises on:
 (i) 23rd March 1965?
 (ii) 22nd March 1973?
 (iii) 1st April 1973?
(3) Has any agreement been reached between landlord and tenant apportioning the rateable value of the demised and other premises? If so please give particulars.
(4) Has a reduced rateable value for the purposes of the Leasehold Reform Act 1967 been agreed or determined? If so, please give particulars.
(5) Has there been a statutory transmission of the tenancy? If so, please give particulars.

L. Rent

(1) Is a rent registered for all or any part of the demised premises? If so, please state:
 (i) amount of rent;
 (ii) amount shown as attributable to services;
 (iii) date of registration, and effective date if different;
 (iv) extent of premises affected;
 (v) any other registered details.
(2) If the current recoverable rent is restricted by the operation of statutory phasing provisions, please state:
 (i) the previous rent limit;
 (ii) the service element

M. Terms of letting

(1) If the present rent contains any amount in respect of the cost, or the increased cost to the landlord or a superior lessor of rates, improvements, furniture, or the provision of services, please give full particulars.

(2) What furniture used by the tenant is supplied by the landlord, and on what terms?

(3) What services is the landlord contractually obliged to supply to the tenant?

N. Resident landlord

If it is considered that the tenancy falls within the Rent Act 1977, s. 12 (lettings by resident landlords):

(1) Did the landlord occupy as his residence (as defined by the Rent Act 1977, Sched. 2, para. 5) another dwellinghouse in the same building when the tenancy was granted to the tenant?

(2) Has the landlord continuously occupied another such dwellinghouse ever since?

(3) If the answer to (1) or (2) is No, please give details of the grounds on which it is believed that the provisions apply.

(4) Immediately before the grant of the current tenancy, did the tenant occupy the demised premises, or some other dwellinghouse in the same building? If so, on what terms?

O. Long tenancies

Where the letting was originally for over 21 years, or is otherwise within the statutory definition for a long tenancy:

(1) How long has the present tenant, and any member of his family from whom he inherited the property, been in possession?

(2) Have terms been agreed with the tenant for a statutory tenancy pursuant to the Landlord and Tenant Act, 1954, Pt I, and if so, on what terms?

(3) Was the lease granted on the exercise of a secure tenant's right to buy?

P. Service charges

If the demised premises are a flat let on a long lease and the tenant pays a service charge as defined by the Housing Act 1980, Sched. 19:

(1) Is there a recognised tenant's association for the tenants of flats in the building containing demised premises?

(2) If so:

(i) was it recognised by the landlord or by a certificate of a rent assessment committee member?

(ii) please give the name and address of its secretary.

(3) Has the tenant, or the secretary of the tenant's association, served a request for a written summary of costs with which the vendor has not yet complied?

(4) Please confirm that on completion the vendor will hand over particulars of the relevant costs, with accounts and receipts to vouch them, competitive estimates obtained and evidence of consultations with tenants and any tenants' association or (as the case may be) of compliance with the requirements for works whose cost exceeded the prescribed amount, for the current and previous accounting years.

(5) In respect of items included in the service charge, the full cost of which has not yet been recovered:

(i) please supply copies of estimates obtained before the liabilities were incurred;

(ii) please supply evidence of compliance with the requirements for works whose cost exceeded the prescribed amount or reasons for non-compliance;

(iii) please supply copies of accounts paid by or rendered to the vendor;

(iv) has the tenant, or tenants' association, expressed dissatisfaction at the standard of, or the amount payable for, any such item?

ADDITIONAL ENQUIRIES

 12-84 F4725

★ ★ ★ ★

Short description of the property

re ....

Parties ....

to ....

Oyez

AGRICULTURAL TENANCY ENQUIRIES

FOR USE WITH ENQUIRIES BEFORE CONTRACT WHERE ALL OR PART OF THE PROPERTY IS LET AS AN AGRICULTURAL HOLDING OR AN AGRICULTURAL TIED COTTAGE

Please strike out enquiries which are not applicable.

Replies are requested to the following additional enquiries.

Please reply separately for each part of the property to be sold which is separately let.

The words 'landlord' and 'tenant' should be construed to include predecessors in title wherever possible.

In the case of an agricultural tied cottage, these enquiries are intended to extend to a licence to occupy. 'Tenancy' and 'tenant' should be read to include 'licence' and 'licensee' where appropriate, and 'landlord' should be given the extended meaning assigned to it by the Rent (Agriculture) Act 1976.

....

Proposed purchaser's solicitors.

Date .... 198 ...

REPLIES

These replies, except in the case of any enquiry expressly requiring a reply from the Vendor's Solicitors, are given on behalf of the proposed Vendor and without responsibility on the part of his solicitors their partners or employees. They are believed to be correct but the accuracy is not guaranteed and they do not obviate the need to make appropriate searches, enquiries and inspections.

The replies are as follows.

....

Proposed vendor's solicitors.

Date .... 198 ....

GENERAL ENQUIRIES

A. Tenant

(1) What are the full names and address of the tenant?

(2) How old is the tenant?

B. Terms of letting

(1) Please supply a copy of the lease, tenancy agreement and any other documents evidencing all or any of the terms of letting.

(2) Unless shown on any copy document supplied:

(i) What part of the property to be sold is let to the tenant, and what rights has the tenant over other parts of the property?

(ii) When was the tenancy originally granted?

(iii) What is the period of the letting?

(iv) How much is the rent, on what days or dates is it payable, in advance or in arrear?

(v) What express repairing and other obligations have been undertaken respectively by the landlord and the tenant?

(3) What licences or consents have been given by the landlord to the tenant?

C. Sub-letting

If the vendor is aware of any sub-letting of all or part of the demised premises, what are:

(i) The full names and address of the sub-tenant?

(ii) The terms of the sub-letting?

D. Insurance

If the tenant insures the demised premises, please give particulars of the existing cover, stating name and address of insurers and any brokers, policy number, insureds' name(s), risks covered, for what amount, premium and date to which the property is insured.

E. Orders, etc.

Please supply copies of any of the following which relate to or affect the terms of the letting or which affect the use of the property when let:

(i) Orders or directions of any court, tribunal or local authority, or arbitration awards;

(ii) Notices served on or by the local authority, and any acknowledgment received from the local authority;

(iii) Undertakings given by the landlord or the tenant.

F. Disputes

(1) Have the terms of the tenancy or any dispute between landlord and tenant been the subject of proceedings before any court, tribunal or arbitrator, or are any such proceedings pending? If so, please give particulars.

(2) Is the tenant now, or has he previously been, in arrear in paying the rent?

(3) Of what other breaches of covenant by the tenant, continuing or past, is the vendor aware?

(4) Has the tenant complained of any breach of the landlord's obligations?

G. Rent revision

Have the landlord and the tenant concluded any agreement as to the rent payable for any future period? If so, please give particulars.

TIED COTTAGE ENQUIRIES

Please reply to enquiries in this section if any part of the property is used for residential purposes.

H. Application of statutory rules

(1) Is the tenancy

(i) a relevant licence or a relevant tenancy (as defined by the Rent (Agriculture) Act 1976, Sched. 2)?

(ii) a statutory tenancy?

(2) What was the rateable value of the demised premises on:

(i) 23rd March 1965?

(ii) 22nd March 1973?

(iii) 1st April 1973?

(3) Is the tenant a qualified worker (as defined by the Rent (Agriculture) Act 1976, Sched. 3), or successor to one?

(4) Have the premises, at any time during the tenancy, been in qualifying ownership (as defined by the Rent (Agriculture) Act 1976, Sched. 3)?

(5) Has there been a statutory transmission of the tenancy? If so, please give particulars.

I. Rent

(1) Please supply a copy of any agreement fixing the rent payable, under the Rent (Agriculture) Act 1976, s. 11.

(2) If the rent is based on rateable value, under the Rent (Agriculture) Act 1976, s. 12, please give particulars.

(3) Is a rent for all or any part of the demised premises registered by the rent officer? If so, please state:

(i) Amount of rent;

(ii) Whether determined by the rent officer or a rent assessment committee;

(iii) Amount shown as attributable to services;

(iv) Date of registration, and effective date if different;

(v) Extent of premises affected;

(vi) Any other registered details.

(4) If the current recoverable rent is restricted by the operation of statutory phasing provisions, please state:

(i) The previous rent limit;

(ii) The service element.

J. Terms of letting

(1) Please supply a copy of any agreement varying any provisions of the statutory tenancy, under the Rent (Agriculture) Act 1976, Sched. 5, para. 12.

(2) What furniture used by the tenant is supplied by the landlord, and on what terms?

(3) What services or facilities is the landlord obliged to supply to the tenant either by contract, or as a term of the statutory tenancy, under the Rent (Agriculture) Act 1976, Sched. 5, para. 5?

K. Rent allowances

(1) Has the tenant been supplied with the statutory particulars of the local rent allowance scheme?

(2) Has the landlord received payment of the tenant's rent allowance direct from the local authority?

L. Rehousing

(1) Has the vendor, or any predecessor in title, applied to the housing authority to rehouse the tenant, under the Rent (Agriculture) Act 1976, s. 27?

(2) If so, what was the result? Please supply copies of the advice of the agricultural dwellinghouse advisory committee and the decision of the authority.

AGRICULTURAL TENANCY ENQUIRIES

Please reply to enquiries in this section if any part of the property constitutes an agricultural holding for the purposes of the Agricultural Holdings Act 1948.

M. Excluding renewal

Before the grant of the tenancy, did the Minister

(i) Approve it for the purposes of the Agricultural Holdings Act 1948, s. 2?

(ii) Approve an agreement that s. 3 should not apply to it, under s. 3B?

If so, please supply a copy of that approval.

N. Improvements and fixtures

(1) (i) Did the tenant carry out any improvements of the classes specified in the Agricultural Holdings Act 1948, Sched. II or Sched. V, which were begun before 1st March 1948?

(ii) If so, was the tenant obliged to carry them out by the terms of a tenancy agreement made before 1st January 1921, did the landlord consent in writing to their execution or did the tenant give notice of intention to carry them out?

(2) (i) Has the tenant carried out any improvements of the classes specified in the Agricultural Holdings Act 1948, Sched. III, Sched. IV, pt. 1, or Sched. V, which were begun on or after 1st March 1948?

(ii) If so, did the landlord give written consent or has the tenant applied for or obtained the consent of the county executive committee or the Agricultural Land Tribunal?

(3) What buildings, engines, machinery, fencing or other fixture was erected or fixed to the property by the tenant (excluding any erected or fixed in pursuance of an obligation, or to replace a building or fixture belonging to the landlord)?

O. Compensation

(1) Have the landlord and the tenant agreed that compensation shall be payable to the tenant for any matter or in any circumstances not covered by the Agricultural Holdings Act 1948 (as amended)?

(2) For the purposes of claiming compensation for tenant right, did the tenant enter into occupation before 1st March 1948?

(3) Is any compensation, or any sum agreed or awarded under the Agricultural Holdings Act 1948, due to the tenant but not paid?

(4) (i) Has any compensation been awarded either to the tenant or to the landlord under the Agriculture (Miscellaneous Provisions) Act 1976? If so, please give particulars.

(ii) Is any such compensation due but unpaid?

P. Tenant's death

(1) Has the tenant, or have all the joint tenants, to whom the tenancy was originally granted died?

(2) If the last tenant of the holding has died and no new tenancy has yet been granted:

(i) On what date did the tenant die?

(ii) On what date did the landlord receive notice of the death?

(iii) Has any notice to quit thereby been rendered ineffective? If so, please supply a copy.

(iv) Is there anyone whom the Vendor believes to be a person eligible to succeed to a tenancy of the holding on the tenant's death?

(v) Has any person made an application to the Agricultural Land Tribunal? If so, please give particulars.

Q. Statutory succession

(1) (i) Was the tenancy granted on or after 12th July 1984?

(ii) If so, does it fall within the Agricultural Holdings Act 1984, s. 2(2) (new tenancies to which statutory succession rights still apply)?

(2) Was either

(i) the present tenancy, or

(ii) the tenancy which preceded it

granted as a result of a tribunal direction under the Agriculture (Miscellaneous Provisions) Act 1976 (succession to deceased tenant) or the Agricultural Holdings Act 1984, Sched. 2, para. 5 (succession on tenant's retirement) or by agreement in lieu thereof?

(3) Has the tenant ever nominated a successor to succeed him on retirement under the Agricultural Holdings Act 1984, Sched. 2? If so, please give particulars.

R. General

(1) Has either the landlord or the tenant required the making of a record in respect of the condition of the holding under the Agricultural Holdings Act 1948, s. 16? If so, please supply a copy.

(2) Has application been made for a certificate of bad husbandry, and, if so, when and with what result?

(3) Who has the right to kill and take wild animals and birds on the property?

(4) Has an agreement been entered into under the Ancient Monuments and Archaeological Areas Act 1979, or legislation replaced thereby, in respect of any part of the property? If so, please supply a copy.

ADDITIONAL ENQUIRIES

oyez

SUPPLEMENTARY ENQUIRIES

BEFORE CONTRACT

To be attached to form **Con 29 (Long)** or form **Con 29 (Short)**

Please strike out enquiries which are not applicable

Property

(a) Please give details of any of the following which have at any time affected the property:

(i) Structural defects;
(ii) Drainage defects;
(iii) Defective foundations;
(iv) Rising damp, dry or wet rot;
(v) Infestation by wood boring insects.

(b) Has the property or the site been subject to:

(i) Flooding?
(ii) Landslip?
(iii) Subsidence or heave?

(c) Is the property situated in an area where mining or underground mineral extraction is carried on?

Services

(d) When was the electrical system:

(i) Last tested and approved by the local electricity board?
(ii) Comprehensively rewired?

(e) Please give details of the service provided by the local authority for emptying any private drainage system.

(f) When the central heating system was last in use, did it function completely satisfactorily?

(g) Will the Vendor give the Purchaser details of any burglar alarm?

(h) Please supply copies of any contracts for regular maintenance or servicing of fixed appliances, which the Purchaser could take over.

Vehicles

(i) Was the garage on the property erected at the same time as the dwelling, or, if later, when?

(j) Do parking restrictions apply to the road in front of the property, or have the police objected to vehicles being parked there?

Chattels and fixtures

(k) A copy of the estate agents' sale particulars is attached. Is any item mentioned there not included in the sale?

(l) Please confirm that no moveable or detachable item included in the sale is subject to any lease, hire, hire purchase or loan agreement, or lien or any other claim by a third party.

(m) Do the telephone instruments on the property belong to British Telecommunications?

Financial

(n) What is the current annual amount payable in respect of the property for:

(i) General rate?

(ii) Water charges (including drainage and environmental charges)?

(o) Does this sale depend on the Vendor contracting to purchase another property?

(p) Please confirm that the Vendor will arrange for the appropriate authorities to read the electric, gas, water and telephone meters on the day of actual completion.

INFORMATION MEMO

FORM Q7

From: (Vendor's Solicitors):- Messrs.

To: Mr/Mrs/Miss/Ms:

re: Sale of:

PART I

Your purchaser has asked a number of questions about the property. We can answer some of them from the Deeds. We enclose their list and would be grateful if you could deal with the question numbers on it listed in this box, and put short answers in the right-hand column against those questions and *return this form and the list to us.* Please also check that any answers we may already have added, are correct to the best of your knowledge.

PLEASE ANSWER QUESTIONS NOS.

[ON THE ANNEXED LIST(S)]

PART II

The further questions below are not on conveyancing matters and you are not obliged to answer them. However the information will obviously be of help to the purchaser. If you choose to answer them, please fill in the information in the right-hand column below.

Telephone

A. (i) Is there a telephone at the property?
(ii) What is the phone number?
(iii) Is it a private or shared line?
(iv) Are you proposing to remove/disconnect the line or to leave it at the property?
(v) What is the name and address of the telephone district authority?

Services

B. Please supply the name and address of the district authority for each of the following supplied to the property:-

SHAW & SONS LTD., Shaway House, London SE26 5AE
LLX 01273-4

(i) Gas

(ii) Electricity

(iii) Water

(iv) We will need your last water rate receipt. Could you please send it to us with this form?

Rates

C. (i) What is the name and address of the local council for rates?

(ii) Do you pay your rates half-yearly or by standing order arrangement?

(iii) If half-yearly, when was your last payment made?

(iv) We will need your last rates receipt. Could you please send it to us with this form?

Burglar alarm

D. Is there a burglar alarm at the property? If so:-

(i) Is it fully owned by you or on rental?

(ii) Do you have the paperwork about the system and how it works to send to us after exchange? (Do not send yet).

Keys

E. (i) How many keys will you be able to hand over on completion?:-

(a) to the front door

(b) to the back door

(ii) Are there any special locks for which you have special registered keys?

Servicing

F. Do you employ a gardener, full or part-time? If so:-

(i) What is his/her name, address and telephone number?

(ii) How many hours per week.

(iii) What do you pay him/her per hour?

G. Do you employ a window cleaner? If so:-

(i) What is his/her name, address and telephone number?

(ii) How often does he/she call?

(iii) What do you normally pay per call?

(iv) Does this cover only outside windows (upstairs and downstairs) or inside as well?

H. (i) Do you have your milk delivered?

(ii) If so, what is the name and local district address of the dairy company?

I. If you use a coal fire/coal boiler:-

(i) What is the name and address of your coal merchant?

(ii) What is the name and address of your chimney sweep?

(iii) When last were your chimneys swept?

J. If you have newspapers delivered, what is the name and address of your newsagent?

K. Although this information is not yet necessary, would you be prepared to draw up a list later which could recommend any of the following local people who could help the Purchasers after they move in?

babysitters;
plumber;
carpenter;
builder;
central heating engineer.

BRISTOL LAW SOCIETY

Additional Enquiries before Contract

For use with Oyez Con 29 (Long) or other form of Enquiries before Contract approved by Bristol Law Society

Short description of the property

re: ....

Parties ....

to: ....

Replies are requested to the following additional enquiries:

....

Proposed Purchaser's Solicitors.

Date .... 198....

The replies are as follows:

....

Proposed Vendor's Solicitors.

Date .... 198....

ADDITIONAL ENQUIRIES

1. Is the Vendor aware of any proposal to develop any adjoining property?

2. Please give details of all carpets and curtains and other chattels included in the purchase price.

3. In respect of the fixtures and fittings being sold separately please confirm that they are in the unencumbered ownership of the Vendor and not subject to any Hire Purchase or Credit Sale Agreement or any claim by any third person.

4. Please confirm that all the items contained in the Estate Agents particulars for the property are included in the purchase price.

5. Please confirm that to the best of the Vendor's knowledge and belief all the main services at the property are in good working order and repair.

6. If there is a central heating system at the property please state:-

(a) the date of installation

(b) the type

(c) supply a copy of the maintenance contract and state the date when last serviced.

7. Is there a burglar alarm? If so please give full details including a copy of the current Maintenance Agreement and the date when last serviced.

8. If a telephone is installed please state who owns it and confirm that it will be available for transfer into the Purchaser's name on completion, subject to British Telecom approval.

9. Please confirm that the Vendor will on completion leave the property in a clean and tidy condition including the removal of rubbish from the loft, garage and outbuildings and that any items left without the consent of the Purchaser can be disposed of by the Purchaser at the Vendor's expense.

REPLIES

1770

BRISTOL LAW SOCIETY

Flat Purchase Enquiries

Short description of the property:

re: ....

Parties ....

to: ....

Replies are requested to the following Flat purchase enquiries:

....

Proposed Purchaser's Solicitors.

Date .... 198....

The replies are as follows:

....

Proposed Vendor's Solicitors.

Date .... 198....

FLAT PURCHASE ENQUIRIES

1. (a) Please supply copy of any Planning Permission or Established Use Certificate.

(b) Please confirm the flat (and as far as the Vendor is aware the other flats in the whole building) fully comply with the permission and its conditions.

(c) If no planning permission or established use certificate exists what evidence is available of the date use as a separate flat commenced and that it has been continuous since then?

(d) Please confirm there has been no further subdivision since the original planning permission or since separate use of the flat became an established use.

2. Please confirm that the whole building complies with Fire Regulations and supply the necessary Fire Officer's Certificate.

3. Have any works been carried out to any part of the whole building requiring Building Regulation Approval or Planning Permission or Listed Building Consent? If so, please supply copies of such Permissions.

4. Please supply details of:-

(a) any Car parking area and/or space allotted

(b) any Dustbin area

(c) any entry phone system

(d) any smoke detector system

(e) provision for secondary means of escape in case of fire

(f) any communal TV aerial serving all the flats

5. Please give details of the positions of the gas and electricity meters serving the flat and the water stop cocks.

6. Please supply details of any work which still remains to be carried out to the flat and the rest of the block including all common parts.

7. How many flats are there in the block and how many have been sold? Are there any flats still tenanted?

8. Please confirm that immediately on completion the Purchaser will receive a share certificate in the Management Company or that the existing share will be transferred to the Purchaser or that, in the case of a company limited by guarantee, the Purchaser will be admitted to membership of it.

REPLIES

9. Are there any holders of shares in (or, in the case of a company limited by guarantee, members of) the Management Company who are not owners of a flat in the Building?

10. Please confirm that each flat owner holds an equal allotment of shares in the Management Company (or, in the case of a company limited by guarantee, is a member of it).

11. Please supply copies of:-
   (a) The Memorandum and Articles of the Management Company
   (b) The concurrent Lease, Conveyance or Transfer to the Management Company
   (c) Minutes of the last AGM of the Management Company
   (d) The Block Insurance Policy on the property and confirm that the Purchaser's interest and that of any Mortgagee will be endorsed on the Policy and that a copy of such endorsement will be supplied upon completion.

12. Please supply details of the names and addresses of the Treasurer and Secretary of the Management Company.

13. Have all the necessary current returns of the Management Company been completed and filed?

14. Please confirm that the Management Company's interest in the property is free of any Charge or other encumbrance.

15. Please confirm that no Winding-Up Order has been made or applied for in connection with the Management Company and that no action for striking off is proposed or contemplated in the future.

16. Please give details of the anticipated maintenance charge for the current year. Has any unusual large expenditure been incurred during the last twelve months or is any such expenditure contemplated?

17. Is the Vendor aware of any disputes with regard to the maintenance charge or of any other matters concerning the management of the flats?

18. Has the Vendor received any notice under the Housing Act 1980 Schedule 19 for expenses to which the Vendor has not yet completed the Vendor's contribution? If so, please supply details.

19. Have any regulations been made by the Landlord as to the use of the flats and the grounds? If so, please supply copies.

20. Please confirm no high alumina cement concrete or calcium chloride additions or other deleterious material were used in the construction or conversion of the building.

21. If there is a lift:-
   (a) Please confirm the Landlord holds a current inspection certificate.
   (b) Please give details of the lift insurance arrangements.
   (c) What are the current maintenance arrangements?
   (d) Are there any plans or reserves for replacement?
   (e) Has the lift failed to operate satisfactorily at any time during the Vendor's ownership?

1982 EDITION

To be submitted in duplicate

ENQUIRIES OF DISTRICT COUNCILS

(NOT LONDON BOROUGHS)

NAME AND ADDRESS OF DISTRICT COUNCIL (IN BLOCK LETTERS) TO WHICH THIS FORM IS TO BE SENT

Description of the Property

RE ....

....

....

....

Relevant roadways, footpaths and footways (see Enquiry 1) in addition to those specified in the above address, on which information is sought.

....

....

....

Fees of ....are enclosed, including fees for an Official Search.

Signed ....
Solicitors.

Dated ....

HEADNOTES

(1) This Form of Enquiry is approved by the Law Society, the Association of County Councils, the Association of District Councils and the Association of Metropolitan Authorities and is published by their authority.
(2) Under the arrangements made between the District Council and the County Council the Replies below to certain Enquiries cover knowledge and actions of both the District Council and the County Council. References to "the Council" are intended to include reference to a predecessor Council and to a Committee or Sub-Committee of the Council or of a predecessor Council acting under delegated powers, and to any other body or person taking action under powers delegated by the Council or a predecessor Council.
(3) The Replies below are furnished after appropriate enquiries and in the belief that they are in accordance with the information at present available to the officers of the respective Councils, but on the distinct understanding that neither the District Council nor the County Council, nor any officer of either Council, is legally responsible therefor, except for negligence. Any such liability for negligence shall extend not only to the person by or on whose behalf these Enquiries are made but also to a person (being a purchaser for the purposes of Section 10(3) of the Local Land Charges Act 1975) who or whose agent had knowledge, before the relevant time as defined in the said Section, of the Replies to these Enquiries.
(4) It is pointed out that so far as the Replies may relate to proposals they may yet change.
(5) References to the property concerned in the Enquiries and Replies are intended to include reference, where appropriate, to any part of the property.
(6) References to any Act, Regulation or Order are intended to include reference to (i) any statutory provision replaced thereby and (ii) any amendment or re-enactment thereof.
(7) References to any Town and Country Planning Act, Order or Regulation are abbreviated, e.g. "T&CP Act 1971".
(8) Where no plan of the property is furnished with the Requisition for Official Search or this Form of Enquiry, neither the District Council nor the County Council can be expected to know the boundaries of the property, and the Replies are given on the basis of the information as to these available to the Councils in their offices. The furnishing of a plan in duplicate will help the Councils to give accurate replies and may save time. The Councils must reserve the right in any particular case to call for a plan in duplicate sufficient to enable the boundaries of the property to be identified on the ordnance survey map before furnishing Replies.

CURRENT FEES

It should be noted that the following fees are liable to change during the currency of this edition. Enquiries submitted on a form which is up-to-date apart from the information concerning fees will be answered provided the current fees are tendered.

	£ p
PART I ENQUIRIES:—	
(a) Where relating to one parcel of land only, as defined in Rule 2(2) of the Local Land Charges Rules, 1977	10.60
(b) Where relating to several parcels of land (which a single Requisition for Official Search would cover) and delivered on a single form:—	
For the first parcel of land	10.60
For each additional parcel of land	2.65
provided that where the fee on that basis would exceed £100, the amount is to be fixed by arrangement between the solicitors and the proper officer of the District Council.	
The above fees cover all the Enquiries in Part I.	
PART II ENQUIRIES:—	
Where relating to one parcel of land only or to several parcels (as above-mentioned) and delivered on a single form:—	
For each printed Enquiry numbered in the form	0.80
For any and each further Enquiry added by solicitors and which the proper officer of the Council is willing to answer	2.00
No maximum fee.	

NAME AND ADDRESS (IN BLOCK LETTERS) TO WHICH THIS FORM IS TO BE RETURNED

SOLICITORS' REFERENCE ....

....

TELEPHONE NUMBER ....

....

TELEX ....

CON. 29A. ENGLAND AND WALES (EXCLUDING LONDON) **GM Set 255**

oyez The Solicitors' Law Stationery Society plc, Oyez House, 237 Long Lane, London SE1 4PU F4865 3.85
★ ★ ★ ★ ★

ENQUIRY **PART I**	REPLY
1. (A) Are all the roadways, footpaths and footways referred to in the Description of the Property maintainable at the public expense within the meaning of the Highways Act 1980? (B) If not, please state whether the Council have passed any resolution either to:— (i) make up any of such roadways, footpaths or footways at the cost of the frontagers, or (ii) adopt any of them without cost to the frontagers. (C) (i) Have the Council entered into any outstanding agreement relating to the adoption of any such roadway, footpath or footway? *(ii) If so, is such an agreement supported by a bond?	1. (A) (B) (i) (ii) (C) (i) *(ii)
2. (A) Have the Council been notified by the appropriate Secretary of State of:— (i) any order, draft order or scheme for the construction of a new trunk or special road, or (ii) any proposals for the alteration or improvement of an existing road, involving the construction, whether or not within existing highway limits, of a subway, underpass, flyover, footbridge, elevated road or dual carriageway the centre line of which in either case is within 200 metres of the property? †(B) Have the Council approved any proposals by themselves for:— (i) the construction of a new road, or (ii) the alteration or improvement of an existing road, involving the construction, whether or not within existing highway limits, of a subway, underpass, flyover, footbridge, elevated road or dual carriageway the limits of construction of which in either case are within 200 metres of the property? (C) Have the Council approved, or have they been notified by the appropriate Secretary of State of, any proposals for highway construction or improvement that involve the acquisition of the property? (D) Has either the Secretary of State or the Council published for the purposes of public consultation any proposals for the construction of a new road indicating a possible route the centre line of which would be likely to be within 200 metres of the property?	2. (A) (i) (ii) †(B) (i) (ii) (C) (D)
3. Are there any outstanding statutory or informal notices (other than notices shown in the Official Certificate of Search and notices served consequent on an order made or a resolution passed to acquire the property recorded in reply to Enquiry 14), which have been issued by the Council under the Public Health Acts, Housing Acts or Highways Acts?	3.
4. Have the Council authorised any proceedings in respect of an infringement of the Building Regulations?	4.

* If the Reply is "yes", the enquirer should satisfy himself of the adequacy of the bond.
† This Enquiry refers to the Council's own proposals and not those of other developers.

REPLY	ENQUIRY
5. (A) (i) (a)*	5. (A) (i) (a)* Does foul drainage from the property drain to a public sewer?
(b)	(b) If the Reply to (a) above is "Yes", please indicate whether the connection to the public sewer is effected by:
(1)	(1) drain and private sewer;
(2)	(2) drain alone.
(ii) (a)	(ii) (a) Does surface water from the property drain to a public sewer?
(b)	(b) Does surface water from the property drain to a highway drain or sewer the subject of an agreement under s.21 (1) (a) of the Public Health Act 1936?
(c)	(c) If the Reply to either (a) or (b) above is "Yes", please indicate whether the connection to the appropriate sewer or highway drain is effected by:
(1)	(1) drain and private sewer;
(2)	(2) drain alone.
(iii)	(iii) Is there in force in relation to any part of the drainage of the property an agreement under s.38 of the Public Health Act 1936?
(B) (i)	(B) (i) To the Council's knowledge is any sewer serving, or which is proposed to serve, the property the subject of an agreement under s.18 of the Public Health Act 1936?
†‡(ii)	†‡(ii) If the Reply to (i) above is "Yes", is the agreement supported by a bond?
(C)	(C) Is any public sewer to which the property drains a sewer of a kind described in s.24(4) of the Public Health Act 1936?
(D)	(D) If the Reply to either Enquiry (A) (i) (a) or (ii) (a) above is "No", do the Council know whether there is a foul or surface water sewer (as appropriate) within 100 feet of the property and at a level which makes it reasonably practicable to construct a drain from the property to that sewer? [N.B. If the Council cannot reply in the affirmative, the applicant must make his own survey.]
‡(E)	‡(E) Are the Council aware of any resolution affecting the property:
(i)	(i) under s.12 or s.13 of the Public Health Act 1961, or
(ii)	(ii) under any local Act as to the recovery from frontagers of the expense of sewering highways?
6. (A)	6. (A) Except as shown in the Official Certificate of Search, or in the Register kept pursuant to s.92A of the T&CP Act 1971, has any enforcement or stop notice under s.87 or s.90 of the T&CP Act 1971 been authorised by the Council for issue or service (other than notices which have been withdrawn or quashed)?
(B)	(B) Are there any entries in the Register kept pursuant to s.92A of the T&CP Act 1971?
(C)	(C) Where can that Register be inspected?
*(D)	*(D) If an enforcement notice has been served or issued, has it been complied with to the satisfaction of the Council?

* This Enquiry will be replied to unless that would necessitate an inspection by the Council's agents. It will be so stated, if it is the case.
† If the Reply is "yes", the enquirer should satisfy himself of the adequacy of the bond.
‡ Even if the Council do reply, enquiry should also be made of the Regional Water Authority.

ENQUIRY	REPLY
*7. (A) (i) What stage has been reached in the preparation of a structure plan for the area which includes the property?	*7. (A) (i)
(ii) Have the Council made public any proposals for the alteration of an approved structure plan?	(ii)
(B) (i) What stage has been reached in the preparation of local plans for the area which includes the property?	(B) (i)
(ii) Have the Council made public any proposals for the alteration of an adopted local plan?	(ii)
(iii) Do any of the proposals made public by the Council in relation to local plans:	(iii)
(a) indicate the primary use for the area which includes the property?	(a)
(b) include any provisions for the property?	(b)
(C) (i) Is an old style development plan in force in the area which includes the property?	(C) (i)
(ii) If so, does the plan:	(ii)
(a) indicate the primary use for the area?	(a)
(b) include any provisions for the property?	(b)
(D) (i) Have the Council made public any proposals for the preparation or modification of a non-statutory plan for the area which includes the property?	(D) (i)
(ii) If so:	(ii)
(a) what stage has been reached?	(a)
(b) do any proposals indicate the primary use of the area or include any provisions for the property?	(b)
(E) Is the property included in any of the categories of land specified in s.71 of the Land Compensation Act 1973?	(E)
8. Except as shown in the Official Certificate of Search, have the Council resolved to make a direction under Article 4 of the T&CP General Development Order 1977 relating to the restriction of permitted development?	8.
9. Except as shown in the Official Certificate of Search, have the Council resolved to make any order under s. 45, s. 51 or s. 60 of the T&CP Act 1971?	9.
10. Has compensation been paid by the Council under s.169 of the T&CP Act 1971?	10.
11. (A) Are there any entries relating to the property in Part I or Part II of the Register kept pursuant to s. 34 of the T&CP Act 1971?	11. (A)
(B) Where can that Register be inspected?	(B)
†12. Is the property within a conservation area designated under s. 277 of the T&CP Act 1971 prior to 31 August 1974?	†12.

* Replies given to Enquiry 2 will not be repeated.
† Conservation areas designated on or after 31/8/74 are registrable as local land charges.

REPLY	ENQUIRY
13.	13. Have the Council authorised the service of a building preservation notice under s.58 of the T&CP Act 1971?
14.	14. Except as shown in the Official Certificate of Search, have the Council made any order (whether or not confirmed by the appropriate Secretary of State) or passed any resolution which is still capable of being implemented for the compulsory acquisition of the property?
15. (A) (B)	15. (A) Is the property included in a programme of slum clearance which has been submitted, or been the subject of a resolution to submit, to the Department of the Environment, or has otherwise been adopted by resolution of the Council? (B) Except as shown in the Official Certificate of Search, have the Council resolved to define the area in which the property is situated as a General Improvement Area.
16.	16. Except as shown in the Official Certificate of Search, is the property included in an area for which the Council have passed a resolution to make or vary a smoke control order under s.11 of the Clean Air Act 1956?
17. (i) (ii) (iii)	17. Is a resolution in force bringing into operation Schedule 1 to the General Rate Act 1967, as to rating of unoccupied property? If so, please specify: (i) the categories of properties affected; (ii) the effective date of the resolution; (iii) the proportion of the rate due.
18.	18. Is the property situated in an area where registration of title under the Land Registration Acts is compulsory on sale? If so, please specify the District Registry and the date of compulsory registration.

ENQUIRY	REPLY
PART II NOTE.—*If the applicant wishes to make any of the following Enquiries, he should place his initials clearly against those concerned. Enquiries not initialled will not be replied to. For fees, see first page.*	
I. Has any public path or road used as a public path or byway which abuts on or crosses the property been shown in a draft, provisional or definitive map or a draft revision or revised map, whichever may be the later, prepared under Part IV of the National Parks and Access to the Countryside Act 1949, Schedule 3 to the Countryside Act 1968 or Part III of the Wildlife and Countryside Act 1981? [N.B. See headnote (8) as to the furnishing of plans.]	I.
II. Have the Council approved any proposals for the stopping up or diversion of any of the roads or footpaths referred to in the Description of the Property?	II.
III. (A) Are there any entries relating to the property in the Register kept by the Council pursuant to the T&CP (Control of Advertisements) Regulations 1969?	III. (A)
(B) Where can that Register be inspected?	(B)
(C) Except as shown in the Official Certificate of Search:	(C)
(i) has any notice been given by the Secretary of State or served under Regulation 15 of the Regulations?	(i)
(ii) have the Council resolved to serve a discontinuance notice under Regulation 16?	(ii)
*(iii) if a discontinuance notice has been served, has it been complied with to the satisfaction of the Council?	*(iii)
(iv) have the Council resolved to make an order defining the area which includes the property as an area of special control under Regulation 26?	(iv)
IV. (A) Have the Council or the Secretary of State granted or refused any listed building consents under s.55 of the T&CP Act 1971?	IV. (A)
(B) Except as shown in the Official Certificate of Search, have the Council resolved to serve a listed building enforcement notice under s.96 of the T&CP Act 1971?	(B)
*(C) If a listed building enforcement notice has been served, has it been complied with to the satisfaction of the Council?	*(C)
V. (A) To the knowledge of the Council, has the service of a repairs notice under s.115 of the T&CP Act 1971 been authorised?	V. (A)
(B) If the Council have authorised the making of an order for the compulsory acquisition of the property under s.114 of the T&CP Act 1971, is a "minimum compensation" provision included, or intended to be included, in the order?	(B)
VI. Have the Council resolved to terminate any of the planning permissions in force by means of a completion notice under s.44 of the T&CP Act 1971?	VI.

*This Enquiry will be replied to unless that would necessitate an inspection by the Council's agents. It will be so stated, if it is the case.

REPLY	ENQUIRY
VII.	VII. Has any order under s.87 of the National Parks and Access to the Countryside Act 1949, been made relating to an area which includes the property?
VIII.	VIII. Has a map been deposited under s.35 of the Pipe-lines Act 1962, or s.39 of the Gas Act 1972, showing a pipe-line within 100 feet of the property?
IX.	IX. Is the property included in a registration of houses scheme (houses in multiple occupation) under s.22 of the Housing Act 1961, containing control provisions as authorised by s.64 of the Housing Act 1969?
X. (A)	X. (A) Have the Council made, or resolved to make, any noise abatement zone order under s.63 of the Control of Pollution Act 1974 for the area which includes the property?
(B)	(B) Is there any entry in relation to the property recorded in the Noise Level Register kept pursuant to s.64 of the Control of Pollution Act 1974?
(C)	(C) Where can that Register be inspected?
*XI.	*XI. If the property is situated in an area designated as an urban development area under Part XVI of the Local Government, Planning and Land Act 1980, please specify the name of the urban development corporation and the address of the principal office.
XII.	XII. Is the property situated in an area designated as an enterprise zone under Part XVIII of the Local Government, Planning and Land Act 1980?
XIII.	XIII. Have the Council resolved to define the area in which the property is situated as an improvement area under s.4 of the Inner Urban Areas Act 1978?
Signed.. *Proper officer* Dated..19.......	

* Information on the functions allocated to an urban development corporation should be sought from that authority.

1982 EDITION (1986 REVISION)

To be submitted in duplicate

LONDON BOROUGH COUNCILS OR THE CORPORATION OF LONDON

ENQUIRIES OF LOCAL AUTHORITY

NAME AND ADDRESS OF LOCAL AUTHORITY (IN BLOCK LETTERS) TO WHICH THIS FORM IS TO BE SENT

Description of the Property

RE ....

....

....

....

Relevant roadways, footpaths and footways (see Enquiry 1) in addition to those specified in the above address, on which information is sought.

....

....

....

Fees of .... are enclosed, including fees for an Official Search.

Signed .... *Solicitors.*

Dated ....

HEADNOTES

(1) This Form of Enquiry is approved by The Law Society, the London Boroughs Association, the Association of Metropolitan Authorities and the Corporation of London, and is published by their authority.
(2) The Replies below are furnished after appropriate enquiries and in the belief that they are in accordance with the information at present available to the officers of the Council, but on the distinct understanding that neither the Common Council, nor the London Borough Council, nor any officer of those Councils is legally responsible therefor, except for negligence. Any such liability for negligence shall extend not only to the person by or on whose behalf these Enquiries are made but also to a person (being a purchaser for the purposes of Section 10(3) of the Local Land Charges Act 1975) who or whose agent had knowledge, before the relevant time as defined in the said Section, of the Replies to these Enquiries.
(3) It is pointed out that so far as the Replies may relate to proposals they may yet change. Where a reply "yes" is given, additional information should be provided where it is implicitly required.
(4) References to the property concerned in the Enquiries and Replies are intended to include reference, where appropriate, to any part of the property.
(5) References to any Act, Regulation or Order are intended to include reference to (i) any statutory provision replaced thereby and (ii) any amendment or re-enactment thereof.
(6) References to "the Council" are intended to include reference to a predecessor Council and to a Committee or Sub-Committee of the Council or of a predecessor Council acting under delegated powers, and to any other body or person taking action under powers delegated by the Council or a predecessor Council.
(7) References to any Town and Country Planning Act, Order or Regulation are abbreviated, e.g. "T&CP Act 1971".
(8) Where no plan of the property is furnished with the Requisition for Official Search or this Form of Enquiry, neither the Borough Council nor the Corporation of London can be expected to know the boundaries of the property, and the Replies are given on the basis of the information as to these available to the Council/Corporation in their offices. The furnishing of a plan in duplicate will help the Council/Corporation to give accurate Replies and may save time. The Council/Corporation must reserve the right in any particular case to call for a plan in duplicate sufficient to enable the boundaries of the property to be identified on the ordnance survey map before furnishing Replies.

CURRENT FEES

It should be noted that the following fees are liable to change during the currency of this edition. Enquiries submitted on a form which is up-to-date apart from the information concerning fees will be answered provided the current fees are tendered.

	£ p
PART I ENQUIRIES:—	
(a) Where relating to one parcel of land only, as defined in Rule 2(2) of the Local Land Charges Rules, 1977.	11.30
(b) Where relating to several parcels of land (which a single Requisition for Official Search would cover) and delivered on a single form:—	
For the first parcel of land	11.30
For each additional parcel of land	2.80
provided that where the fee on that basis would exceed £100, the amount is to be fixed by arrangement between the solicitors and the proper officer of the Council.	
The above fees cover all the Enquiries in Part I.	
PART II ENQUIRIES:—	
Where relating to one parcel of land only or to several parcels (as above-mentioned) and delivered on a single form:—	
For each printed Enquiry numbered in the form	0.85
For any and each further Enquiry added by solicitors and which the proper officer of the Council is willing to answer	2.15
No maximum fee.	

NAME AND ADDRESS (IN BLOCK LETTERS) TO WHICH THIS FORM IS TO BE RETURNED

SOLICITORS' REFERENCE ....

....

TELEPHONE NUMBER ....

....

TELEX ....

CON. 29D. LONDON ONLY **GM Set 255**

Oyez The Solicitors' Law Stationery Society plc, Oyez House, 27 Crimscott Street, London SE1 5TS

7.86 F6322

5033052

ENQUIRY **PART I**	REPLY
1. (A) Are all the roadways, footpaths and footways referred to in the Description of the Property maintainable at the public expense within the meaning of the Highways Act 1980?	1. (A)
(B) If not, please state whether the Council have passed any resolution either to:—	(B)
(i) make up any of such roadways, footpaths or footways at the cost of the frontagers, or	(i)
(ii) adopt any of them without cost to the frontagers.	(ii)
(C) (i) Have the Council entered into any outstanding agreement relating to the adoption of any such roadway, footpath or footway?	(C) (i)
*(ii) If so, is such an agreement supported by a bond?	*(ii)
2. (A) Have the Council been notified by the appropriate Secretary of State of:—	2. (A)
(i) any order, draft order or scheme for the construction of a new trunk or special road, or	(i)
(ii) any proposals for the alteration or improvement of an existing road, involving the construction, whether or not within existing highway limits, of a subway, underpass, flyover, footbridge, elevated road or dual carriageway the centre line of which in either case is within 200 metres of the property?	(ii)
†(B) Have the Council approved any proposals by themselves for:—	†(B)
(i) the construction of a new road, or	(i)
(ii) the alteration or improvement of an existing road, involving the construction, whether or not within existing highway limits, of a subway, underpass, flyover, footbridge, elevated road or dual carriageway the limits of construction of which in either case are within 200 metres of the property?	(ii)
(C) Have the Council approved, or have they been notified by the appropriate Secretary of State, of any proposals for highway construction or improvement that involve the acquisition of the property?	(C)
(D) Has either the Secretary of State or the Council published for the purposes of public consultation any proposals for the construction of a new road indicating a possible route the centre line of which would be likely to be within 200 metres of the property?	(D)
3. Are there any outstanding statutory or informal notices (other than notices shown in the Official Certificate of Search and notices served consequent on an order made or a resolution passed to acquire the property recorded in reply to Enquiry 14), which have been issued by the Council under the Public Health Acts, Housing Acts or Highways Acts or (Inner London Boroughs only) London Building Acts?	3.
4. Have the Council authorised any proceedings in respect of an infringement of the Building Regulations?	4.

* If the Reply is "yes", the enquirer should satisfy himself of the adequacy of the bond.
† This Enquiry refers to the Council's own proposals and not those of other developers.

REPLY	ENQUIRY
5. (A) (i) (a)*	5. (A) (i) (a)* Does foul drainage from the property drain to a public sewer?
(b)	(b) If the Reply to (a) above is "Yes", please indicate whether the connection to the public sewer is effected by:
(1)	(1) drain and private sewer;
(2)	(2) drain alone.
(ii) (a)	(ii) (a) Does surface water from the property drain to a public sewer?
(b)	(b) Does surface water from the property drain to a highway drain or sewer the subject of an agreement under s.21(1)(a) of the Public Health Act 1936?
(c)	(c) If the Reply to either (a) or (b) above is "Yes", please indicate whether the connection to the appropriate sewer or highway drain is effected by:
(1)	(1) drain and private sewer;
(2)	(2) drain alone.
(iii)	(iii) Is there in force in relation to any part of the drainage of the property an agreement under s.38 of the Public Health Act 1936?
(B) (i)	(B) (i) To the Council's knowledge is any sewer serving, or which is proposed to serve, the property the subject of an agreement under s.18 of the Public Health Act 1936?
†‡(ii)	†‡(ii) If the Reply to (i) above is "Yes", is the agreement supported by a bond?
(C)	(C) Is any public sewer to which the property drains a sewer of a kind described in s.24(4) of the Public Health Act 1936?
(D)	(D) If the Reply to either Enquiry (A) (i) (a) or (ii) (a) above is "No", do the Council know whether there is a foul or surface water sewer (as appropriate) within 100 feet of the property and at a level which makes it reasonably practicable to construct a drain from the property to that sewer? [N.B. If the Council cannot reply in the affirmative, the applicant must make his own survey.]
‡(E)	‡(E) Are the Council aware of any resolution affecting the property:
(i)	(i) under s.12 or s.13 of the Public Health Act 1961, or
(ii)	(ii) under any local Act as to the recovery from frontagers of the expense of sewering highways?
6. (A)	6. (A) Except as shown in the Official Certificate of Search, or in the Register kept pursuant to s.92A of the T&CP Act 1971, has any enforcement or stop notice under s.87 or s.90 of the T&CP Act 1971 been authorised by the Council for issue or service (other than notices which have been withdrawn or quashed)?
(B)	(B) Are there any entries in the Register kept pursuant to s.92A of the T&CP Act 1971?
(C)	(C) Where can that Register be inspected?
*(D)	*(D) If an enforcement notice has been served or issued, has it been complied with to the satisfaction of the Council?

* This Enquiry will be replied to unless that would necessitate an inspection by the Council's agents. It will be so stated, if it is the case.
† If the Reply is "yes", the enquirer should satisfy himself of the adequacy of the bond.
‡ Even if the Council do reply, enquiry should also be made of the Regional Water Authority.

[The reference in enquiry 5A(iii) to s.38 of the Public Health Act 1936 is to be changed to s.22 of the Building Act 1984, when the form is next printed.]

ENQUIRY	REPLY
*7. (A) (i) Has Part I of Schedule I to the Local Government Act 1985 come into force in the borough?	*7. (A) (i)
(ii) If so, what stage has been reached in the preparation of a Unitary Development Plan?	(ii)
(iii) Does any such Unitary Development Plan:	(iii)
(a) indicate the primary use for the area that includes the property?	(a)
(b) include any provisions for the property?	(b)
(c) include the property in an action area?	(c)
(iv) Have the Council or the Secretary of State made any proposal for the alteration or replacement of a Unitary Development Plan?	(iv)
(v) Has the Secretary of State revoked any part of the Greater London Development Plan in relation to any part of the borough?	(v)
(B) (i) If Part I of Schedule I to the Local Government Act 1985 has not come into force, which local plans and old Development Plans (if any) remain in force?	B (i)
(ii) Are there any local plans in the course of preparation for the area that includes the property? If so, what stage has been reached?	(ii)
(iii) Have the Council made public any proposals for the alteration of an adopted local plan?	(iii)
(iv) Does any adopted local plan, or any proposal made public by the Council for the alteration of an adopted local plan:	(iv)
(a) indicate the primary use for the area which includes the property?	(a)
(b) include any provisions for the property?	(b)
(C) (i) Is the Initial Development Plan for Greater London still in force in the area which includes the property?	(C) (i)
(ii) If so, does that Plan:	(ii)
(a) indicate the primary use for the area?	(a)
(b) include any provisions for the property?	(b)
(D) (i) Have the Council made public any proposals for the preparation or modification of a non-statutory plan for the area which includes the property?	D (i)
(ii) If so:	(ii)
(a) what stage has been reached?	(a)
(b) do any of the proposals indicate the primary use of the area or include any provisions for the property?	(b)
(E) Is the property included in any of the categories of land specified in Section 71 of the Land Compensation Act 1973?	E
8. Except as shown in the Official Certificate of Search, have the Council resolved to make a direction under Article 4 of the T&CP General Development Order 1977 relating to the restriction of permitted development?	8.
9. Except as shown in the Official Certificate of Search, have the Council resolved to make any order under s.45, s.51 or s.60 of the T&CP Act 1971?	9.
10. Has compensation been paid by the Council under s.169 of the T&CP Act 1971?	10.
11. (A) Are there any entries relating to the property in Part I or Part II of the Register kept pursuant to s.34 of the T&CP Act 1971?	11. (A)
(B) Where can that Register be inspected?	(B)
†12. Is the property within a conservation area designated under s.277 of the T&CP Act 1971 prior to 31 August 1974?	12.

* Replies given to Enquiry 2 will not be repeated.
† Conservation areas designated on or after 31/8/74 are registrable as local land charges.

REPLY	ENQUIRY
13. *(See note opposite.)*	13. Have the Council authorised the service of a building preservation notice under s.58 of the T&CP Act 1971? [NOTE:— The Historic Buildings and Monuments Commission also have power to issue this type of notice. Separate enquiry should be made of them, if considered necessary.]
14. *(See note opposite.)*	14. Except as shown in the Official Certificate of Search, have the Council made any order (whether or not confirmed by the appropriate Secretary of State) or passed any resolution which is still capable of being implemented for the compulsory acquisition of the property? [NOTE: This enquiry will not elicit information regarding Compulsory Purchase actions by the many other authorities having such Powers.]
15. (A) (B)	15. (A) Is the property included in a programme of slum clearance which has been submitted, or been the subject of a resolution to submit, to the Department of the Environment, or has otherwise been adopted by resolution of the Council? (B) Except as shown in the Official Certificate of Search, have the Council resolved to define the area in which the property is situated as a General Improvement Area?
16. (A) (B)	16. (A) Except as shown in the Official Certificate of Search, is the property included in an area for which the Council have passed a resolution to make or vary a smoke control order under s.11 of the Clean Air Act 1956? (B) If the property is in the City of London, please supply particulars of any order made under s.4(2) of the City of London (Various Powers) Act 1954 affecting the property and state whether any exemption from, or deferment of, the provisions of s.4 has been made under s.4(6) or (7).
17. (A) (i) (ii) (iii) (B)	17 (A) Is a resolution in force bringing into operation Schedule 1 to the General Rate Act 1967, as to rating of unoccupied property? If so, please specify: (i) the categories of properties affected; (ii) the effective date of the resolution; (iii) the proportion of the rate due. (B) If the property is in the City of London (in addition to replying to (A) above), is it liable to be rated under s.177 of the City of London Sewers Act 1848, as amended by s.42 of the City of London Sewers Act 1851 and the City of London (Union of Parishes) Act 1907?
18.	18. As the property is situated in an area where registration of title under the Land Registration Acts is compulsory on sale, please specify the District Registry and the date of compulsory registration.

ENQUIRY	REPLY
PART II NOTE.—*If the applicant wishes to make any of the following Enquiries, he should place his initials clearly against those concerned. Enquiries not initialled will not be replied to. For fees, see first page.*	
I. Has any public path or road used as a public path or byway which abuts on or crosses the property been shown in a draft, provisional or definitive map or a draft revision or revised map, whichever may be the later, prepared under Part IV of the National Parks and Access to the Countryside Act 1949, Schedule 3 to the Countryside Act 1968 or Part III of the Wildlife and Countryside Act 1981? [N.B. See headnote (8) as to the furnishing of plans.]	I.
II. Have the Council approved any proposals for the stopping up or diversion of any of the roads or footpaths referred to in the Description of the Property?	II.
III. (A) Are there any entries relating to the property in the Register kept by the Council pursuant to the T&CP (Control of Advertisements) Regulations 1969?	III. (A)
(B) Where can that Register be inspected?	(B)
(C) Except as shown in the Official Certificate of Search:	(C)
(i) has any notice been given by the Secretary of State or served under Regulation 15 of the Regulations?	(i)
(ii) have the Council resolved to serve a discontinuance notice under Regulation 16?	(ii)
*(iii) if a discontinuance notice has been served, has it been complied with to the satisfaction of the Council?	*(iii)
(iv) have the Council resolved to make an order defining the area which includes the property as an area of special control under Regulation 26?	(iv)
IV. (A) Have the Council or the Secretary of State granted or refused any listed building consents under s.55 of the T&CP Act 1971?	IV. (A)
(B) Except as shown in the Official Certificate of Search, have the Council resolved to serve a listed building enforcement notice under s.96 of the T&CP Act 1971?	(B)
*(C) If a listed building enforcement notice has been served, has it been complied with to the satisfaction of the Council?	*(C)
V. (A) To the knowledge of the Council, has the service of a repairs notice under s.115 of the T&CP Act 1971 been authorised?	V. (A)
(B) If the Council have authorised the making of an order for the compulsory acquisition of the property under s.114 of the T&CP Act 1971, is a "minimum compensation" provision included, or intended to be included, in the order?	(B)

*This Enquiry will be replied to unless that would necessitate an inspection by the Council's agents. It will be so stated, if it is the case.

REPLY	ENQUIRY
VI.	VI. Have the Council resolved to terminate any of the planning permissions in force by means of a completion notice under s.44 of the T&CP Act 1971?
VII.	VII. Has any order under s.87 of the National Parks and Access to the Countryside Act 1949, been made relating to an area which includes the property?
VIII.	VIII. Has a map been deposited under s.35 of the Pipe-lines Act 1962, or s.39 of the Gas Act 1972, showing a pipe-line within 100 feet of the property?
IX.	IX. Is the property included in a registration of houses scheme (houses in multiple occupation) under s.22 of the Housing Act 1961, containing control provisions as authorised by s.64 of the Housing Act 1969?
X. (A)	X. (A) Have the Council made, or resolved to make, any noise abatement zone order under s.63 of the Control of Pollution Act 1974 for the area which includes the property?
(B)	(B) Is there any entry in relation to the property recorded in the Noise Level Register kept pursuant to s.64 of the Control of Pollution Act 1974?
(C)	(C) Where can that Register be inspected?
•XI.	•XI. If the property is situated in an area designated as an urban development area under Part XVI of the Local Government, Planning and Land Act 1980, please specify the name of the urban development corporation and the address of the principal office.
XII.	XII. Is the property situated in an area designated as an enterprise zone under Part XVIII of the Local Government, Planning and Land Act 1980?
XIII.	XIII. Have the Council resolved to define the area in which the property is situated as an improvement area under s.4 of the Inner Urban Areas Act 1978?

•Information on the functions allocated to an urban development corporation should be sought from that authority.

Signed...
Proper officer

Dated..19........

The Law Society's Code for Completion by Post (1984 Edition)

Preamble The code provides a procedure for postal completion which practising solicitors may adopt by reference.

First, each solicitor must satisfy himself that no circumstances exist that are likely to give rise to a conflict between this code and the interests of his own client (including where applicable a mortgagee client).

The code, where adopted, will apply without variation except so far as recorded in writing beforehand.

The Code

1. Adoption hereof must be specifically agreed by all the solicitors concerned and preferably in writing.

2. On completion the vendor's solicitors will act as agent for the purchaser's solicitor without fee or disbursements.

3. The vendor's solicitor undertakes that on completion, he:

(1) will have the vendor's authority to receive the purchase money; and

(2) will be the duly authorised agent of the proprietor of any charge upon the property to receive the part of the money paid to him which is needed to discharge such charge.

4. The purchaser's solicitor shall send to the vendor's solicitor instructions as to:

(1) documents to be examined and marked;

(2) memoranda to be endorsed;

(3) deeds, documents, undertakings and authorities relating to rents, deposits, keys, *etc*; and

(4) any other relevant matters.

In default of instructions, the vendor's solicitor shall not be under any duty to examine, mark or endorse any documents.

5. The purchaser's solicitor shall remit to the vendor's solicitor the balance due on completion specified in the vendor's solicitor's completion statement or with written notification; in default of either, the balance shown due by the contract. If the funds are remitted by transfer between banks, the vendor's solicitor shall instruct his bank to advise him by telephone immediately the funds are received. The vendor's solicitor shall hold such funds to the purchaser's solicitor's order pending completion.

6. The vendor's solicitor, having received the items specified in paras 4 and 5, shall forthwith, or at such later times as may have been agreed, complete. Thereupon he shall hold all documents and other items to be sent to the purchaser's solicitor as agent for such solicitor.

7. Once completion has taken place, the vendor's solicitor shall as soon as possible thereafter on the same day confirm the fact to the purchaser's solicitor by telephone or telex and shall also as soon as possible send by first class post or document exchange written confirmation to the purchaser's solicitor, together with the enclosures referred to in para 4 hereof. The vendor's solicitor shall ensure that such title deeds and any other items are correctly committed to the post or document exchange. Thereafter, they are at the risk of the purchaser's solicitor.

8. If either the authorities specified in para 3 or the instruc-

tions specified in para 4 or the funds in para 5 have not been received by the vendor's solicitor by the agreed completion date and time, he shall forthwith notify the purchaser's solicitor and request further instructions.

9. Nothing herein shall override any rights and obligations of parties under the contract or otherwise.

10. Any dispute or difference which may arise between solicitors that is directly referable to a completion agreed to be carried out in accordance herewith, whether or not amended or supplemented in any way, shall be referred to an arbitrator to be agreed, within one month of any such dispute or difference arising between the solicitors who are party thereto, and, in default of such agreement, on the application of any such solicitor, to an arbitrator to be appointed by the President of The Law Society.

11. Reference herein to vendor's solicitor and purchaser's solicitor shall, where appropriate, be deemed to include solicitors acting for parties other than vendor and purchaser.

IMPORTANT
This is a technical document, designed to create specific legal rights and obligations. It is recommended for use only in accordance with the advice of your solicitors.

THE LAW SOCIETY'S CONTRACT FOR SALE (1984 REVISION)

AGREEMENT made the day of 198

BETWEEN

Vendor

Purchaser

IT is agreed that the Vendor shall sell and the Purchaser shall purchase in accordance with the following special conditions the property described in the particulars below at the price of

---

PARTICULARS—ALL THAT freehold/leasehold property

SPECIAL CONDITIONS OF SALE SEE BACK PAGE

Purchase money *less* deposit paid		SIGNED
Chattels, fittings etc.		
Balance		Vendor/Purchaser

Vendor's Solicitors Ref.

Purchaser's Solicitors Ref.

Local Authorities

THE LAW SOCIETY'S GENERAL CONDITIONS OF SALE (1984 REVISION)

1 DEFINITIONS

In these conditions—

(*a*) "completion notice" means a notice served under condition 23 (2)

(*b*) "the contract rate" means the rate specified in a special condition or, if none is so specified, the rate prescribed from time to time under section 32 of the Land Compensation Act 1961 for interest payable thereunder

(*c*) "contractual completion date" has the meaning given in condition 21

(*d*) "conveyance" includes an assignment and a transfer under the Land Registration Acts

(*e*) "lease" includes underlease

(*f*) "normal deposit" means the sum which, together with any preliminary deposit paid by the purchaser, amounts to ten per centum of the purchase money (excluding any separate price to be paid for any chattels, fixtures or fittings)

(*g*) "working day" means any day from Monday to Friday (inclusive) other than—

(i) Christmas Day, Good Friday and any statutory bank holiday, and

(ii) any other day specified in a special condition as not a working day

(*h*) a reference to a statute includes any amendment or re-enactment thereof.

2 SERVICE AND DELIVERY

(1) Section 196 of the Law of Property Act 1925 applies to any notice served under the contract, save that—

(*a*) a notice shall also be sufficiently served on a party if served on that party's solicitors

(*b*) a reference to a registered letter shall include a prepaid first class ordinary letter

(*c*) if the time at which a letter containing a notice would in the ordinary course be delivered is not on a working day, the notice shall be deemed to be served on the next following working day

(*d*) a notice shall also be sufficiently served if—

(i) sent by telex or by telegraphic facsimile transmission to the party to be served, and that service shall be deemed to be made on the day of transmission if transmitted before 4 p.m. on a working day, but otherwise on the next following working day

(ii) when the addressee is a member of a document exchange (as to which the inclusion of a reference thereto in the solicitors' letterhead shall be conclusive evidence) delivered to that or any other affiliated exchange, and that service shall be deemed to have been made on the first working day after that on which the document would, in the ordinary course, be available for collection by the addressee.

(2) Sub-condition (1) applies to the delivery of documents as it applies to the service of notices.

3 MATTERS AFFECTING THE PROPERTY

(1) In this condition—

(*a*) "competent authority" means a local authority or other body exercising powers under statute or Royal Charter

(*b*) "requirement" includes (whether or not subject to confirmation) any notice, order or proposal

(*c*) "relevant matter" means any matter specified in sub-condition (2) whenever arising.

(2) The property is sold subject to—

(*a*) all matters registrable by any competent authority pursuant to statute

(*b*) all requirements of any competent authority

(*c*) all matters disclosed or reasonably to be expected to be disclosed by searches and as a result of enquiries formal or informal, and whether made in person, by writing or orally by or for the purchaser or which a prudent purchaser ought to make

(*d*) all notices served by or on behalf of a reversioner, a tenant or sub-tenant, or the owner or occupier of any adjoining or neighbouring property.

(3) (*a*) Notwithstanding sub-condition (2), the vendor warrants that he has informed the purchaser of the contents of any written communication received by, or known to, the vendor on or before the working day preceding the date of the contract relating to any relevant matter. Failure to give such information before the contract is made shall be deemed to be an omission in a statement in the course of the negotiations leading to the contract, but shall give rise to no right to compensation to the extent that the purchaser has a claim for damages against a competent authority

(*b*) In the event of any conflict or variation between information in fact received from any competent authority relating to any relevant matter and any statement made by the vendor in respect of the same matter, the purchaser shall rely on the information received from the competent authority to the exclusion of that given by the vendor

(*c*) The vendor shall forthwith inform the purchaser of the contents of any written communication received by him after the working day preceding the date of the contract and before the day of actual completion which if received on or before the former day would have fallen within paragraph (*a*).

(4) The purchaser (subject to any right or remedy arising under sub-condition (3)) will indemnify the vendor in respect of any liability under any requirement of a competent authority (whether made before or after the date of the contract), including the reasonable cost to the vendor of compliance after reasonable notice to the purchaser of the vendor's intention to comply, such sum to be payable on demand. The provisions of this sub-condition shall prevail in the event of conflict with any other condition.

4 OPPORTUNITY TO RESCIND

(1) This condition only applies if a special condition so provides.

(2) Within such period as is specified in a special condition or, if none is so specified, within twenty working days from the date of the contract (as to which, in either case, time shall be of the essence), the purchaser shall be entitled, notwithstanding condition 3 (2), to rescind the contract by service of notice on the vendor specifying a matter to which this condition applies affecting the property.

(3) This condition applies to any of the following matters of which the purchaser had no knowledge on or before the working day preceding the date of the contract—

(*a*) a financial charge which the vendor cannot or has not at the purchaser's written request agreed to discharge on or before actual completion

(*b*) a statutory provision prohibiting, restricting or imposing adverse conditions upon the use or the continued use of the property for such purpose as is specified in a special condition or, if none is so specified, the purpose for which the vendor used it immediately before the date of the contract

(*c*) a matter which is likely materially to reduce the price which a willing purchaser could otherwise reasonably be expected to pay for the relevant interest in the property in the open market at the date of the contract.

(4) For the purposes of this condition, the purchaser's knowledge—

(*a*) includes everything in writing received in the course of the transaction leading to the contract by a person acting on his behalf from the vendor, a person acting on the vendor's behalf, or a competent authority (as defined in condition 3 (1) (*a*))

(*b*) does not include anything solely because a statute deems that registration of a matter constitutes actual notice of it.

5 EASEMENTS, RESERVATIONS, RIGHTS AND LIABILITIES

(1) The vendor warrants that he has disclosed to the purchaser the existence of all easements, rights, privileges and liabilities affecting the property, of which the vendor knows or ought to know, other than the existence of those known to the purchaser at the date of the contract, or which a prudent purchaser would have discovered by that date.

(2) Without prejudice to the generality of sub-condition (1)—

(*a*) the purchaser shall purchase with full notice of the actual state and condition of the property and shall take it as it stands, save where it is to be constructed or converted by the vendor

(*b*) the property is sold, and will if the vendor so requires be conveyed, subject to all rights of way, water, light, drainage and other easements, rights, privileges and liabilities affecting the same.

(3) (*a*) In this sub-condition "the retained land" means land retained by the vendor—

(i) adjoining the property, or

(ii) near to the property and designated as retained land in a special condition.

(*b*) The conveyance of the property shall contain such reservations in favour of the retained land and the grant of such rights over the retained land as would have been implied had the vendor conveyed both the property and the retained land by simultaneous conveyances to different purchasers.

6 TENANCIES

(1) This condition applies if the property is sold subject to any lease or tenancy and shall have effect notwithstanding any partial, incomplete or inaccurate reference to any lease or tenancy in the special conditions or the particulars of the property.

(2) Copies or full particulars of all leases or tenancies not vested in the purchaser having been furnished to him, he shall be deemed to purchase with full knowledge thereof and shall take the property subject to the rights of the tenants thereunder or by reason thereof. The purchaser shall indemnify the vendor against all claims, demands and liability in respect of such rights, notwithstanding that they may be void against a purchaser for want of registration.

(3) The vendor gives no warranty as to the amount of rent lawfully recoverable from any tenant, as to the effect of any legislation in relation to any lease or tenancy or as to the compliance with any legislation affecting the same.

(4) The vendor shall inform the purchaser of any change in the disclosed terms and conditions of any lease or tenancy.

(5) If a lease or tenancy subject to which the property is sold terminates for any reason, the vendor shall inform the purchaser and, on being indemnified by the purchaser against all consequential loss, expenditure or liability, shall act as the purchaser may direct.

7 ERRORS, OMISSIONS AND MISSTATEMENTS

(1) No error, omission or misstatement herein or in any plan furnished or any statement made in the course of the negotiations leading to the contract shall annul the sale or entitle the purchaser to be discharged from the purchase.

(2) Any such error, omission or misstatement shown to be material shall entitle the purchaser or the vendor, as the case may be, to proper compensation, provided that the purchaser shall not in any event be entitled to compensation for matters falling within conditions 5 (2) or 6 (3).

(3) No immaterial error, omission or misstatement (including a mistake in any plan furnished for identification only) shall entitle either party to compensation.

(4) Sub-condition (1) shall not apply where compensation for any error, omission or misstatement shown to be material cannot be assessed nor enable either party to compel the other to accept or convey property differing substantially (in quantity, quality tenure or otherwise) from the property agreed to be sold if the other party would be prejudiced by the difference.

(5) The purchaser acknowledges that in making the contract he has not relied on any statement made to him save one made or confirmed in writing.

8 LEASEHOLDS

(1) This condition applies if the property is leasehold.

(2) In all cases the immediate title to the property shall begin with the lease. Where the lease, unless registered with absolute title, is dated not more than fifteen years before the date of the contract and was granted for a term exceeding twenty-one years, the freehold title and all other titles superior to the lease shall be deduced for a period beginning not less than fifteen years prior to the date of the contract and ending on the date of the lease.

(3) A copy of the lease and a copy of, sufficient extract from, or abstract of, all superior leases, the contents of which are known to the vendor, having been supplied or made available to the purchaser, he shall be deemed to purchase with full notice of the contents thereof, whether or not he has inspected the same.

(4) Where any consent to assign is necessary—

(*a*) the vendor shall forthwith at his own cost apply for and use his best endeavours to obtain such consent

(*b*) the purchaser shall forthwith supply such information and references as may reasonably be required by the reversioner before granting such consent

(*c*) if any such consent is not granted at least five working days before contractual completion date, or is subject to any condition to which the purchaser reasonably objects, either party may rescind the contract by notice to the other.

(5) Any statutory implied covenant on the part of the vendor shall not extend to any breach of the terms of the lease as to the state and condition of the property and the assignment shall so provide. This sub-condition applies notwithstanding that a special condition provides for the vendor to convey as beneficial owner.

(6) Where the property is sold subject to an apportioned rent specified as such in a special condition, the purchaser shall not require the consent of the reversioner to be obtained, or the rent to be otherwise legally apportioned.

(7) The purchaser shall assume that any receipt for the last payment due for rent under the lease before actual completion was given by the person then entitled to such rent or his duly authorised agent.

9 DEPOSIT

(1) The purchaser shall on or before the date of the contract pay by way of deposit to the vendor's solicitors as stakeholders the normal deposit, or such lesser sum as the vendor shall have agreed in writing. On a sale by private treaty, payment shall be made by banker's draft or by cheque drawn on a solicitors' bank account.

(2) Upon service by the vendor of a completion notice, the purchaser shall pay to the vendor any difference between the normal deposit and any amount actually paid (if less).

(3) If any draft, cheque or other instrument tendered in or towards payment of any sum payable under this condition is dishonoured when first presented the vendor shall have the right by notice to the purchaser within seven working days thereafter to treat the contract as repudiated.

10 OPTIONAL METHODS OF EXCHANGE

(1) Exchange of contracts may be effected by a method authorised by condition 2 for the service of notices. If so effected, the contract shall be made when the last part is, as the case may be, posted or delivered to a document exchange.

(2) Where contracts have not been exchanged, the parties' solicitors may agree by telephone or telex that the contract be immediately effective and thereupon the solicitors holding a part of the contract signed by their client shall hold it irrevocably to the order of the other party.

11 INSURANCE

(1) If the property is destroyed or damaged prior to actual completion and the proceeds of any insurance policy effected by or for the purchaser are reduced by reason of the existence of any policy effected by or for the vendor, the purchase price shall be abated by the amount of such reduction.

(2) Sub-condition (1) shall not apply where the proceeds of the vendor's policy are applied towards the reinstatement of the property pursuant to any statutory or contractual obligation.

(3) This condition takes effect in substitution for section 47 of the Law of Property Act 1925.

(4) The vendor shall be under no duty to the purchaser to maintain any insurance on the property, save where the property is leasehold and the vendor has an obligation to insure.

12 ABSTRACT OF TITLE

(1) Forthwith upon exchange of contracts the vendor shall deliver to the purchaser—

(*a*) where the title is not registered, an abstract of the title to the property or an epitome of the title together with photocopies of the relevant documents

(*b*) where the title is registered—

(i) the documents, particulars and information specified in sub-sections (1) and (2) of section 110 of the Land Registration Act 1925, save that copies of the entries on the register, the filed plan and any documents noted on the register and filed in the registry shall be office copies, and

(ii) such additional authorities to inspect the register as the purchaser shall reasonably require for any sub-purchaser or prospective mortgagee or lessee.

(2) Where the title is not registered, the vendor shall at his own expense produce the relevant documents of title or an abstract, epitome of title or copy thereof (bearing in each case original markings of examination of all relevant documents of title or of examined abstracts thereof).

(3) Where before the date of the contract any abstract, epitome or document has been delivered to the purchaser, he shall not, save as provided by conditions 6 (2) or 8 (3), be deemed to have had notice before the date of the contract of any matter of title thereby disclosed.

13 IDENTITY AND BOUNDARIES

(1) The vendor shall produce such evidence as may be reasonably necessary to establish the identity and extent of the property, but shall not be required to define exact boundaries, or the ownership of fences, ditches, hedges or walls, nor, beyond the evidence afforded by the information in his possession, separately to identify parts of the property held under different titles.

(2) If reasonably required by the purchaser because of the insufficiency of the evidence produced under sub-condition (1), the vendor shall at his own expense provide and hand over on completion a statutory declaration as to the relevant facts, in a form agreed by the purchaser, such agreement not to be unreasonably withheld.

14 MORTGAGES IN FAVOUR OF FRIENDLY AND OTHER SOCIETIES

Where the title includes a mortgage or legal charge in favour of trustees on behalf of a friendly society, a building society or a society registered under the Industrial and Provident Societies Acts, the purchaser shall assume that any receipt given on the discharge of any such mortgage or legal charge and apparently duly executed was in fact duly executed by all proper persons and is valid.

15 REQUISITIONS

(1) In this condition "abstract" means all the documents, particulars and information required to be delivered by the vendor under condition 12.

(2) Subject to sub-condition (4), the purchaser shall deliver any requisitions or objections relating to the title, evidence of title or the abstract, in writing within six working days of receipt of the abstract (or, in the case of an abstract delivered before the date of the contract, within six working days of the date of contract). Within four working days of such delivery the vendor shall deliver his replies in writing.

(3) The purchaser shall deliver any observations on any of the vendor's replies in writing within four working days of their receipt.

(4) Where some but not all parts of the abstract have been delivered, and defects in title are not disclosed by such parts of the abstract as have been delivered, then in respect only of the undelivered parts or undisclosed defects (as the case may be) the abstract shall be deemed to be received for the purpose of sub-condition (2) at the time or respective times when any previously undelivered part is delivered.

(5) Time shall be of the essence for the purposes of this condition.

16 RESCISSION

(1) If the vendor is unable, or on some reasonable ground unwilling, to satisfy any requisition or objection made by the purchaser, the vendor may give the purchaser notice (specifying the reason for his inability or the ground of his unwillingness) to withdraw the same. If the purchaser does not withdraw the same within seven working days of service, either party may thereafter, notwithstanding any intermediate negotiation or litigation, rescind the contract by notice to the other.

(2) Upon rescission under any power given by these conditions or any special condition—

(*a*) the vendor shall repay to the purchaser any sums paid by way of deposit or otherwise under the contract, with interest on such sums at the contract rate from four working days after rescission until payment

(*b*) the purchaser shall forthwith return all documents delivered to him by the vendor and at his own expense procure the cancellation of any entry relating to the contract in any register.

17 PREPARATION OF CONVEYANCE

(1) The purchaser shall deliver the draft conveyance at least twelve working days before contractual completion date, and within four working days of such delivery the vendor shall deliver it back approved or revised.

(2) The purchaser shall deliver the engrossment of the conveyance (first executed by him, where requisite) at least five working days before contractual completion date.

(3) The purchaser shall not, by delivering the draft conveyance or the engrossment, be deemed to accept the vendor's title or to waive any right to raise or maintain requisitions.

(4) Save to the extent that a covenant for indemnity will be implied by statute, the purchaser shall in the conveyance covenant to indemnify the vendor and his estate (and any estate of which the vendor is personal representative or trustee) against all actions, claims and liability for any breach of any covenant, stipulation, provision or other matter subject to which the property is sold and in respect of which the vendor or any such estate will remain liable after completion.

(5) The vendor shall give an acknowledgment for production and, unless in a fiduciary capacity, an undertaking for safe custody of documents of title retained by him. Where any such document is retained by a mortgagee, trustee or personal representative, the vendor shall procure that such person shall give an acknowledgment for production, and the vendor, unless in a fiduciary capacity, shall covenant that if and when he receives any such document he will, at the cost of the person requiring it, give an undertaking for safe custody.

(6) The vendor shall be entitled on reasonable grounds to decline to convey the property to any person other than the purchaser, by more than one conveyance, at more than the contract price or at a price divided between different parts of the property.

18 OCCUPATION BEFORE COMPLETION

(1) This condition applies if the vendor authorises the purchaser to occupy the property before actual completion, except—

(*a*) where the purchaser already lawfully occupies any part of the property, or

(*b*) where the property is a dwellinghouse and the authority for the occupation is only for the purpose of effecting works of decoration, repair or improvement agreed by the vendor.

(2) The purchaser occupies the property as licensee and not as tenant. The purchaser may not transfer his licence or authorise any other person save members of his immediate family to occupy any part of the property.

(3) The purchaser shall not, by taking such occupation, be deemed to accept the vendor's title or to waive any right to raise or maintain requisitions.

(4) While the purchaser is in occupation of the whole or any part of the property under this condition, he shall—

(*a*) pay and indemnify the vendor against all outgoings and any other expenses in respect of the property and pay to the vendor in respect of such occupation a sum calculated at the contract rate on the amount of the purchase money (less any deposit paid)

(*b*) be entitled to receive any rents and profits from any part of the property not occupied by him

(*c*) insure the property in a sum not less than the purchase price against all risks in respect of which premises of the like nature are normally insured.

(5) The purchaser's licence to occupy the property shall end—

(*a*) on contractual completion date, or

(*b*) upon termination of the contract, or

(*c*) upon the expiry of five working days' notice given by either party to the other,

and thereupon the purchaser shall give up occupation of the property and leave the same in as good repair as it was in when he went into occupation.

(6) If the purchaser, after his licence has ended under sub-condition 5(*a*), remains in occupation with the express or implied consent of the vendor, he shall thereafter occupy on the other terms of this condition and on the further term that the vendor's rights under condition 22 shall not thereby be affected.

19 APPORTIONMENTS

(1) In this condition—

(*a*) "the apportionment day" means—

(i) if the property is sold with vacant possession of the whole, the date of actual completion

(ii) in any other case, contractual completion date

(*b*) "payment period" means one of the periods for which a sum payable periodically is payable, whether or not such periods are of equal length.

(2) This condition shall not apply to any sum if—

(*a*) the purchaser cannot, by virtue only of becoming the owner of the property, either enforce payment of it or be obliged to pay it, or

(*b*) it is an outgoing paid in advance, unless the vendor cannot obtain repayment and the purchaser benefits therefrom or is given credit therefor against a sum that would otherwise be his liability.

(3) On completion the income and outgoings of the property shall, subject to sub-condition (2) and conditions 3 and 22(4) and to any adjustment required by condition 18(4), be apportioned as at the apportionment day.

(4) For the purposes of apportionment only, it shall be assumed—

(*a*) that the vendor remains owner of the property until the end of the apportionment day, and

(*b*) that the sum to be apportioned—

(i) accrues from day to day

(ii) is payable throughout the relevant period at the same rate as on the apportionment day.

(5) Sums payable periodically shall be apportioned by charging or allowing—

(*a*) for any payment period entirely attributable to one party, the whole of the instalment payable therefor

(*b*) for any part of a payment period, a proportion on an annual basis.

(6) (*a*) This sub-condition applies to any sum payable in respect of any period falling wholly or partly prior to the apportionment day, the amount of which is not notified to either party before actual completion

(*b*) A provisional apportionment shall be made on the best estimate available. Upon the amount being notified, a final apportionment shall be made and one party shall thereupon make to the other the appropriate balancing payment.

20 ENDORSEMENT OF MEMORANDUM

Where the vendor does not hand over all the documents of his title, he shall at completion endorse a memorandum of the sale to the purchaser on the last such document in each relevant title and thereupon produce the endorsed documents for inspection.

21 COMPLETION

(1) Contractual completion date shall be as stated in the special conditions but if not so stated shall be the twenty-fifth working day after the date of the contract. Completion shall take place in England or Wales either at the office of the vendor's solicitors or, if required by the vendor at least five working days prior to actual completion, at the office of the vendor's mortgagee or his solicitors.

(2) The vendor shall not be obliged to accept payment of the money due on completion otherwise than by one or more of the following methods—

(*a*) legal tender

(*b*) a banker's draft drawn by and upon a settlement bank for the purposes of the Clearing House Automated Payments System or any other bank specified in a special condition

(*c*) an unconditional authority to release any deposit held by a stakeholder

(*d*) otherwise as the vendor shall have agreed before actual completion.

(3) If completion is effected otherwise than by personal attendance the time for completion is when on a working day

(*a*) the money due on completion is paid to the vendor or his solicitors, and

(*b*) the vendor's solicitors hold to the order of the purchaser all the documents to which he is entitled on completion.

(4) For the purposes of this condition money is paid when the vendor receives payment by a method specified in sub-condition (2). Where the parties have agreed upon a direct credit to a bank account at a named branch, payment is made when that branch receives the credit.

(5) (*a*) This sub-condition applies if the money due on completion is not paid by 2.30 p.m. on the day of actual completion or by such other time on that day as is specified in a special condition

(*b*) For the purposes of condition 22 only, completion shall be deemed to be postponed by reason of the purchaser's delay from the day of actual completion until the next working day

(*c*) The purchaser shall not as a result of the deemed postponement of completion be liable to make any payment to the vendor unless the vendor claims such payment by giving notice at completion or within five working days thereafter (as to which period time shall be of the essence). Payment shall be due five working days after receipt of such notice.

22 COMPENSATION FOR LATE COMPLETION

(1) For the purposes of this condition—

(*a*) "delay" means failure to perform or lateness in performing any obligation of the contract which causes or contributes to lateness in completion

(*b*) a party is "in default" if and to the extent that the period, or the aggregate of the periods, of his delay exceeds the period, or the aggregate of the periods, of delay of the other party

(*c*) "the period of default" means the length of the excess defined in paragraph (*b*) or, if shorter, the period from contractual completion date to the date of actual completion.

(2) If the sale shall be completed after contractual completion date, the party in default (if any) shall be liable to compensate the other for loss occasioned to him by reason of that default.

(3) Before actual completion, or within five working days thereafter (as to which period time shall be of the essence), the party entitled to compensation may, by notice to the other party, opt to be paid or allowed a sum calculated at the contract rate on the amount of the purchase money (less any deposit paid) for the period of default as liquidated damages in settlement of his claim for compensation.

(4) If the vendor is entitled to compensation, he may, before actual completion, by notice to the purchaser, opt to take the net income of the property for the period of default in lieu of such compensation.

(5) The right to recover any compensation under this condition shall not be prejudiced by completion of the sale, whether before or after the commencement of proceedings.

23 COMPLETION NOTICE

(1) This condition applies unless a special condition provides that time is of the essence in respect of contractual completion date.

(2) If the sale shall not be completed on contractual completion date, either party, being then himself ready able and willing to complete, may after that date serve on the other party notice to complete the transaction in accordance with this condition. A party shall be deemed to be ready, able and willing to complete—

(*a*) if he could be so but for some default or omission of the other party

(*b*) notwithstanding that any mortgage on the property is unredeemed when the completion notice is served if the aggregate of all sums necessary to redeem all such mortgages (to the extent that they relate to the property) does not exceed the sum payable on completion.

(3) Upon service of a completion notice it shall become a term of the contract that the transaction shall be completed within fifteen working days of service and in respect of such period time shall be of the essence.

(4) If the purchaser does not comply with a completion notice—

(*a*) the purchaser shall forthwith return all documents delivered to him by the vendor and at his own expense procure the cancellation of any entry relating to the contract in any register

(*b*) without prejudice to any other rights or remedies available to him, the vendor may—

(i) forfeit and retain any deposit paid and/or

(ii) re-sell the property by auction, tender or private treaty.

(5) If on any such re-sale contracted within one year after contractual completion date the vendor incurs a loss and so elects by notice to the purchaser within one month after the contract for such re-sale, the purchaser shall pay to the vendor liquidated damages. The amount payable shall be the aggregate of such loss, all costs and expenses reasonably incurred in any such re-sale and any attempted re-sale and interest at the contract rate on such part of the purchase money as is from time to time outstanding (giving credit for all sums received under any re-sale contract on account of the re-sale price) after contractual completion date.

(6) If the vendor does not comply with a completion notice, the purchaser, without prejudice to any other rights or remedies available to him, may give notice to the vendor forthwith to pay to the purchaser any sums paid by way of deposit or otherwise under the contract and interest on such sums at the contract rate from four working days after service of the notice until payment. On compliance with such notice the purchaser shall not be entitled to specific performance of the contract, but shall forthwith return all documents delivered to him by the vendor and at the expense of the vendor procure the cancellation of any entry relating to the contract in any register.

(7) Where after service of a completion notice the time for completion shall have been extended by agreement or implication, either party may again invoke the provisions of this condition which shall then take effect with the substitution of "seven working days" for "fifteen working days" in sub-condition (3).

24 CHATTELS

The property in any chattels agreed to be sold shall pass to the purchaser on actual completion.

25 AUCTIONS

(1) This condition applies if the property is sold by auction.

(2) The sale is subject to a reserve price for the property and, when the property is sold in lots, for each lot.

(3) The vendor reserves the right—

(*a*) to divide the property into lots and to sub-divide, re-arrange or consolidate any lots

(*b*) to bid personally or by his agent up to any reserve price

(*c*) without disclosing any reserve price, to withdraw from the sale any property or lot at any time before it has been sold, whether or not the sale has begun.

(4) The auctioneer may—

(*a*) refuse to accept a bid

(*b*) in the case of a dispute as to any bid, forthwith determine the dispute or again put up the property or lot at the last undisputed bid.

(5) The purchaser shall forthwith complete and sign the contract and pay, but not necessarily by the means specified in condition 9(1), the normal deposit.

SPECIAL CONDITIONS

A. The property is sold subject to The Law Society's General Conditions of Sale (1984 Revision) ("general conditions") printed within so far as they are not varied by or inconsistent with these special conditions but general condition 8(5) shall apply in any event.

B. For the purposes of the following general conditions—

1(*b*) the contract rate is % per annum above the base rate from time to time of

1(c) contractual completion date is 198

21(2)(*b*) the specified bank is

21(5)(a) the latest time is am/pm

1(g) the following are not working days

5(3) the retained land is

C. General condition 4 shall not apply. [For the purposes of general condition 4(2) the period shall be from the date hereof and for the purposes of general condition 4(3)(*b*) the specified use is .]

D. The Vendor shall convey as

E. The Vendor's title is registered with title under Title No. in the District Land Registry.
The Vendor authorises the Purchaser's solicitors to inspect the register and to obtain office copies thereof.

(or) E. The abstract of title shall begin with

F. The property is sold with vacant possession on completion.

(or) F. The property is sold subject to the following leases or tenancies

G. The property is sold subject to

CONTRACT OF SALE

The National Conditions of Sale, Twentieth Edition

Vendor

Purchaser

Registered Land	Purchase price	£
District Land Registry:	Deposit	£
Title Number:	Balance payable	£
Agreed rate of interest:	Price fixed for chattels or valuation money (if any)	£
	Total	£

Property and interest therein sold

Vendor sells as

Completion date:

AGREED that the Vendor sells and the Purchaser buys as above, subject to the Special Conditions endorsed hereon and to the National Conditions of Sale Twentieth Edition so far as the latter Conditions are not inconsistent with the Special Conditions.

* *Signed*

Date 19

*** This is a form of legal document. Neither the form nor the National Conditions of Sale which the form embodies, were produced or drafted for use, without technical assistance, by persons unfamiliar with the law and practice of conveyancing.**

The National Conditions of Sale

20th Edition first published December 1981

Construction of the conditions

In these conditions, where the context admits--
(1) The "vendor" and the "purchaser" include the persons deriving title under them respectively
(2) "Purchase money" includes any sum to be paid for chattels, fittings or other separate items
(3) References to the "Special Conditions" include references to the particulars of sale and to the provisions of the contract which is made by reference to the conditions
(4) The "prescribed rate" means the agreed rate of interest or, if none, then the rate of interest prescribed from time to time under Land Compensation Act 1961, s. 32
(5) "Solicitor" includes a barrister who is employed by a corporate body to carry out conveyancing on its behalf and is acting in the course of his employment
(6) "Working day" means a day on which clearing banks in the City of London are (or would be but for a strike, lock-out, or other stoppage, affecting particular banks or banks generally) open during banking hours Except in condition 19(4), in which "working day" means a day when the Land Registry is open to the public
(7) "Designated bank" means a bank designated by the Chief Registrar under Building Societies Act 1962, s. 59
(8) The "Planning Acts" means the enactments from time to time in force relating to town and country planning
(9) On a sale by private treaty references to the "auctioneer" shall be read as references to the vendor's agent
(10) On a sale in lots, the conditions apply to each lot
(11) "Abstract of title" means in relation to registered land such documents as the vendor is required by Land Registration Act 1925, s. 110, to furnish.

The conditions

1. The Sale: by Auction: by Private Treaty
(1) Paragraphs (2) to (5) of this condition apply on a sale by auction and paragraphs (6) and (7) on a sale by private treaty
(2) Unless otherwise provided in the Special Conditions, the sale of the property and of each lot is subject to a reserve price and to a right for the vendor or any one person on behalf of the vendor to bid up to that price
(3) The auctioneer may refuse any bid and no person shall at any bid advance less than the amount fixed for that purpose by the auctioneer
(4) If any dispute arises respecting a bid, the auctioneer may determine the dispute or the property may, at the vendor's option, either be put up again at the last undisputed bid, or be withdrawn
(5) Subject to the foregoing provisions of this condition, the highest bidder shall be the purchaser and shall forthwith complete and sign the contract, the date of which shall be the date of the auction
(6) Where there is a draft contract, or an arrangement subject to contract, or a negotiation in which there are one or more outstanding items or suspensory matters (which prevent there being yet a concluded agreement of a contractual nature), a solicitor, who holds a document signed by his client in the form of a contract of sale in writing and embodying this condition, shall (unless the other party or his solicitor is informed to the contrary) have the authority of his client to conclude, by formal exchange of contracts, or by post, or by telex or other telegraphic means, or by telephone, and in any case with or without involving solicitors' undertakings, a binding contract in the terms of the document which his client has signed
(7) The date of the contract shall be--
(i) the date, if any, which is agreed and put on the contract, but if none, then
(ii) on an exchange of contracts by post (unless the parties' solicitors otherwise agree), the date on which the last part of the contract is posted, or
(iii) in any other case, the date on which, consistently with this condition, a binding contract is concluded.

2. Deposit
(1) Unless the Special Conditions otherwise provide, the purchaser shall on the date of the contract pay a deposit of 10 per cent. of the purchase price, on a sale by auction, to the auctioneer, or on a sale by private treaty, to the vendor's solicitor and, in either case, as stakeholder
(2) In case a cheque taken for the deposit (having been presented, and whether or not it has been re-presented) has not been honoured, then and on that account the vendor may elect--
either (i) to treat the contract as discharged by breach thereof on the purchaser's part
or (ii) to enforce payment of the deposit as a deposit, by suing on the cheque or otherwise.

3. Purchaser's short right to rescind
(1) This condition shall have effect if the Special Conditions so provide, but not otherwise
(2) If the property is affected by any matter to which this condition applies, then the purchaser may by notice in writing (hereinafter referred to as a "Condition 3 Notice") given to the vendor or his solicitor and expressly referring to this condition and the matter in question, and notwithstanding any intermediate negotiation, rescind the contract on the same terms as if the purchaser had persisted in an objection to the title which the vendor was unable to remove
(3) A Condition 3 Notice shall not be given after the expiration of 16 working days from the date of the contract, time being of the essence of this condition
(4) This condition applies to any matter materially affecting the value of the property, other than--
(i) a matter which was not yet in existence or subsisting at the date of the contract
(ii) a specific matter to which the sale was expressly made subject, or
(iii) a matter of which the purchaser had at the date of the contract express notice or actual knowledge, not being notice or knowledge imputed to the purchaser by statute solely by reason of a registration of such matter, or notice or knowledge which the purchaser is only deemed to have had by the conditions
(5) This condition and condition 15 are additional to each other.

4. Chattels, etc., and separate items
If the sale includes chattels, fittings or other separate items, the vendor warrants that he is entitled to sell the same free from any charge, lien, burden, or adverse claim.

5. Date and manner of completion
(1) The completion date shall be the date specified for the purpose in the contract or, if none, the 26th working day after the date of the contract or the date of delivery of the abstract of title, whichever be the later
(2) Unless the Special Conditions otherwise provide, in respect of the completion date time shall not be of the essence of the contract, but this provision shall operate subject and without prejudice to--
(i) the provisions of condition 22 and
(ii) the rights of either party to recover from the other damages for delay in fulfilling his obligations under the contract
(3) The purchaser's obligations to pay money due on completion shall be discharged by one or more of the following methods--
(i) authorisation in writing to release a deposit held for the purposes of the contract by a stakeholder
(ii) banker's draft issued by a designated bank
(iii) cheque drawn on and guaranteed by a designated bank
(iv) telegraphic or other direct transfer (as requested or agreed to by the vendor's solicitor) to a particular bank or branch for the credit of a specified account
(v) legal tender
(vi) any other method requested or agreed to by the vendor's solicitor
(4) Completion shall be carried out, either formally at such office or place as the vendor's solicitor shall reasonably require, or (if the parties' solicitors so arrange) by post, or by means of solicitors' undertakings concerning the holding of documents or otherwise Provided that on a sale with vacant possession of the whole or part of the property, if the conveyance or transfer will not, by overreaching or otherwise, discharge the property from interests (if any) of persons in, or who may be in, actual occupation of the property or such part of it, then (subject always to the rights of the purchaser under Law of Property Act 1925, s. 42 (1)), the purchaser may, by giving reasonable notice, require that on, or immediately before the time of, completion possession of the property or part be handed over to the purchaser or his representative at the property
(5) The date of actual completion shall be the day on which, the contract being completed in other respects, the purchaser has discharged consistently with the provisions of this condition the obligations of the purchaser to pay the money due on completion Provided that--
(i) for the purposes only of conditions 6, 7 and 8, if but for this proviso the date of actual completion would be the last working day of a week (starting on Sunday) and the purchaser is unable or unwilling to complete before 2.15 p.m. on that day, then the date of actual completion shall be taken to be the first working day thereafter
(ii) a remittance sent by post or delivered by hand shall be treated as being made on the day on which it reaches the vendor's solicitor's office, unless that day is not a working day in which case the remittance shall be treated as being made on the first working day thereafter.

6. Rents, outgoings and apportionments
The purchase being completed (whether on the completion date or subsequently), the income and outgoings shall be apportioned as follows (the day itself in each case being apportioned to the vendor):—
(1) In a case to which proviso (i) to condition 7 (1) applies apportionment shall be made as at the date of actual completion
(2) In a case in which the purchaser is in possession of the whole of the property as lessee or tenant at a rent apportionment shall be made as at the date of actual completion unless proviso (ii) to condition 7 (1) applies, when apportionment shall be made as at the date of the purchaser's notice under that proviso
(3) In any other case apportionment shall be made as from the completion date Provided nevertheless that, if delay is attributable to the vendor's failure to obtain the reversioner's licence, where necessary, or if the vendor remains in beneficial occupation of the property after the completion date, the purchaser may by notice in writing before actual completion elect that apportionment shall be made as at the date of actual completion
(4) Rates shall be apportioned according to the period for which they are intended to provide and rents (whether payable in advance or in arrear) according to the period in respect of which they have been paid or are payable; and apportionment of yearly items (whether or not the same are payable by equal quarterly, monthly or other instalments) shall be according to the relevant number of days relatively to the number of days in the full year
(5) Service charges under leases, in the absence of known or readily ascertainable amounts, shall be apportioned according to the best estimate available at the time of completion and, unless otherwise agreed, the vendor and the purchaser shall be and remain mutually bound after completion to account for and pay or allow to each other, within 15 working days after being informed of the actual amounts as ascertained, any balances or excesses due.

7. Interest
(1) If the purchase shall not be completed on the completion date then (subject to the provisions of paragraph (2) of this condition) the purchaser shall pay interest on the remainder of his purchase money at the prescribed rate from that date until the purchase shall actually be completed Provided nevertheless--
(i) That (without prejudice to the operation of proviso (ii) to this paragraph) the vendor may by notice in writing before actual completion elect to take the income of the property (less outgoings) up to the date of actual completion instead of interest as aforesaid
(ii) That, if the delay arises from any cause other than the neglect or default of the purchaser, and if the purchaser (not being in occupation of the property in circumstances to which condition 8 applies) places the remainder of his purchase money (at his own risk) at interest on a deposit account in England or Wales with any designated bank,and gives written notice thereof to the vendor or his solicitor, then in lieu of the interest or income payable to or receivable by the vendor as aforesaid, the vendor shall from the time of such notice be entitled to such interest only as is produced by such deposit
(iii) That the vendor shall in no case be or become entitled in respect of the same period of time both to be paid interest and to enjoy income of the property, or to be paid interest more than once on the same sum of money
(2) The purchaser shall not be liable to pay interest under paragraph (1) of this condition—
(i) so long as, or to the extent that, delay in completion is attributable to any act or default of the vendor or his mortgagee or Settled Land Act trustees
(ii) in case the property is to be constructed or converted by the vendor, so long as the construction or conversion is unfinished.

8. Occupation pending completion
(1) If the purchaser (not being already in occupation as lessee or tenant at a rent) is let into occupation of the property before the actual completion of the purchase, then, as from the date of his going into occupation and until actual completion, or until upon discharge or rescission of the contract he ceases to occupy the property, the purchaser shall--
(i) be the licensee and not the tenant of the vendor
(ii) pay interest on the remainder of the purchase money at the prescribed rate
(iii) keep the property in as good repair and condition as it was in when he went into occupation
(iv) pay, or otherwise indemnify the vendor against, all outgoings and expenses (including the cost of insurance) in respect of the property, the purchaser at the same time taking or being credited with the income of the property (if any)
(v) not carry out any development within the meaning of the Planning Acts
(2) Upon discharge or rescission of the contract, or upon the expiration of 7 working days' or longer notice given by the vendor or his solicitor to the purchaser or his solicitor in that behalf, the purchaser shall forthwith give up the property in such repair and condition as aforesaid
(3) A purchaser going into occupation before completion shall not be deemed thereby to have accepted the vendor's title
(4) Where the purchaser is allowed access to the property for the purpose only of carrying out works or installations, the purchaser shall not be treated as being let into occupation within the meaning of this condition.

9. Abstract, requisitions and observations
(1) The vendor shall deliver the abstract of title not later than 11 working days after the date of the contract but, subject and without prejudice as mentioned in condition 5 (2), that time limit shall not be of the essence of the contract
(2) Subject always to the rights of the purchaser under Law of Property Act 1925, s. 42(1), the vendor may be required by the purchaser to deal with requisitions and observations concerning persons who are or may be in occupation or actual occupation of the property, so as to satisfy the purchaser that the title is not, and that the purchaser will not be, prejudicially affected by any interests or claims of such persons.

(3) The purchaser shall deliver in writing his requisitions within 11 working days after delivery of the abstract, and his observations on the replies to the requisitions within 6 working days after delivery of the replies
(4) In respect of the delivery of requisitions and observations, time shall be of the essence of the contract, notwithstanding that the abstract may not have been delivered within due time
(5) The purchaser shall deliver his requisitions and observations on the abstract as delivered, whether it is a perfect or an imperfect abstract, but for the purposes of any requisitions or observations which could not be raised or made on the information contained in an imperfect abstract, time under paragraph (3) of this condition shall not start to run against the purchaser, until the vendor has delivered the further abstract or information on which the requisitions or observations arise
(6) Subject to his requisitions and observations, the purchaser shall be deemed to have accepted the title.

10. Vendor's right to rescind
(1) If the purchaser shall persist in any objection to the title which the vendor shall be unable or unwilling, on reasonable grounds, to remove, and shall not withdraw the same within 10 working days of being required so to do, the vendor may, subject to the purchaser's rights under Law of Property Act 1925, ss. 42 and 125, by notice in writing to the purchaser or his solicitor, and notwithstanding any intermediate negotiation or litigation, rescind the contract
(2) Upon such rescission the vendor shall return the deposit, but without interest, costs of investigating title or other compensation or payment, and the purchaser shall return the abstract and other papers furnished to him.

11. Existing leaseholds
(1) Where the interest sold is leasehold for the residue of an existing term the following provisions of this condition shall apply
(2) The lease or underlease or a copy thereof having been made available, the purchaser (whether he has inspected the same or not) shall be deemed to have bought with full notice of the contents thereof
(3) On production of a receipt for the last payment due for rent under the lease or underlease, the purchaser shall assume without proof that the person giving the receipt, though not the original lessor, is the reversioner expectant on the said lease or underlease or his duly authorised agent
(4) No objection shall be taken on account of the covenants in an underlease not corresponding with the covenants in any superior lease
(5) The sale is subject to the reversioner's licence being obtained, where necessary. The purchaser supplying such information and references, if any, as may reasonably be required of him, the vendor will use his best endeavours to obtain such licence and will pay the fee for the same. But if the licence cannot be obtained, the vendor may rescind the contract on the same terms as if the purchaser had persisted in an objection to the title which the vendor was unable to remove
(6) Where the property comprises part only of the property comprised in a lease or underlease, the rent, covenants and conditions shall, if the purchaser so requires, be legally apportioned at his expense, but completion shall not be delayed on that account and in the meantime the apportionment by the auctioneer shall be accepted, or the property may at the option of the vendor be sub-demised for the residue of the term, less one day, at a rent apportioned by the auctioneer and subject to the purchaser executing a counterpart containing covenants and provisions corresponding to those contained in the lease or underlease aforesaid
(7) Any statutory covenant to be implied in the conveyance on the part of a vendor shall be so limited as not to affect him with liability for a subsisting breach of any convenant or condition concerning the state or condition of the property, of which state and condition the purchaser is by paragraph (3) of condition 13 deemed to have full notice, and where Land Registration Act 1925, s. 24, applies the purchaser, if required, will join in requesting that an appropriate entry be made in the register.

12. Vendor's duty to produce documents
(1) If an abstracted document refers to any plan material to the description of the property, or to any covenants contained in a document earlier in date than the document with which the title commences, and such plan or earlier document is in the possession or power of the vendor or his trustees or mortgagee, the vendor shall supply a copy thereof with the abstract
(2) If the property is sold subject to restrictive covenants, the deed imposing those covenants or a copy thereof having been made available, the purchaser (whether he has inspected the same or not) shall be deemed to have purchased with full knowledge thereof
(3) The vendor shall not be required to procure the production of any document not in his possession or not in the possession of his mortgagee or trustees, and of which the vendor cannot obtain production, or to trace or state who has the possession of the same.

13. Identity: boundaries: condition of property
(1) The purchaser shall admit the identity of the property with that comprised in the muniments offered by the vendor as the title thereto upon the evidence afforded by the descriptions contained in such muniments, and of a statutory declaration, to be made (if required) at the purchaser's expense, that the property has been enjoyed according to the title for at least twelve years
(2) The vendor shall not be bound to show any title to boundaries, fences, ditches, hedges or walls, or to distinguish parts of the property held under different titles further than he may be able to do from information in his possession
(3) The purchaser shall be deemed to buy with full notice in all respects of the actual state and condition of the property and, save where it is to be constructed or converted by the vendor, shall take the property as it is.

14. Property sold subject to easements, etc.
Without prejudice to the duty of the vendor to disclose all latent easements and latent liabilities known to the vendor to affect the property, the property is sold subject to any rights of way and water, rights of common, and other rights, easements, quasi-easements, liabilities and public rights affecting the same.

15. Town and Country Planning
(1) In this condition, where the context admits, references to "authorised use" are references to "established use", or to use for which permission has been granted under the Planning Acts, or to use for which permission is not required under those Acts, as the case may be
(2) The purchaser shall be entitled to deliver, with his requisitions in respect of the title, requisitions concerning the authorised use of the property for the purposes of the Planning Acts. The vendor in reply shall give all such relevant information as may be in his possession or power
(3) Where the property is in the Special Conditions expressed to be sold on the footing of an authorised use which is specified, then if it appears before actual completion of the purchase that the specified use is not an authorised use of the property for the purposes of the Planning Acts, the purchaser may by notice in writing rescind the contract, and thereupon paragraph (2) of condition 10 shall apply. But, subject to the foregoing provisions of this condition, the purchaser shall be deemed to have accepted that the specified use is an authorised use of the property for the purposes of the Planning Acts
(4) Save as mentioned in the Special Conditions, the property is not to the knowledge of the vendor subject to any charge, notice, order, restriction, agreement or other matter arising under the Planning Acts, but (without prejudice to any right of the purchaser to rescind the contract under paragraph (3) of this condition) the property is sold subject to any such charges, notices, orders, restrictions, agreements and matters affecting the interest sold
(5) Subject as hereinbefore provided, and without prejudice to the obligations of the vendor to supply information as aforesaid, the purchaser shall be deemed to buy with knowledge in all respects of the authorised use of the property for the purposes of the Planning Acts.

16. Requirements by local authority
(1) If after the date of the contract any requirement in respect of the property be made against the vendor by any local authority, the purchaser shall comply with the same at his own expense, and indemnify the vendor in respect thereof: in so far as the purchaser shall fail to comply with such requirement, the vendor may comply with the same wholly or in part and any money so expended by the vendor shall be repaid by the purchaser on completion
(2) The vendor shall upon receiving notice of any such requirement forthwith inform the purchaser thereof.

17. Errors, mis-statements or omissions
(1) Without prejudice to any express right of either party, or to any right of the purchaser in reliance on Law of Property Act 1969, s. 24, to rescind the contract before completion and subject to the provisions of paragraph (2) of this condition, no error, mis-statement or omission in any preliminary answer concerning the property, or in the sale plan or the Special Conditions, shall annul the sale, nor (save where the error, mis-statement or omission relates to a matter materially affecting the description or value of the property) shall any damages be payable, or compensation allowed by either party, in respect thereof
(2) Paragraph (1) of this condition shall not apply to any error, mis-statement or, omission which is recklessly or fraudulently made, or to any matter or thing by which the purchaser is prevented from getting substantially what he contracted to buy
(3) In this condition a "preliminary answer" means and includes any statement made by or on behalf of the vendor to the purchaser or his agents or advisers, whether in answer to formal preliminary enquiries or otherwise, before the purchaser entered into the contract.

18. Leases and tenancies
(1) Abstracts or copies of the leases or agreements (if in writing) under which the tenants hold having been made available, the purchaser (whether he has inspected the same or not) shall be deemed to have notice of and shall take subject to the terms of all the existing tenancies and the rights of the tenants, whether arising during the continuance or after the expiration thereof, and such notice shall not be affected by any partial or incomplete statement in the Special Conditions with reference to the tenancies, and no objection shall be taken on account of there not being an agreement in writing with any tenant
(2) Where a lease or tenancy affects the property sold and other property, the property sold will be conveyed with the benefit of the apportioned rent (if any) mentioned in the Special Conditions or (if not so mentioned) fixed by the auctioneer, and no objection shall be taken on the ground that the consent of the tenant has not been obtained to the apportionment and the purchaser shall not require the rent to be legally apportioned
(3) The purchaser shall keep the vendor indemnified against all claims by the tenant for compensation or otherwise, except in respect of a tenancy which expires or is determined on or before the completion date or in respect of an obligation which ought to have been discharged before the date of the contract
(4) Land in the occupation of the vendor is sold subject to the right (hereby reserved to him) to be paid a fair price for tillages, off-going and other allowances as if he were an outgoing tenant who had entered into occupation of the land after 1st March 1948, and as if the purchaser were the landlord, and in case of dispute such price shall be fixed by the valuation of a valuer, to be nominated in case the parties differ by the President of the Royal Institution of Chartered Surveyors.

19. Preparation of conveyance: priority notices: indemnities
(1) Where the interest sold is leasehold for a term of years to be granted by the vendor, the lease or underlease and counterpart shall be prepared by the vendor's solicitor in accordance (as nearly as the circumstances admit) with a form or draft annexed to the contract or otherwise sufficiently identified by the signatures of the parties or their solicitors
(2) In any other case the conveyance shall be prepared by the purchaser or his solicitor and the following provisions of this condition shall apply
(3) The draft conveyance shall be delivered at the office of the vendor's solicitor at least 6 working days before the completion date and the engrossment for execution by the vendor and other necessary parties (if any) shall be left at the said office within 3 working days after the draft has been returned to the purchaser approved on behalf of the vendor and other necessary parties (if any)
(4) Where the property is unregistered land not in an area of compulsory registration and the conveyance is to contain restrictive covenants, and the purchaser intends contemporaneously with the conveyance to execute a mortgage or conveyance to a third party, he shall inform the vendor of his intention and, if necessary, allow the vendor to give a priority notice for the registration of the intended covenants at least 15 working days before the contract is completed
(5) Where the property is sold subject to legal incumbrances, the purchaser shall covenant to indemnify the vendor against actions and claims in respect of them; and the purchaser will not make any claim on account of increased expense caused by the concurrence of any legal incumbrancer
(6) Where the property is sold subject to stipulations, or restrictive or other covenants, and breach thereof would expose the vendor to liability, the purchaser shall covenant to observe and perform the same and to indemnify the vendor against actions and claims in respect thereof
(7) Paragraphs (5) and (6) of this condition shall have effect without prejudice to the provisions of Law of Property Act 1925, s. 77, and Land Registration Act 1925, s. 24, where such provisions respectively are applicable, and in respect of matters covered by a covenant implied under either of those sections no express covenant shall be required.

20. Severance of properties formerly in common ownership
Where the property and any adjacent or neighbouring property have hitherto been in common ownership, the purchaser shall not become entitled to any right to light or air over or in respect of any adjacent or neighbouring property which is retained by the vendor and the conveyance shall, if the vendor so requires, reserve to him such easements and rights as would become appurtenant to such last-mentioned property by implication of law, if the vendor had sold it to another purchaser at the same time as he has sold the property to the purchaser.

21. Insurance
(1) With respect to any policy of insurance maintained by the vendor in respect of damage to or destruction of the property, the vendor shall not (save pursuant to an obligation to a third party) be bound to keep such insurance on foot or to give notice to the purchaser of any premium being or becoming due
(2) The purchaser shall be entitled to inspect the policy at any time
(3) The vendor shall, if required, by and at the expense of the purchaser obtain or consent to an endorsement of notice of the purchaser's interest on the policy, and in such case the vendor (keeping the policy on foot) may require the purchaser to pay on completion a proportionate part of the premium from the date of the contract

22. Special notice to complete
(1) At any time on or after the completion date, either party, being ready and willing to fulfil his own outstanding obligations under the contract, may (without prejudice to any other right or remedy available to him) give to the other party or his solicitor notice in writing requiring completion of the contract in conformity with this condition
(2) Upon service of such notice as aforesaid it shall become and be a term of the contract, in respect of which time shall be of the essence thereof, that the party to whom the notice is given shall complete the contract within 16 working days after service of the notice (exclusive of the day of service): but this condition shall operate without prejudice to any right of either party to rescind the contract in the meantime
(3) In case the purchaser refuses or fails to complete in conformity with this condition, then (without prejudice to any other right or remedy available to the vendor) the purchaser's deposit may be forfeited (unless the court otherwise directs) and, if the vendor resells the property within twelve months of the expiration of the said period of 16 working days, he shall be entitled (upon crediting the deposit) to recover from the purchaser hereunder the amount of any loss occasioned to the vendor by expenses of or incidental to such resale, or by diminution in the price

Re: : to

SPECIAL CONDITIONS OF SALE

A. Condition 3 of the National Conditions of Sale shall [not] have effect [But it shall not apply to a matter or matters affecting the value of the property by less than £ or to the following:—

]

B. Title shall be deduced and shall commence as follows:—

C. The sale is with vacant possession/subject to the existing tenancy of which details have been supplied to the Purchaser/subject to the following tenancies:—

D. The property is sold on the footing that the authorised use thereof for the purposes of the Planning Acts is the use (if any) specified in the particulars of sale/use as

E. The sale includes the chattels fittings and separate items specified in the inventory annexed which are to be taken by the Purchaser for a sum (additional to the purchase price of the property) of £ / to be ascertained by a valuation to be made by
at the expense of

F. The property is sold subject so far as they are subsisting and capable of being enforced or of taking effect to the restrictions and stipulations

oyez
THE SOLICITORS' LAW STATIONERY SOCIETY plc
Oyez House, 237 Long Lane, London SE1 4PU
F3419 BM35871 8/83
Form Con 14 —with special conditions
★ ★ ★

INDEX

Access. *See* Easement; Path; Road.
Additional Enquiries,
  Bristol area, in, *re* limestone quarrying, 115
  canals, *re*, 118
  caravan site,
    site licence, planning permission and relevant agreements, 70
  "chain", to establish whether a conveyancing, 69, 135, 152
  chattels, *re*, 69, 151, 157,
    no hire purchase, etc. agreement *re*, 138, 151, 157
  coal mines,
    areas of, in, 113, 151. *See also* Subsidence.
    proposed, 113
  condition of property, 68, 151
  Cornwall, in,
    clay working, *re*, 115
    tin mining, *re* subsidence from, 115
  Derbyshire, in, *re* limestone quarrying, 114
  development, proposed, 70, 157
  Devon, in, *re* clay working, 115
  discharge effluent, licence to, 117
  drain,
    route of, 117. *See also* Drainage.
  Dudley, properties in, *re* subsidence, 114
  duty to make, 4
  electric cables and installations *re*, 118
  fee for, proposed, 6
  garage, 69, 151
  gas pipes, location of, 119. *See also* Gas.
  heating appliances complying with smokeless zone order, 80
  information memo, 69, 138, 153–156
    useful addresses, 155–156
    keys, 154
Additional Enquiries—*cont.*
  limestone working, *re*, 114. *See also* Subsidence.
  local authority, of, 174–176
    building regulation consents, copies of, 87
  parking restrictions, 69, 151
  pipelines, *re*, 122. *See also* Pipeline.
  pond or lake,
    permission to obstruct watercourse to make, 117
  potato quota, *re*, 70
  railway,
    fences abutting on, 115–116
    tunnels, 116
  river,
    maintenance of bank, 116
  Sandwell, properties in, *re* subsidence, 114
  services, further details of, 68, 69, 151, 157. *See also* Services.
  sewer,
    route of, 117. *See also* Drainage.
  subsidence, *re* possibility of. *See* Subsidence.
  telecommunications,
    location of equipment, 120
  vendor, of,
    special, 70
    standard, 68–70, 151, 157
    subsidence, *re*, 68
  Walsall, properties in, *re* subsidence, 114
  water authority, of, 116–118. *See also* Water.
  water, licence to abstract, 117
  water pipe,
    building work proposed over, 117
    route of, 117
  watercourse, permission to obstruct, 117

Additional Enquiries—*cont.*
 Wolverhampton, properties in,
  re subsidence, 114
Adverse Possession,
 driveway, of, 28–30
 garage, of, 30
 squatters,
  inspection to ascertain rights of, 111
  overriding interest, can have. *See* Occupation, Persons in.
  rights of, against purchaser, 111
Adverse Rights. *See also* Easement; Overriding Interest; Restrictions; Restrictive Covenant.
 beneficial interest, owner of a,
  receipt for purchase money, must join in, 38
  separate legal advice, should have, 39
 disclose, duty to. *See also* Disclose, Duty to.
  latent defect in title, amounting to, 5
  standard conditions of sale, under, 5, 19, 30, 180, 185
 easements as, 30, 31. *See also* Easements.
 examples of, 31
 inspection to ascertain, 111
 notice of, 32, 34–36, 40–41
  inspection to ascertain, 111
  tenant and intermediate landlord, of, 40–41
 minor interests. *See* Minor Interest.
 mutual benefit and burden, 32
 occupation, rights of persons in. *See* Occupation, Persons in.
 overriding interests. *See* Overriding Interest.
 preliminary enquiries *re*, 30–42, 128, 132, 137
 rent charges burdening property, 30, 31
 rents and profits, belonging to persons in receipt of, 40–42
Adverse Rights—*cont.*
 sale subject to,
  standard conditions of sale, under, 30, 180, 185
 squatters' rights, 42
 washing, right to hang, 31
 water, right to extract,
  burdening property, 30, 31, 132
Advertisements, Control of Display, 98–99, 112, 166, 174
 area of special control, 99, 166, 174
 deemed consent, 99, 166, 174
 discontinuance notice, 99, 166, 174
 register of consents for, 98
  inspection of, 112, 166, 174
Agent,
 completion by post,
  vendor's solicitor as, 53, 177
 misrepresentation by, 8, 11–12, 13
  indemnity for vendor, 14
  innocent, 14
 vendor of,
  authority, no,
   representations, to make, 11
Agreement,
 adversely affecting land, 30–42
 ancient monument, *re*, 30, 128
 burdening land, 30–42
  inspection to ascertain, 111
 informal, use of land, for, 30–42
  inspection to ascertain, 111
 local authority and builder, between,
  drainage and sewers, contruction and maintenance of, s.18 Public Health Act 1936, 23–24, 82, 127, 163, 171
  roads, construction and maintenance of, s.38 Highways Act 1980, 20, 23–24, 77, 127, 137, 162, 170

Agent—*cont.*
local authority, with,
combined drainage for, under s.38 Public Health Act 1936, 82, 163, 171
Agriculture,
potato quota, basic area for, 70
Agricultural Tenancy. *See also* Leasehold Properties; Tenancy, Property Subject to a.
agricultural holding, 147 *et seq.*, 149–150
breach of covenant, 148
copies of relevant documents, 147
disputes with landlord, 148
insurance, 147
notices of or to local authority, 147
orders of court, local authority, etc., 147
preliminary enquiries *re*, 67, 147
rent revision, 148
subletting, 147
tenant, identity of, 147
tied cottage, 67, 147 *et seq.*, 148–149
Alterations to Property,
building regulation consent, requiring, 42, 128, 131, 138
consents necessary for, 42, 128, 131, 138
leasehold property, 57, 130, 140
disclose building work, generally no duty to, 24
guarantees for work. *See* Guarantees.
inspection to check, 111
neighbouring property, proposed, 70, 157
planning permission, requiring, 43 *et seq.*, 131, 138
permitted development, 89–90
rateable value liable to alteration, 50–52, 129, 131
Boundaries,
canal, 118
dispute *re*, 17–18, 127, 131, 137
inspection before contract to avoid, 111
fences,
new properties, 54, 131
railway, abutting on, 115–116
permitted development, 90
inspection to confirm description and plan, 111
maintenance of, 15–16
new properties,
dimensions of plot, confirmation of, 131
ownership of, 15–16, 127, 131, 136
party walls, 16–17, 131
agreement *re*, 27, 28
plan of, 16, 30, 131
inspection to check, 111
Land Registry, 16
local authority enquiries, for, 161
misrepresentation where inaccurate, 16
preliminary enquiries *re*, 15 *et seq.*, 127, 131, 136
walls,
permitted development, 90
Building Regulations,
cavity wall insulation, 111
consent,
preliminary enquiry *re*, 42, 128, 131, 138
copies of, 87, 129, 159
duty of care of local authority, owners and subsequent owners, to, 87
infringement of, 87
negligence of inspector in inspecting foundations, 87
proceedings for, 86, 162, 170
London Building Acts,
notices served under, 109, 173
N.H.B.C. supervision, 47
notice of building works to local authority, 87
purpose of, 87

Building Regulations—*cont.*
  sewer or drain, building work proposed over, 117
  water pipe, building work proposed over, 117
Building Work. *See* Alterations to Property.

Caravan Site, 70
Central Heating. *See* Services.
"Chain" Transaction,
  misrepresentation in replies to preliminary enquiries,
    damages to third parties, 13
  misstatement, negligent, vendor's solicitor, by,
    third parties, liability to, 15
  preliminary enquiry to ascertain whether, 69, 135, 152
Charges, Annual or Periodic,
  preliminary enquiries *re*, 50–52, 129, 138
    rent charges, 30–31
Chattels, 48–50, 129. *See also* Fixtures and Fittings.
  additional preliminary enquiries *re*, 69, 157
  hire purchase, etc. agreements, no, 138, 151, 157
  stock in trade,
    apportionment of purchase price, 112
Coal Mining. *See* Subsidence.
Common, Rights of,
  Commons Registration Search, 31–32
  preliminary enquiries *re*, 30, 31–32, 128, 132, 133
Completion,
  date of, 54, 135
  meter readings on day of, 69, 152
  post, by, 52–53
    Law Society's code for, 52–53, 177–178
  preliminary enquiries *re*, 52–54, 69, 129, 133, 135
  time of, 54, 133
Completion—*cont.*
  undertaking by vendor's solicitor,
    documents of title, to forward, 53
    mortgage, to discharge, 53
  vacant possession, 52–54, 129, 132, 133, 157
Compulsory Acquisition,
  compensation,
    reduced where paid on previous refusal of planning permission, 98
  enquiries of other statutory bodies *re*, 74
  highway construction, necessitated by, 76, 162, 170, 174
  listed building, of, 99, 103
  local authority enquiry *re*, 74, 162, 165, 170, 173, 174
Condition of Property,
  additional enquiries of vendor, 68, 151
  disclose, no duty to, 5, 122
    leasehold, 59
  guarantee *re*. *See* Guarantee.
Conditions of Sale,
  Law Society's, 179–182
  National, 183–186
Conservation Area, 104–105
  local authority enquiry *re*, 164, 172
  local land charge, registrable as, 105
  trees, 105
Conveyancers, Licensed, 1
Conveyancing,
  process, chart of, 1–2
  speeding up,
    delay before contract,
      solicitor's negligence, 5
    replies to preliminary enquiries with draft contract, 3, 6
Covenants. *See also* Adverse Rights; Facilities; Restrictions.

Covenants—*cont.*
benefiting property, 20, 23, 27–28, 127, 128, 132, 136
breach of, 128, 137. *See also* Disputes.
leasehold property. *See* Leasehold Properties.
burdening property, 20, 23, 30, 31, 127, 128, 132, 137
consent required by,
preliminary enquiry *re*, 42, 128
disclosure of, 30–31. *See* Disclose, Duty to.
latent defects in title, 5
preliminary enquiry *re*, 30–31, 127, 128, 132, 137
standard conditions of sale, 5, 19, 30
disputes *re*, 17–18, 127, 137. *See also* Disputes.
leasehold properties. *See* Leasehold Properties.
positive,
maintenance of access, 20, 23, 27–30, 127
preliminary enquiry, 20, 23, 27–28, 30–31, 127, 128, 132, 137

Damages,
misrepresentation, for, 7–8, 12–13
Bain v. *Fothergill*, rule in, 12
loss of bargain, for, 12–13
third parties in "chain", 13
replies to preliminary enquiries incorrect, 7–8, 12–13
Development Land Tax, 54
Development, Proposed. *See also* Alterations to Property.
enquiry *re* neighbouring property, 70, 157
notice to building control officer, 87
planning permission for. *See* Planning.
planning policy. *See* Planning.
Disclose, Duty to,
building work, generally no, 24

Disclose, Duty to—*cont.*
caveat emptor, 5
condition, physical, of property, no, 5, 122
leasehold, 59
easements and liabilities, certain,
standard conditions of sale, under, 5, 19, 30, 180, 185
latent defect in title, 5
planning matter amounting to, 43
none, generally, 5
except latent defects in title, 5
planning matters,
latent defect in title amounting to, 43
national conditions of sale, under, 20, 43, 185
none, generally, 43
use, authorised, no warranty that, 43
title, defect in,
latent, 5
preliminary enquiry, 135
use,
no warranty that authorised, 43
written communications, relevant, received by or known to vendor,
Law Society's conditions of sale, under, 19–20, 43, 180
Disputes,
inspection before contract to avoid, 111
landlord, with. *See* Agricultural Tenancies; Leasehold Properties; Tenancy, Property Subject to a.
preliminary enquiry, 17, 127, 137
boundaries, 17–18, 127, 131, 137
covenants, *re*, 17–18, 127, 137
easements, *re*, 17–18, 27, 127, 128, 137
facilities, *re*, 27, 137

Disputes—*cont.*
preliminary enquiry—*cont.*
neighbours, with, 17–18, 127, 131
Drainage,
adoption by local authority, 82, 163, 171
charges for, 20, 23–24, 127
agreement for combined drainage under s.38 Public Health Act 1936, 82, 163, 171
agreement for construction and connection of, under s.18 Public Health Act 1936, 23–24, 82, 127, 163, 171
bond *re*, 24, 127, 163, 171
charges for, 25, 50–52, 128, 137
combined drainage, 82
construction and connection of new properties, 23–24, 54, 127
public sewer, work on, 82, 163, 171
combined, agreement for, 82, 163, 171
construction and connection of new properties, 20, 23–24, 54, 82, 127
defective, 81
claim under s.18 agreement, 20, 127
discharge effluent, licence to, 117
drain,
building work proposed over, 117
meaning of, 81
easement, right, etc. *re*, 25, 26, 27–28, 128, 132. *See also* Easement.
emptying of private system, enquiry *re*, 68, 151
local authority enquiries *re*, 163, 171
mains, 25, 128, 132, 137, 163, 171
maintenance of, agreement for, 24, 82, 127, 137, 163, 171
bond *re*, 24, 127, 137, 163, 171

Drainage—*cont.*
new properties,
agreement for construction and connection by builder, 23–24, 54, 82, 127, 163, 171
preliminary enquiries *re*, 20, 23–24, 25–26, 127, 128, 129, 132, 137
importance of, 81
new properties, 54, 129
private sewer, whether a, 81, 163, 171. *See also* Easement.
public sewer,
connection to, 25, 132, 137, 163, 171
recovery of cost of certain work by Water Authority, 82, 163, 171
rates for, 25, 50–52, 133
rights adversely affecting property, 30–31, 128, 132, 137. *See also* Adverse Rights.
overriding interests, 32
route of sewers, pipes, 25, 117, 128, 132
sewer,
building work proposed over, 117
meaning of, 81
route of, 25, 117, 128, 132
surface water, of, 25, 163, 171

Easement,
access for maintenance, right of, 27–30, 31, 128
burdening property, 20, 27–33, 128, 132. *See also* Adverse Rights.
disclose, duty to,
latent defect in title, if, 5
standard conditions of sale, under, 5, 19, 30, 180, 185
disputes *re*, 17–18, 27, 127, 128
drainage, of, 25–26, 27–28, 128, 132, 137. *See also* Drainage.
equitable, 32–33
overriding interest, can be, 33

Easement—*cont.*
inspection of property to ascertain, 111
light, right of, 27, 128, 132
maintenance of, 28, 128
way, right of, 20, 23, 27, 28, 75, 127, 128, 136
maintenance, right of access for, 27–30, 31, 128
overriding interest, as, 32–33, 42
pipes and wires, for, 25–26, 27, 128, 132. *See also* Services.
preliminary enquiries *re*, 20, 25–26, 27–33, 127, 128, 132, 133
repair, right to enter for, 27–30, 31, 128
sale subject to all,
standard conditions of sale, under, 30, 180, 185
services, *re*, 25–26, 27–28, 128, 132, 137. *See also* Drainage; Services.
adequacy of, 26
title to convey or grant,
services, for, 25–26, 128, 132
way, right of, 27–30, 127, 128, 132, 133, 136. *See also* Path; Road.
adopt, local authority's resolution to, 75
adverse possession of driveway, 28–30
agreement or covenant *re*, 20, 23, 127
claim *re*, 20, 28, 127
inspection to check, 111
maintenance of, 20, 23, 27, 28, 75, 127, 128, 136
shared, 28–30, 136
title to, 75
water. *See* Water.
weatherproofing, of, 17
Electric Fittings, 48–49. *See* Fixtures and Fittings.
Electricity. *See* Services.
Enquiries After Contact, 4
Enquiries Before Contact of Vendor. *See* Preliminary Enquiries; Replies to Preliminary Enquiries.
Enquiries of Local Authorities. *See* Local Authority Enquiries; Replies to Local Authority Enquiries.
Enterprise Zone, 107–108, 167, 175
enquiry *re* functions transferred to the authority, 108
planning, relaxation of control, 107
rates benefits, 107–108
tax benefits, 107–108
Equitable Interest. *See also* Adverse Rights, Overriding Interest.
beneficial interest, owner of,
receipt for purchase money, must join in, 38
separate advice, should have, 38–39
non-spouse, of,
restriction of circumstances where acquired in another's property, 37
notice of, 34–36
occupation, person in,
notice of, 34–36. *See* Occupation, Persons in.
overriding interest, as, 30, 32 *et seq*. *See also* Overriding Interest.
preliminary enquiry to disclose, 30 *et seq*., 128, 132, 137
Estate Agent. *See* Agent.
Estoppel,
licence protected by, 32
Extensions. *See* Alterations to Property.

Facilities. *See also* Agreement; Covenant; Drainage; Easement; Services.
benefiting property, 27 *et seq*., 128, 132, 133, 136–137

Facilities—*cont.*
burdening property, 27 *et seq.*, 128, 132–133, 136, 137. *See also* Adverse Rights.
inspection to check, 111
disputes *re*, 27, 127, 128, 131, 137
footpath, *re*, 136
flat, for, 159
inspection to check, 111
maintenance of, 28, 128, 136
footpath, 136
payments for, 28, 128, 132, 136–137
footpath, 136
services, 132
preliminary enquiries *re*, 27–30, 128, 132–133, 136–137
water, licence to abstract, 25, 26–27, 31, 128
Fences. *See* Boundaries.
Fire Certificate, 43, 48, 129, 159
Fixtures and Fittings. *See also* Chattels.
apportionment of purchase price, 111
central heating,
vendor's unencumbered property, 138
garden plants and furniture, 48–50, 129
greenhouse, 49, 129
inspection of, 111
meaning of, 48–50
no hire purchase or other rights existing over, 138, 151, 157
burglar alarm, 154
preliminary enquiries *re*, 48–50, 129, 133, 138, 151, 157
Flat,
freehold,
mortgage for, 55
leasehold. *See* Leasehold Properties.
Footpath. *See* Path.
Fraud,
misrepresentation,
replies to preliminary enquiries, in, 7
Fraud—*cont.*
misstatement,
solicitor's, in replies to preliminary enquiries, 14

Garage,
erection of,
preliminary enquiry *re*, 69, 138, 151,
Garden Ornaments, 49–50, 129. *See* Chattels; Fixtures and Fittings.
Gas. *See also* Services.
exploration area for,
preliminary enquiry, 132
pipes, location of, 119
General Improvement Area, 81, 165, 173
Greenhouse, 49, 129. *See* Fixtures and Fittings.
Guarantee. *See also* National House-Building Council.
assignment of, 21, 23, 132, 137
bond supporting agreement with local authority,
drainage and sewers,
construction and maintenance, for, 20, 23–24, 82, 127, 163, 171
road, construction and maintenance, for, 20, 23–24, 77, 127, 137, 162, 170
building work, for, 20 *et seq.*, 127, 132. *See also* National House-Building Council.
claim under, 20, 24, 127, 137
damp proofing, for, 23, 127, 132, 137
flooding, 137
N.H.B.C. scheme. *See* National House-Building Council.
preliminary enquiries *re*, 20 *et seq.*, 127, 132, 137
title for, 23, 127. *See also* Insurance.
woodworm, etc., against, 23, 127, 132, 137

Highway. *See* Road.

Housing,
 hostel,
  registration of, 80–81, 167, 175
 general improvement area, 81, 165, 173
  grants for improvement, 81
 lodging house,
  registration of, 80–81, 167, 175
 multiple occupation,
  registration of, 80–81, 167, 175
 slum clearance area, 81, 165, 173

Indemnities. *See* Guarantee; Insurance.
Informal Arrangements Affecting Land. *See* Adverse Rights.
Inspection of Property, 111–112
 rights apparent on, disclosure of, 30
 surveyor, by, 122–124
Insurance. *See also* Guarantee.
 assignment of policy,
  preliminary enquiry *re*, 20, 21, 23, 136
 claims under, 20, 24, 127, 137
 flooding, against, 24, 137
 N.H.B.C. scheme, 21, 127. *See* National House-Building Council.
 preliminary enquiry *re*, 20–23, 127, 136
  tenancy, property subject to a, 143, 147
 restrictive covenant, breach of, for, 23, 127, 136
 title, defective, for, 23, 127, 136

Landlord. *See also* Agricultural Tenancy; Leasehold Properties; Tenancy, Property Subject to a.
 assignee, covenant with, 57
 identity of, 56, 130
 overriding interest may have, 40–42
 purchaser, rights against, 40–42

Leasehold Properties. *See also* Agricultural Tenancy; Tenancy, Property Subject to a.
 alterations, consent for, 57, 130, 140
 assign licence to, 57, 130, 139
 assignee and landlord, covenant between, 57, 139
 breach of covenant,
  landlord, by, 59, 60–61, 111, 130
  other tenants, by, 60–61
  tenant, by, 59–60, 130, 140
 condition of, 59, 111
 construction of, 160
 covenants,
  breach of. *See* breach of covenant.
  enforcement of, 59–61
 enfranchisement, 54, 59
 flat,
  preliminary enquiries *re*, 159–160
 forfeiture, 56
  service charge, failure to pay, 58
 inspection of,
  condition of premises to ascertain, 111
 insurance, 63–65, 141
  flats, block of, 64, 141
  interest of mortgagee noted on policy, 64, 160
  landlord's obligation, 64
  mortgagee's requirements, 64, 160
  preliminary enquiries *re*, 63, 130, 141, 160
  tenant's obligation, 63–64
 landlord,
  identity of, 56, 61, 130, 139
 Leasehold Reform Act 1967, 59
 licence to assign, 57, 130, 139
 licences granted by landlord, 56, 57, 130, 139
 lift, 160
 maintenance of, 55, 59–63. *See* service charge.
  inspection to check, 111

Leasehold Properties—*cont.*
maintenance of—*cont.*
problems of, 59–61, 160
management companies, 61, 141, 159–160
managing agents, 61
identity of, 139
preliminary enquiries *re*, 54 *et seq.*, 130, 139–141
problems of, 55–56
reform, proposals for, 55–56
regulations *re*, 160
rent,
enquiries *re*, 57–58, 140
receipt, production of, 58, 59, 140
Rent Act, whether applies, 58
repair covenants,
breach of, 59–61
inspection to check performance of, 111
purchaser takes property as it is, 59, 111
reversion, disposal of,
problems of enforcing landlord's covenants, 60–61
services, 58
problems *re*, 55, 60–61. *See also* service charge.
service charge, 62–63, 130, 140, 160
amount of, 62, 130, 140, 160
apportionment of, 63, 140
information, right to obtain, 62, 130
sinking fund, 63, 160
tenants' associations, 61, 141
consultation with, 63
title to, 56, 65–67, 130, 139
underlease, 56, 130, 139
covenant to observe head lease, 56
registration with superior landlords, 139
superior landlords, identity of, 139
title to, 65–66, 139
use, change of, consent for, 57, 130

Leasehold Properties—*cont.*
wasting asset, 55
Licence,
assign, to. *See* Leasehold Properties.
contractual,
inspection to ascertain rights, 111
rights under, not overriding interest, 41–42
disclosure of, 30–33, 128, 132, 137
estoppel, proprietary, protected by, 32
overriding interest, as, 32
preliminary enquiries *re*, 30–33, 67, 128, 132, 137, 143–145, 147–150
service occupant, 111
subject to, buying property,
inspection to ascertain rights of licencee, 111
preliminary enquiries *re*, 67, 143–145, 147–150
Licensed Conveyancers, 1
Listed Building,
building preservation notice, 99, 103–104, 165, 173
compensation where not listed, 104
certificate of intention not to list, 101
compensation,
compulsory acquisition, on, 99, 103
not listed after building preservation notice, 104
refusal of or conditions on consent, 101–102
compulsory acquisition of, 99, 103
compensation, basis of assessment, 99, 103, 166, 175
consent, 99, 101, 159, 166, 174
conditions, subject to, 101
finance, availablility of, relevant consideration, 101

Listed Building—*cont.*
consent—*cont.*
planning permission, separate from, 101
refusal of, 99, 101, 166, 174
effect of listing, 100 *et seq.*
value of property, 100
enforcement notice, 99, 102, 166, 174
purchaser, position of, 102
grading, significance of, 100
local authority enquiries *re*, 99, 165, 166, 173, 174
local land charge, registration of, 100
procedure for listing, 100
purchase notice, 102
refusal of consent, 99, 101
compensation, 101–102
purchase notice, 102
repairs notice, 99, 102–103, 166, 175
"spot listing", 100, 103–104
Local Authority,
building regulation consent, 42. *See* Building Regulations.
notice served by,
preliminary enquiry *re*, 18–20, 127, 131, 137
inspection at offices of, 112
Local Authority Enquiries, 71 *et seq.*, 161 *et seq.*
after contract, 4
description of property, 72
forms, 71, 161 *et seq.*
fees, 72, 161, 169
when submitted, 71–72
plan with, 72, 161, 169
replies to. *See* Replies to Local Authority Enquiries.
Local Searches, 71, 72
notices *re* property,
copies of, from vendor, 18
tree preservation order,
unregistered, 19. *See also* Tree Preservation Order.

Mining. *See* Subsidence.
Minor Interest,
disclosure of, 30, 33–34
Minor Interest—*cont.*
unregistered, 33–34
Misrepresentation,
agent, by, 8, 11–12, 13
boundaries inaccurate on plan, 16
"chain", conveyancing, effect on, 13
damages for, 12–13
Bain v. *Fothergill*, rule in, 12
loss of bargain, 12–13
disclaimer, effect of, 8 *et seq.*
exclude liability for, attempts to, 6 *et seq.*, 10–11
fraudulent, 7
innocent, 7
agent, by, 14
negligent, 7 *et seq.*
plan with inaccurate boundaries, 16
remedies for, 7–8
damages, 12–13
replies to preliminary enquiries, in, 7 *et seq.*
third parties, liability to, 13
vendor, by, 6 *et seq.*
Misstatement,
negligent,
replies to preliminary enquiries, in, 7, 14
Mortgage,
beneficial interest, owner of,
receipt, should join in, 38
separate advice, should have, 38–39
discharge of, undertaking for, 53, 136
insurance policy noting interest of mortgagee, 64
preliminary enquiry *re*, 136
receipt,
owner of a beneficial interest should join in, 38

National House-Building Council,
claim against, defect in property, for,
notification of vendor, 19, 24
preliminary enquiry *re*, 19, 127, 137

National House-Building
Council—*cont.*
guarantees by,
preliminary enquiries *re*,
20–23, 24, 127, 132,
137
Negligence,
disclaimer, effect of,
local authority replies, in, 73,
74, 161
replies to preliminary
enquiries, in, 6 *et seq.*,
14–15, 127, 131, 135,
143, 147
local authority, of,
inspection of foundations by
building inspector, 87
replies to enquiries, in, 73–74
misrepresentation in replies to
preliminary enquiries, 7 *et
seq.*
misstatement in replies to
preliminary enquiries,
solicitor's liability, 14–15
replies to preliminary enquiries,
in 6 *et seq.*
solicitor, of, 3–4
commons registration search,
failure to make, 32
completion by post, 52–53
delay before contract, 5
disclaimer, effect of, 6 *et seq.*,
14–15
duty to third parties, 4, 15
indemnity for vendor, 14
lease, failure to check, 67
matrimonial home, right to
occupy, failure to
protect, 3
misrepresentation in replies to
preliminary enquiries, 6
et seq., 13–14
misstatement in replies to
preliminary enquiries,
14
planning permission, failure
to check, 3
procedure for complaints, 1
rateable value, failure to
check, 3, 52

Negligence—*cont.*
solicitor, of—*cont.*
replies to preliminary
enquiries, in, 6 *et seq.*,
13–15
surveyor, of, 123–124
duty to third parties, 123–124
vendor, of,
replies to preliminary
enquiries, in 6 *et seq.*
Neighbouring Property,
development, proposed,
whether any, 70, 157
dispute with neighbours, 17–18,
127, 131
notice *re*, 19, 131, 137
information *re*,
register of planning
applications, inspection
of, 89
terraced and semi-detached,
improvements to, which may
affect property, 133
New Properties,
drainage, construction and
connection of,
agreement by builder for,
23–24, 82, 127, 163, 171
charges for, 23–24, 54, 127
preliminary enquiry *re*, 54,
129
fencing of, 54, 129
garden, clearing and levelling of,
54, 129
inspection for faults,
N.H.B.C., claim against, 111
N.H.B.C. scheme protects
against defects, 21–23
paths and drives, 54, 129
preliminary enquiries *re*, 54, 129
roads, construction and
maintenance of, 77
agreement under s.38
Highways Act 1980 and
performance bond, 20,
23–24, 77, 127, 137, 162,
170
services for, 54. *See also*
Drainage, Construction and
Connection of.

New Properties—*cont.*
sewers. *See* Drainage, Construction and Connection of.
Noise Abatement Zone,
consent to exceed noise level, 80
cost of reducing noise levels, 80
order made, 79–80, 167, 175
planning permission for noisy development may be unlikely, 79
Notice,
building preservation, 99, 103–104
building works, of, to local authority, 87
completion notice from local planning authority, 92–93
copy of those given and received, request in preliminary enquiries, 18, 127, 131
disclosure of,
planning matters, *re*, National Conditions of Sale, in, 20, 43
preliminary enquiries, in, 18–20, 127, 131, 137
written, Law Society's Conditions of Sale, in, 19–20, 43
discontinuance,
advertisements, *re* display of, 99
disrepair, of, water authority, from,
maintenance of river banks, *re*, 116–117
doctrine of. *See* Adverse Rights.
enforcement, 93–96
listed building, 99, 102
Highway Acts, under, 109, 162, 170, 173
Housing Acts, under, 109, 162, 170, 173
informal, whether any served by local authority, 109, 162, 170, 173
London Building Acts, under, 109, 173
Notice—*cont.*
N.H.B.C., claim against, 19, 24, 127, 137
planning, *re*
disclosure of, 18–20, 43
preliminary enquiries *re*, 18–20, 127, 131, 137
local searches, connection with, 18
Public Health Acts, under, 109, 162, 170, 173
purchase, 91–92
listed building, of, 102
repairs,
listed building, of, 99, 102
stop, 95–96
support, withdrawing, for coal mining purposes, 113
tenancy, property subject to a, *re*, 143, 147

Occupation, Persons in,
equitable interest in another's property,
restriction of cases where non-spouses acquire, 37
examples of, 39–40
inquiry addressed to relevant persons, 34, 38
inspection to check, 39, 111
meaning of, 35–36, 41
minor interest, person with, 36
minors, 37–38
notice to vendor of rights, 34–36, 40
overriding interest of, 34 *et seq.*
preliminary enquiry as to, 30, 34 *et seq.*, 128, 130, 137
effectiveness of, 37–38
rights of, 41–42
notice of, 34–36, 40
reform, proposals for, 36–37
separate advice for, 39
spouse, not limited to, 34, 36–37
Oil. *See also* Services.
exploration area for,
preliminary enquiry, 132
Outgoings,
preliminary enquiries *re*, 50–52, 129, 133, 138

Outgoings—*cont.*
rateable value, alteration to, 50–52. *See* Rates.
Overriding Interest. *See also* Adverse Rights.
beneficial interest, owner of,
receipt for purchase money, must join in, 38–39
restriction of cases in which non-spouse can acquire, 37
separate legal advice, should have, 39
disclosure of, 30, 32 *et seq.*, 128, 132, 137
easement as, 32–33
equitable, 33
examples of, 42
occupation, coupled with, 39–40
inquiry of relevant person, 34, 38, 40–41
inspection to check, 39, 111
licence as, 32, 39
minor interest as, 36
occupation, persons in. *See* Occupation, Persons in.
preliminary enquiries *re*, 30, 33, 34 *et seq.*, 128, 132, 137
effectiveness of, 37–38
receipt of rent and profits, person in, 40–42
inquiry addressed to relevant person, 40–41
reform, proposals for, 36–37
rights of persons in occupation, 41–42
spouse, not limited to, 34, 36–37
undertaking not to enforce, 137

Parking Restrictions,
additional preliminary enquiry *re*, 69, 151
Party Wall,
agreements, 27, 28
enquiry *re*, 16–17. *See also* Boundaries.
Path. *See also* Easement; Road.
adoption, local authority's resolution to, 76, 162, 170
Path—*cont.*
closure of, proposal for, 78, 166, 174
dispute over use of, 136
diversion of, 78, 166, 174
planning permission for development not authority for, 78
local authority enquiries, named on, 72, 162, 170
maintenance of, 136
maintainable at public expense, enquiry whether, 75, 162, 170
public, 79
definitive map, shown on, 79, 132, 166, 174
interference with public's enjoyment of, 79
preliminary enquiry *re*, 30, 31, 132, 136
Pipeline,
enquiry of local authority *re*, 112, 122, 167, 175
supplementary enquiry of authority for exact location, 122
permission to build within 10 feet of, 122
Pipes. *See* Drainage; Easement; Services; Water.
Plan,
approval of, required, restriction under, 42, 128
boundaries, of, 16
misrepresentation where inaccurate, 16
identification, 135
local authority enquiries, with, 72
local search with, 72
Planning,
advertisements. *See* Advertisement, Control of Display.
authorised use, 45
conditions of sale *re*, 43–44
warranty, no, that, 43
blight, 91–92, 164, 172
caravan site, 70

Planning—*cont.*
change of use, 42, 44
proposed, 46–47, 86
compensation for loss,
conditions on permission, 96–98, 164, 172
refusal of permission, 96–98, 164, 172
revocation or modification of permission, 91
stop notice, 96
completion notice, 92–93, 166, 175
contents of, 92–93
effect of, 93
purchaser's response to, 93
conditional permission,
breach of condition, 137
compensation for loss, 96–98
conservation area, 104–105, 164, 172
demolition order, 91, 164, 172
developer, purchaser a property,
structure and local plans, relevance of, 86, 112
development,
meaning of, 88
development plan, 85–86, 164, 172
development proposed,
history, enquiry as to planning, 46–47, 112
disclose matters,
preliminary enquiries *re*, 18, 42–43
disclose matters, duty to,
some, in standard conditions of sale, 19, 30
latent defect in title, 43
no, 5
discontinuance order, 91, 164, 172
enforcement notice, 44, 89, 93–96, 163, 171
appeal against, 94–95
contents of, 93
effect of, 93–94
four-year rule, 44, 93
listed building, 102. *See* Listed Building.

Planning—*cont.*
enforcement notice—*cont.*
purchaser's possible response to, 94–95
registration of, 94, 112, 163, 171
enterprise zone, 107–108, 167, 175
established use, 44–45
certificate, 159
extension of house,
permitted development, may be, 47, 89
history, enquiry as to, 42–47, 128, 138
improvement area, 108, 167, 176
industry, purchaser requires property for,
enterprise zone, importance of, 107–108
structure and local plans, relevance of, 86
listed buildings. *See* Listed Buildings.
local plan, 83, 85–86
challenging a, 85, 86
content of, 83, 85
local authority enquiries *re*, 164, 172
procedure for, 85
purpose of, 85
local planning authority, 88
neighbouring properties, information *re*, 89, 112
noise abatement zone, proposed development in, 79
outstanding natural beauty, area of, 105–106, 167, 175
relevance to purchaser, 106
permission,
attaches to land, 90
completion notice, effect of, 93
copies of, 43, 45, 88, 129, 159
detailed, 88
diversion of road or path, not authority for, 78
expiry date, 3, 5
failure to check, 3, 5
failure to obtain, 89

Planning—*cont.*
permission—*cont.*
listed building consent separate, 101
need for, 44
outline, 88
permitted development under General development Order, 89–90
revocation or modification of, 91, 164, 172
permitted development, 89–90
general permission withdrawn, 90, 164, 172
policy for area, long-term, 83–86
local plan, 83, 85–86
structure plan, 83–86
preliminary enquiries *re*, 42 *et seq.*, 128–129, 131, 138, 159
purchase notice, 91–92
refusal of permission,
compensation for, 96–98
register, inspection of, 88–89, 112, 164, 172
neighbouring property, for information *re*, 89, 112
stop notice, 95–96, 163, 171
cessation of, 95
compensation for loss, 96
effect of, 95
purchaser's response to, 96
structure plan, 83–86
challenging a, 84, 86
content of, 83–84
local authority enquiries *re*, 164, 172
procedure for adopting, 84–85
purpose of, 85–86
relevance to purchaser of, 86
trees,
conservation area, 105
tree preservation order, 96, 164, 172
unauthorised use not "lawful", 45–46
urban development area, 106, 107
use, change of, 42, 44
proposed, 46–47, 86

Pollution,
noise. *See* Noise Abatement Zone.
smoke, smokeless zone, 80, 165, 173
Positive Covenants. *See* Covenants.
Preliminary Enquiries,
additional to standard. *See* Additional Enquiries.
after contract, 4
flat, *re*, 159–160
leasehold enquiries, 54 *et seq.*, 130, 139–141
purpose of, 5
replies to. *See* Replies to Preliminary Enquiries.
standard, 6 *et seq.*, 127–129, 131–133, 135–138
replies supplied with draft contract, 3, 6
Purchaser,
caveat emptor, 5
fraud, effect of, 5
Public Highway. *See* Road.
Public Health Acts,
notices under. *See* Notice.
Public Path. *See* Path.
Public Rights,
affecting land, 30, 31–32, 128

Railway,
fences, responsibility for maintaining,
enquiry as to, 115–116
tunnels, rights *re*, 116
Rates,
amount of, 69, 133, 152
apportionment of, 50, 52
enterprise zone, in, 108
information memo *re*, 154
preliminary enquiries *re*, 50–52, 129, 133, 138
rateable value, 129, 138
alteration to, 50–52, 129
enfranchisement, relevance for, 59
failure to check, 3
unoccupied property, on, 108–109, 165, 173

Reform, Proposals for,
additional enquiries, fee for, 6
boundaries, *re*, 18
leasehold properties, 55–56
occupation, rights of persons in, 36–37
overriding interests, 36–37
preliminary enquiries,
Law Society guidelines for, 6
preliminary enquiries, standard,
replies supplied with draft contract, 3, 6
Registered Land,
compulsory registration, area of, 83, 135, 165, 173
Public Index Map, search of, 83
Rent Charges. *See* Adverse Rights.
Replies to Local Authority Enquiries,
contract subject to satisfactory, 4
draft contract, supplied with, 3
liability for, 73–74
disclaimer, effect of, 73, 74, 161
negligent, 73–74
priority period, confers no, 73
satisfactory, contract subject to, 4
value of, 73
Replies to Preliminary Enquiries,
accuracy, importance of, 13
contract subject to satisfactory, 4
disclaimer, effect of, 6 *et seq.*, 127, 131, 135, 143, 147
disclose defects, no duty to, 5
caveat emptor, 5
fraud, effect of, 5
latent defects in title, 5
material facts adversely affecting property, 5
patent easements and other rights, 5
draft contract, supplied with, 3, 6
incorrect, 6 *et seq.*
misrepresentation in, 7 *et seq.*
misstatement in, 7 *et seq.*
satisfactory, contract subject to, 4
Rescission,
"authorised use" unauthorised, 43
misrepresentation for,
replies to preliminary enquiries, in, 7–8
Residence,
preliminary enquiry *re* vendor's, 133
Restrictions. *See also* Adverse Rights; Covenants.
preliminary enquiry *re*, 42, 128,
breach of, 128, 137
Restrictive Covenants. *See* Covenants; Restrictions.
Rights Over Property. *See* Adverse Rights; Drainage; Easement; Facilities; Services; Water.
River. *See* Water.
Road,
adopt, local authority's resolution to, 75, 162, 170
agreement between builder and local authority,
construct and maintain, to, 20, 23–24, 77, 127, 137, 162, 170
closure of, proposal for, 78
construction of,
agreement for, 20, 23–24, 77, 127, 137, 162, 170
proposed, 76, 162, 170, 174
defective,
claim under s.38 agreement, 20, 24, 77, 127
diversion of, 78
planning permission for development not authority for, 78
maintenance of, 75
agreement and bond *re*, 20, 23–24, 77, 127, 137, 162, 170
public expense, at, 75, 162, 170
new housing development,
agreement under s.38 Highways Act with performance bond, 20, 23–24, 77, 127, 137, 162, 170

Road—*cont.*
proposed construction of, near property, 76, 162, 170, 174
subways, flyovers, etc., 76, 162, 170
public highway, enquiry whether, 75, 162, 170
widening scheme,
informal notice of, 109
notice *re*, 18–19

Services,
burglar alarm, 68, 151, 157
fully owned by vendor, 154
information memo *re*, 154
central heating,
functioning of, 68, 151, 157
service contract for, 132, 137, 151, 157
vendor's unencumbered property, 138
claim *re*, 137
compulsory acquisition of property by statutory bodies, enquiries as to, 74
construction and connection of, to new properties, 20, 23–24, 77, 82, 127, 137, 162, 170
drainage. *See* Drainage.
easement, right, etc. *re*, 25–26, 27–28, 128, 132, 137
adequacy of, 26
title to grant, 25–26, 128, 132
electrical system, testing and rewiring of, 68, 151
electricity, 118
compensation for interference by supply lines, 118
inspection of records *re* proposed and existing cables and installations, 118
right to enter and maintain, 118
gas, 119
location of pipes, 119
right to enter and maintain, 119
information memo *re*, 153–154

Service—*cont.*
lease, under. *See* Leasehold Properties.
mains, 25, 128, 137
maintaining property, information *re*. 155–156
meter readings on completion day, 69, 152
payment for, 137
contributions by, 132
pipeline,
proposal to construct near property, 109–110
preliminary enquiries *re*, 25–27, 128, 132, 137
additional enquiries, 68, 69, 151, 157
route of, 25–26, 128, 132
inspection to ascertain, 111
service contracts for appliances, 68, 151
telecommunications, 69, 120–121, 151, 157
information memo *re*, 153
location of equipment, 120
right to enter and repair or construct, 120
telephone. *See* Telecommunications.
water. *See* Water.
wayleave *re*, 25
working order, in, 157
Sewers. *See* Drainage.
Shed. *See* Fixtures and Fittings.
Slum Clearance Area, 81, 165, 173
Smokeless Zone,
exemption for, 80
heating appliances, whether comply, 80
order, local land charges search reveals, 80
resolution for order, enquiry *re*, 80, 165, 173
Solicitor,
completion by post,
vendor's, as agent for purchaser's, 53, 177
complaint against,
procedures for, 1

Solicitor—*cont.*
- duty of care to third parties in "chain",
  - replies to preliminary enquiries, in, 15
- duty to make enquiries, 3–4
  - additional enquiries, 4. *See* Additional Enquiries.
  - tenancy, terms of, as to, 5
  - usual, 5
- misrepresentation by,
  - innocent, 14
  - negligent. *See* Negligence.
  - replies to preliminary enquiries, in, 6 *et seq.*, 13–14
- misstatement by,
  - replies to preliminary enquiries, in, 14
- negligence of. *See* Negligence.
- third parties, duty to,
  - replies to preliminary enquiries, in, 15, 18
- undertaking,
  - documents of title, to forward, 53
  - discharge mortgage, to, 53

Spouse,
- equitable interest, with,
  - receipt for purchase money, should join in, 38
  - separate advice, should have, 38–39

Standard Preliminary Enquiries, 3, 6 *et seq.*, 15 *et seq.*, 127–129, 131–133, 135–138
- disclaimer in replies, 6 *et seq.*
- draft contract, replies with, 3, 6

Subsidence,
- clay working, due to,
  - enquiries *re*, 115
- coal mining, due to, 112–113
  - building works, precautions for, 113
  - compensation for, 113
  - notice withdrawing support, 113
- compensation, 133
  - coal mining, for, 113

Subsidence—*cont.*
- guarantee or insurance policy *re*, 137. *See also* Guarantee; Insurance.
- limestone mining, due to, 114
  - enquiries for Walsall, Sandwell, Dudley and Wolverhampton, 114
- preliminary enquiry of vendor *re*, 68, 132, 151
- salt mining, 132
- tin mining, due to,
  - enquiries *re*, 115, 132

Survey,
- before exchange of contracts, 123
- full structural, 123, 124
- intermediate, 123, 124
- mortgage valuation report, 123, 124
- negligent, 123–124
- purpose of, 122

Tenancy, Property Subject to a. *See also* Agricultural Tenancy; Leasehold Properties.
- breach of covenant, 144
- business tenancy, 144
- copy documents supplied, 66, 143
  - notice, full, contents and legal consequences of, 67
- disputes with landlord, 144
- failure to check lease negligent, 67
- inspection to ascertain,
  - occupancy, 111
  - rights of tenants, 111
- insurance, 143
- notices from or to local authority, 143
- order of court, local authority, etc., *re*, 143
- overriding interest,
  - inspection to ascertain occupancy and rights, 111
  - intermediate landlord may have, 40–41
  - tenant may have, 40–41

Tenancy, Property Subject to a—*cont.*
preliminary enquiries *re*, 66–68, 136, 143–145
rent,
no warranty as to, 67
revision, 144
residential tenancy, 144
sub-tenancy, 143
tenant's rights against purchaser,
inspection to ascertain, 111
notice of, 40–41
Tied Cottage. *See* Agricultural Tenancy.
Timber, Right to Extract, 132
Title,
defective,
insurance for, 23, 127, 136
defects in, disclosure of. *See* Disclose, Duty to.
documents,
custody of, after exchange, 135
undertaking to forward in postal completion, 53, 177
insurance of defective, 23, 127, 136
leasehold, 56, 65–66, 130, 139
office copies, before exchange, 135
Tree Preservation Order,
conservation area, 105
effect of, 96
local land charge, registrable as, 96
not registered, 19, 164, 172
purpose of, 96
registered as local land charge, not, 19, 164, 172

Urban Development Area, 106–107, 167, 175
effect on planning control, 106–107
enquiry *re* functions transferred to corporation, 107, 167, 175
purpose of, 106

Use,
authorised, sale with specified, 43
change of,
consent required for, 57, 130
planning permission for, 42 *et seq.*, 88, 90
inspection to check, 112

Vacant Possession, 52–54
meaning, 53
preliminary enquiry, 52, 129, 132, 133, 157
rubbish, 53, 133, 157
standard conditions of sale,
must state whether, 66
Vendor,
indemnity from solicitor,
misrepresentation, negligent, for, 14
misrepresentation by, 7 *et seq.*

Water,
authority, 116–118
drainage. *See* Drainage.
building work proposed over waterpipe,
building regulation consent for, 117
canals, enquiries *re*, 118
compulsory acquisition, enquiry of Authority as to proposals for, 74
discharge effluent, licence to, 117
easement, right etc. *re*, 25–26, 27, 128, 132
impoundment licence, 117
licence to abstract, 25, 26, 128
disclosure of, 31
fees for, 50, 52, 133
notice to authority of change in ownership, 117
licence to discharge effluent, 117
mains, 25, 128, 132, 137
meter, 25, 26, 128
obstruct watercourse,
permission to, 117

Water—*cont.*
pipe,
building work proposed over route of, 117
proposal to construct near property, 109–110
pond or lake,
permission to obstruct watercourse to make, 117
preliminary enquiries *re*, 25–27, 128, 132, 137
rates, 50–52, 133. *See also* Rates.
last receipt, request for, 154
right to extract,
burdening property, 30, 31, 132. *See also* Adverse Rights.

Water—*cont.*
rights as overriding interests, 32
river or stream crosses or borders property,
maintenance of banks, 116–117
mooring rights, 131
notice of disrepair, 116–117
route of pipes, 25, 128
surface, drainage of, 25. *See* Drainage.
Way, Right of. *See* Easement.
Wayleave,
preliminary enquiry *re*,
benefiting property, 25, 128, 132, 137
burdening property, 30, 128, 132, 137